MW01299634

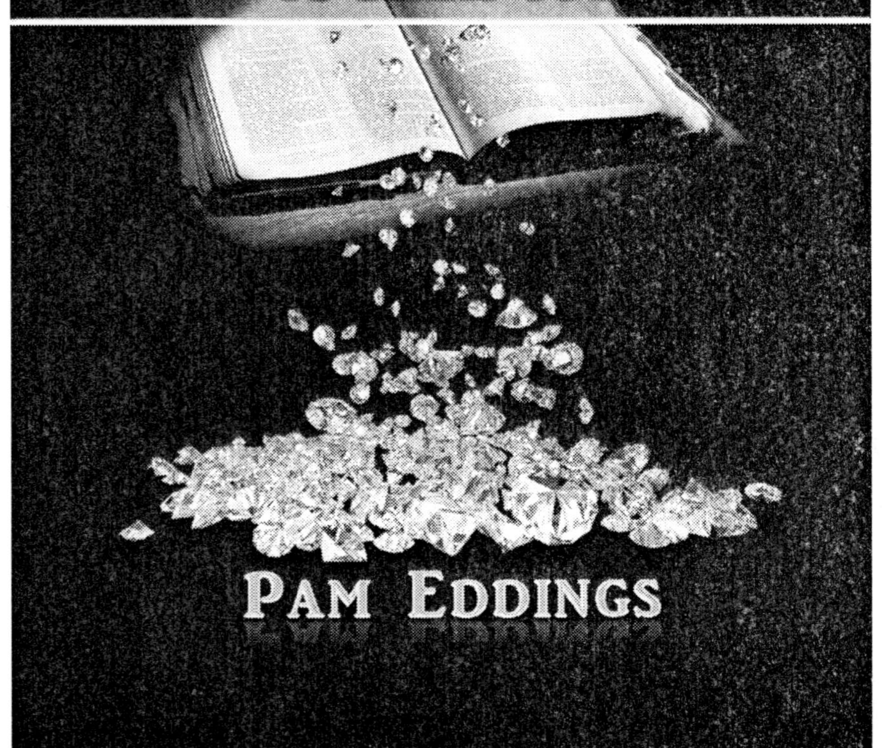
BIBLE
Gems
TO START YOUR DAY
PAM EDDINGS

Gary & Pam
I pray that my discoveries will provide a launching pad for you to discover some of the abundant "gems" in God's precious Word.
Love You!
Pam
12/5/14
2 Tim 2:15

Bible Gems To Start Your Day

By: Pam Eddings

ISBN-13: 978-1503313637
ISBN-10: 1503313638

All scripture quotations in this book are from the Authorized King James Version of the Bible unless otherwise noted.

Quotes by Don Wyrtzen come from his devotional book, *"A Musician Looks at the Psalms,"* (Grand Rapids, MI: Daybreak Books, 1988)

Quotes by Robert Morgan come from his devotional book, *"All to Jesus,"* (Nashville, TN: B & H Publishing Group, 2008)

Cover Design by Ken Raggio
Image: Open Bible, © Sean Nel, Dreamstime.com
Image: Diamonds Falling, © Whitehoun, 123RF.com

For Information, Contact:
eddingspam@gmail.com

FOLLOW ME on TWITTER: pameddings
FRIEND ME on FACEBOOK: Pam Eddings

Dedication

To my parents, Hubert & Gloria Nixon,
who instilled a love for God and His Word into my life from the time of my birth until I started my own family.

To my late husband, Ron Eddings,
whose well-worn Bible left a legacy to all who knew him of his love for that precious book.

To my sons Russell, Raymond and Rodney,
with whom their dad and I shared many evenings of playing Bible Trivia in addition to hundreds of hours of memorizing scriptures during their years of participating in Bible quizzing events.

To my daughters-in-law, Ashley, Desiree, and Jazmin,
who have joined in with our family tradition of being students of the Bible.

To my very precious grandchildren,
Kevin, Ryder, Molly, Bethany, and Kristen,
I pass on the legacy of loving God and His Word.

And finally, to Pastors, Sunday School teachers, and a host of family and friends who have influenced me to become a student and lover of God and His Word, I owe a great debt of gratitude.

Foreword

As I was preparing this new book for publication,
I sent previews of it to my sons and daughter-in-laws
as well as selected family members and close friends.
I have included their comments below. ~ **Pam**

To an incredible spiritual leader and an excellent resource for support! We are blessed to call you Mom and Grandma!

~ Russell, Ashley, Kevin, Ryder and Molly Eddings
Marionville, MO

We are thankful for the godly heritage Mom has provided for us and our children. We are looking forward to reading her daily insights and hope they will be an inspiration for many others.

~ Raymond, Desiree, Bethany and Kristen Eddings
Springfield, MO

We are beneficiaries of a lifetime of learning from my Mom. Her writing showcases the investment of years of Biblical study, and teaching. The insights gleaned from her life and devotion included in this new book are only surpassed by her consistent example of a Christian Mom.

~ **Rodney and Jazmin Eddings**
Brooklyn, NY

This scripture from Psalms 42:7 reminds me of Pam. "Deep calleth unto deep." It is consecration calling for deeper consecration. From a dedicated person to the ones who desire the meat of God's Word, Pam's writing is designed for those who hunger for righteousness and a closer walk with God.

~ Rev. Carroll & Linda Bushnell
Former Pastor, Church Planter, Evangelist
Kinder, LA

We feel honored that God smiled down upon us and gave us this beautiful daughter, now a beautiful woman, who loves God with all her heart. He gave her musical talents, teaching talents and now a talent for putting her spiritual insights into words to share with others. Her books are an inspiration and provide instruction to all who read them. She is a wonderful Mother, Grandmother, Daughter and Child of God. Thank you Pam, for giving your all to the Lord. We love you and are "proud" to call you our Daughter!

~ ***Hubert & Gloria Nixon***
Baton Rouge, LA

I have known Pam for almost 40 years, and she is a true Christian lady. Her writings come from years of experience as wife, mother, grandmother and teacher. She has lived her life in total devotion to God and His Word. Her knowledge comes from the daily study of God's Word. Her wisdom comes from the many challenges that life has thrown at her. As you read her writings, your heart and mind will be blessed and enriched.

~ **Rev. Glenn Murphy**
Pastor Grace Church of Central
Baton Rouge, LA

I am so glad to see Pam writing books! Her musings and writings have been a source of inspiration to so many over the years. I think it is great that she is gathering her "gems" together and putting them into this volume. I have received strength and encouragement as I meditate on the scriptures that have come from her heart, and on her elaborations. Thank you, Pam, and keep up the good work!

~ **Rev. Lynda Allison Doty, Ph.D**
Author of the book, "Help Me Heal"
Sponsor of "Help Me Heal Conferences for Women"
Columbia, SC

Jesus said in Matthew 13:44, *"The Kingdom of Heaven is like unto treasure hid in a field."* In her new book, Pam has dug out many gems from God's Word and shared them in written form with her readers. What a beautiful array of inspiring and uplifting exhortations that will make a godly difference every day of the year! Thank you Pam! Once again your love for God and His Word comes "sparkling" through.

~ Rev. Ben L. and Rebecca Medlin
Ministers of the Gospel
Mount Vernon, MO

I have enjoyed reading Pam's daily devotions on her Facebook page over the past year, and I am happy that she has decided to publish them for others to enjoy. Pam's first book, *"One-Year Bible Quiz"* has been a blessing to many people, and I expect her new *"Bible Gems"* book will also fill a need in people's lives. I appreciate her dedication to God, her burden to reach the lost, and her desire to bless God's people with her writing. The Lord surely has His hand on her.

~ Rev. Billy Hughey
Evangelist
Poplar Bluff, MO

I love the format of this book. Not only is a daily "Gem" of scripture given, but also words of encouragement as well as a quote to tie it all together. Anyone who will spend the time each day to absorb the "Gems" will surely find themselves not only feeling the Lord, but will also look forward to the next day's reading. Thank you Pam for your love of the Lord and your willingness to share that love.

~ Cindy Henshaw
Bartlesville, OK

Introduction

From the time I was a very young girl, the importance of daily devotions was so ingrained into my spirit that starting my day with devotions has become a lifelong habit. When I was growing up, churches promoted Bible reading by asking Sunday School teachers to keep records of how many chapters were read each week, and prizes were given at the end of each quarter to the ones who had read the most. I soon discovered that Psalms had dozens of short chapters, so I would read them over and over in order to report higher numbers of chapters read to my teachers. A benefit received from reading the Psalms so much was that I memorized dozens of verses and even whole chapters. Today, Psalms is still one of my favorite books in the Bible, and a significant number of the scriptures used in this book come from the book of Psalms.

In recent years I have added the reading of a daily devotional book to my daily devotions. For the past two years I have done in-depth studies of the scripture or thought for the day in my devotional books. Then I have written my own devotional thoughts based on my daily studies, and I have posted them on my Facebook page. About mid-way through this year, I decided to create a one-year devotional book containing the "gems" I had discovered during my reflections and research over the past two years. The topics I have included in this book are not the traditional "encouraging-thought-for-your-day" type of fare that is normally found in a daily devotional book. My quest for information has taken me on a journey through Heaven and Hell topics, Conversion and Discipleship topics, Relationship with God and others topics, Prayer and Worship topics, and the necessity for knowing and obeying the Word topics. I have included numerous scriptures to promote further research by my readers. It is my prayer that you will not only read the daily selections in this book, but that you will also use them as a launching pad to dig deeper into God's Holy Word and discover more of the "gems" that are hidden inside its pages.

Pam Eddings

Pam Eddings
November 2014

Therefore I love thy commandments above gold; yea, above fine gold.
Psalms 119:127

Gem #1 **January 1**

Whoso offereth praise glorifieth me: and to him that ***ordereth his conversation*[1] *aright*** *will I shew the salvation of God.*
Psalms 50:23

Order my steps in thy word:
and let not any iniquity have dominion over me.
Psalms 119:103

Let all things be done decently and in ***order****.*
1 Corinthians 14:40

~~~~~

The Bible contains hundreds of examples of very specific instructions for the building of altars and houses of worship, preparations for sacrifice, establishing positions of authority and leadership, proper methods of worship, instructions for daily living, etc. Failure to follow God's orders often resulted in serious consequences. David inadvertently caused the death of a man because he failed to follow God's order for transporting the Ark of the Covenant on the shoulders of the priests.

God gets no glory out of haphazardly-run church business, worship services or Christian lifestyles. As we embark on a New Year, now is a good time to order our lives according to the Word. Haphazard, hit-or-miss reading will not get the job done. To live an ordered Christian lifestyle requires disciplined scheduling of time every day for prayer and reading of the Word; not just reading, but also studying and applying its teachings to our life. Start this New Year out right for **God likes ORDER.**

---

[1] Strong's Hebrew and Chaldee Dictionary defines "conversation" as a course of life, journey, or pathway, meaning that those whose lives are in order will be shown the salvation of God.
~~~~~

Gem #2 **January 2**

Also I heard the voice of the Lord, saying,
Whom shall I send, and who will go for us*?*
Then said I, Here am I; send me.
Isaiah 6:8

~~~~~

"**Lord, send me** anywhere, only go with me.
Lay any burden on me, only sustain me.
Sever me from every tie,
except the tie that binds me to you and your love."
David Livingstone

~~~~~

Today's Church puts great emphasis on ***ability***. How well can you sing or play an instrument? How capable are you at leading worship or overseeing a ministry? What are your credentials for being chosen for a special position in the church? While ***ability*** is helpful in getting a job accomplished, God is more concerned with our ***availability***. If we make ourselves available to spend time in His presence through prayer and study of His Word, He will create in us the abilities He needs to get His Kingdom work accomplished.

~~~~~

"The Church is looking for better methods.
God is looking for better Men.
The Holy Ghost does not flow through methods, but through Men.
He does not come on machinery, but on Men.
He does not anoint plans, but Men.
...Men of prayer."
E.M. Bounds

~~~~~

The urgent need of the hour is for Men and Women of Prayer.

Are You Available?

Gem #3 **January 3**

Deliver me from mine enemies, O my God:
defend me from them that rise up against me.
*But **I will sing** of thy power; yea, **I will sing aloud** of thy mercy in the morning: for thou hast been my defense and refuge in the day of my trouble. Unto thee, O my strength, **will I sing:***
for God is my defence, and the God of my mercy.
Psalms 59:1, 16-17

***I will sing** of the mercies of the LORD for ever:*
*with my mouth will **I** make known thy faithfulness to all generations.*
Psalms 89:1

***I will sing** unto the LORD as long as I live:*
***I will sing** praise to my God while I have my being.*
Psalms 104:33

~~~~~

"The Church knew what the Psalmist knew. **Music praises God**.
Music is well or better able to praise Him than the
building of the Church and all its decoration.
It is the Church's greatest ornament."
Igor Stravinsky (1882-1971)
Russian composer, pianist and conductor

~~~~~

If we only focus on the darkness and sin around us, we could very easily give in to despair, but there is something very powerful about **singing to the LORD**. Music can lift my spirits to the heights of Heaven and usher me into His Presence. I love to sit down at the piano and sing to God during my prayer and devotion time each day. Are you fearful of the violence and wars and trouble on every hand? Instead of giving in to despair…

Lift your voice to God and SING.

Gem #4 **January 4**

The Lord is nigh unto them that are of a ***broken heart;***
and saveth such as be of a ***contrite spirit.***
Psalms 34:18

The sacrifices of God are a ***broken spirit:***
a ***broken and a contrite heart,*** *O God, thou wilt not despise.*
Psalms 51:17

For thus saith the high and lofty One that inhabiteth eternity,
whose name is Holy;
I dwell in the high and holy place,
with him also that is of a ***contrite and humble spirit,***
to revive the spirit of the humble,
and to revive the heart of the ***contrite ones.***
Isaiah 57:15

~~~~~

If given the chance to choose between ***blessing and brokenness,*** most all of us would choose blessing. Although God blesses His people abundantly, He has chosen the path of ***pain and brokenness*** to draw near to His people and prepare them to inhabit eternity in the high and holy place with Him.

Lord, help me to accept the heartaches and disappointments life brings so that You may heal me and one day bring me into Your presence forever.

~~~~~

"Most Christians pray to be blessed; few pray to be ***broken***."
Leonard Ravenhill

"If your life is ***broken*** when given to Jesus, it may be because pieces will feed a multitude, when a loaf would satisfy only a little lad."
Elisabeth Elliot

Gem #5 **January 5**

He healeth the broken in heart*, and bindeth up their wounds.*
Psalms 147:3

I will seek that which was lost,
and bring again that which was driven away,
and ***will bind up that which was broken****,*
and will strengthen that which was sick…
Ezekiel 34:16

The Spirit of the Lord is upon me,
because he hath anointed me to preach the gospel to the poor;
he hath sent me to ***heal the brokenhearted****,*
to preach deliverance to the captives,
and recovering of sight to the blind,
to set at liberty them that are bruised,
Luke 4:18

"Everyone in life is somehow ***broken***.
But there are three ways in which people respond.
1. They find healing and become healers.
2. They remain broken and give up.
3. They become so bitter that they become breakers,
and repeat the pattern."
Johnathan Nazarian

~~~~~

The Spirit of the Lord has been placed in the Church for the express purpose of empowering the saints to witness, preach, teach, heal, deliver and liberate all who are enslaved by the enemy of their souls.

I want to choose #1 and help others find healing.
~~~~~

Gem #6 **January 6**

For this is my ***blood*** *of the new testament,*
which is shed for many for the remission of sins.
Matthew 26:28

And almost all things are by the law purged with ***blood;***
and without shedding of ***blood*** *is no remission.*
Hebrews 9:22

But if we walk in the light, as he is in the light,
we have fellowship one with another,
and the ***blood*** *of Jesus Christ his Son cleanseth us from all sin.*
1 John 1:7

And from Jesus Christ, who is the faithful witness,
and the first begotten of the dead, and the prince of the kings of the earth.
Unto him that loved us, and washed us from our sins in his own ***blood,***
Revelation 1:5

~~~~~

"There is a dearth of preaching on the ***blood*** of Christ. It is not a wonder to me there is so little victory, because we have not taught people to plead the ***blood,*** to stand on the ***blood,*** to believe in the value of this ***blood.*** Our preaching must take on the preaching of the ***blood*** so the confidence of the people can be restored in the value of the **blood** of Jesus Christ."

B.H. Clendennen

~~~~~

I am thankful today for the ***blood*** of Jesus. I'm also thankful that my pastor still teaches about the ***blood,*** and that we still sing songs about the ***blood.***

What can wash away my sin? Nothing but the ***blood*** of Jesus.
What can make me whole again? Nothing but the ***blood*** of Jesus.[2]

[2] Published in 1976. Words and music by Robert Lowry, 1826-1899

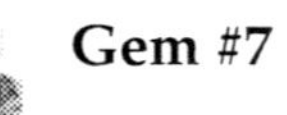

Gem #7 **January 7**

*And God said unto Noah,... **Make thee an ark of gopher wood;** rooms shalt thou make... and shalt pitch it within and without with pitch. Thus did Noah; according to all that God commanded him, so did he.*

Genesis 6:13-14, 22

*And the Lord said unto [Ananias], Arise, and go into the street which is called Straight, and **enquire in the house of Judas for one called Saul, of Tarsus**: for, behold, he prayeth, Then Ananias answered, Lord, I have heard by many of this man, how much evil he hath done to thy saints at Jerusalem:*

Acts 9:11, 13

*While Peter thought on the vision, the Spirit said unto him, Behold, **three men seek thee. Arise therefore, ...and go with them,** doubting nothing: for I have sent them. And he said unto [Cornelius' household], Ye know how that it is an unlawful thing for a man that is a Jew to keep company, or come unto one of another nation; but God hath shewed me that I should not call any man common or unclean.*

Acts 10:19-20, 28

~~~~~

Noah obeyed all of God's instructions for building the Ark and preparing food for his family and the animals even though he had never seen rain (Hebrews 11:7). No doubt he was ridiculed by his friends for his actions. ***Ananias obeyed*** God's voice to go and pray for Saul even though Saul was a well-known persecutor of Christians. ***Peter obeyed*** God's command to go to Cornelius' house and preach the Gospel to them even though it was against Jewish tradition to keep company with Gentiles. He even got called on the carpet for his actions when he returned home.

So what does it take today to be totally obedient to God? The Bible gives us examples of total obedience in spite of the ridicule of others, the possibility of imprisonment, or even the possibility of being reprimanded by Church authorities. We are commanded to
~~~~~

go into all the world and preach the Gospel to every creature. (Mark 16:15) It doesn't say to only preach when the weather is nice and it is convenient to do so. We are commanded to share the Gospel every time we have an opportunity. So on these cold, snowy mornings in the winter, my preference would be to stay inside and enjoy my warm house, yet the Word of God compels me to leave my comfort zone and teach my class at a local jail, for souls are perishing everyday without the Gospel, and I must tell everyone I can that there's hope in Jesus.

Gem #8 **Jan 8**

Then Peter said, ***Silver and gold have I none;***
but such as I have give I thee:
In the name of Jesus Christ of Nazareth rise up and walk.
And he leaping up stood, and walked, and entered with them
into the temple, walking, and leaping, and praising God.
Acts 3:6, 8

And [Moses] said, I beseech thee, ***shew me thy glory.***
Exodus 33;18

~~~~~

"The Apostles had no gold, but lots of glory.
We have lots of gold, but no glory."
Leonard Ravenhill

~~~~~

Many of today's churches put more emphasis on acquiring gold than on acquiring God's glory.

Lord Jesus, help me not to seek the riches of this world, but to be rich in the things of the Spirit which can change me and minister to the physical and spiritual needs of those around me.

Gem #9

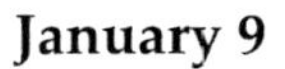

January 9

He chose David also his servant, and took him from the sheepfolds:
From following the ewes great with young he brought him
to feed Jacob his people, and Israel his inheritance.
*So he fed them according to the **integrity** of his heart;*
and guided them by the skilfulness of his hands.
Psalms 78:70-72

*Let **integrity** and uprightness preserve me; for I wait on thee.*
Psalms 25:21

*The **integrity** of the upright shall guide them:*
but the perverseness of transgressors shall destroy them.
Proverbs 11:3

*The just man walketh in his **integrity**: his children are blessed after him.*
Proverbs 20:7[3]

~~~~~

During my morning Bible reading of Psalms 78, the word ***integrity*** jumped out at me. I did some research on that word in the Bible and the dictionary. It means to "adhere to moral and ethical principles; be honest and sound in moral character." The Psalmist said that in times of trouble in our lives, our ***integrity*** will preserve us. David led Israel with ***integrity*** and skill. His son, Solomon wrote that ***integrity*** is a guide for the upright, and a lifestyle of ***integrity*** will bring blessings upon the children of the just man.

May my life be sound in moral and ethical principles and character so that my children and those I influence can follow that example and reap rich blessings from God.

---

[3] Scriptures for additional study: Genesis 20:5-6; 1 Kings 9:4; Job 2:3, 9; Job 27:5; Job 31:6; Psalms 7:8; Psalms 26:1, 11; Psalms 41:12; Proverbs 19:1.
~~~~~

Gem #10 **January 10**

For ever O LORD, thy ***word is settled*** *in heaven.*
Psalms 119:89

The grass withereth, the flower fadeth:
but the ***word of our God shall stand for ever.***
Isaiah 40:8

For verily I say unto you, Till heaven and earth pass, ***one jot or one tittle shall in no wise pass from the law****, till all be fulfilled.*
Matthew 5:18

Heaven and earth shall pass away,
but my ***words shall not pass away.***
Matthew 24:35; Mark 13:31; Luke 21:33

Being born again, not of corruptible seed, but of incorruptible,
by the ***word of God, which liveth and abideth for ever.***
For all flesh is as grass,
and all the glory of man as the flower of grass.
The grass withereth, and the flower thereof falleth away:
But the ***word of the Lord endureth for ever.***
And this is the word which by the gospel is preached unto you.
1 Peter 1:23-25

~~~~~

Men have tried to burn God's Word, outlaw it and water down its teachings, but it has outlasted all its detractors and continues to be the best-selling book of all times.

In a world of uncertainty, instability, broken promises and changing laws, I am thankful for the ***Word of God*** which never changes and contains everything I need to live a life pleasing unto God.
~~~~~

Gem #11 **January 11**

Blessed be God, even the Father of our Lord Jesus Christ,
the Father of mercies, and the ***God of all comfort;***
Who ***comforteth us*** *in all our tribulation,*
that we may be able to ***comfort them which are in any trouble,***
by the comfort wherewith we ourselves are comforted of God.
For as the sufferings of Christ abound in us,
so our consolation also aboundeth by Christ.
And whether we be afflicted,
it is for your ***consolation and salvation,***
which is effectual in the enduring of the same sufferings which we also suffer: or whether we be comforted,
it is for your ***consolation and salvation.***
2 Corinthians 1:3-6

~~~~~

God is my ***comfort*** in all of my tribulations and afflictions. However, it is my responsibility to endure those difficult times in such a way that they will result in the ***consolation and salvation*** of others who are watching me go through hard times. My hard times are actually object lessons to bring comfort and salvation to others who experience similar things. I never knew how to relate to someone who had lost a spouse to death until I lost mine. As a result, my experience of grieving and healing from that terrible loss has equipped me to empathize with others who are experiencing the same loss.

Who is watching you today?

May you exhibit those qualities of character that will bring comfort and salvation to others who are searching for answers to their difficult dilemmas in life.
~~~~~

Gem #12 **January 12**

Wait *on the Lord: be of good courage, and he shall strengthen thine heart:*
wait*, I say, on the Lord.*
Psalms 27:14

But they that ***wait*** *upon the LORD shall renew their strength;*
they shall mount up with wings as eagles; they shall run,
and not be weary; and they shall walk, and not faint.
Isaiah 40:31

~~~~~

"We'd like for God to work 'presto' (at a rapid rate) when the tempo of His plan may be 'largo' (slow and dignified). But God always moves to accomplish His purposes...with precise timing."
Don Wyrtzen

~~~~~

Waiting for God's timing is often difficult. Due to our "microwave mentality" and "time management" training, we want everything done quickly and efficiently. I constantly have to rein in my impatience and listen for that 'still, small voice' to say proceed, be still, listen, or forget that. So while I **wait** to see prayers answered and dreams come to pass, I will seek Him whom my soul loveth and serve Him to the best of my ability, for as I **wait** and spend time in His presence and in His Word, my strength, hope and faith is renewed.

~~~~~

Let all those that seek thee rejoice and be glad *in thee: and let such as love thy salvation say continually, Let God be magnified.*
Psalms 70:4
~~~~~

Gem #13 **January 13**

Confirming the souls of the disciples, and exhorting them to
continue in the faith...
Acts 14:22

For as the body without the spirit is dead,
so faith without works is dead also.
James 2:26

And beside this, giving all diligence, ***add*** *to your faith virtue;*
and to virtue knowledge; And to knowledge temperance;
and to temperance patience; and to patience godliness;
And to godliness brotherly kindness;
and to brotherly kindness charity.
For if these things be in you, and abound,
they make you that ye shall neither be barren nor unfruitful
in the knowledge of our Lord Jesus Christ.
2 Peter 1:5-8

~~~~~

It is not enough to simply believe in Jesus and become born again. That is only the beginning of the beautiful Christian walk. The Apostles exhorted the converts to ***continue in the faith*** and add moral characteristics to their lifestyle. If these added characteristics abound in my life, then they will produce knowledge of the Lord that bears fruit. Even though it's been over 49 years since my new birth occurred, it is still a daily requirement that I continue to add Biblical character traits to my faith. I'm working toward the goal of hearing my Lord say...

"Well done, thou good and faithful servant.
Enter thou into the joy of thy Lord."
~~~~~

Gem #14 **January 14**

Bless the Lord, O my soul, and forget not all his ***benefits****:*
Who ***forgiveth*** *all thine iniquities;*
who ***healeth*** *all thy diseases;*
Who ***redeemeth*** *thy life from destruction;*
who ***crowneth*** *thee with lovingkindness and tender mercies;*
Who ***satisfieth*** *thy mouth with good things;*
so that thy youth is renewed like the eagle's.
The Lord is merciful and gracious, slow to anger,
and plenteous in mercy.
He hath not dealt with us after our sins;
nor rewarded us according to our iniquities.
For as the heaven is high above the earth,
so great is his mercy toward them that fear him.
Like as a father pitieth his children,
so the Lord pitieth them that fear him.
But the mercy of the Lord is from everlasting to everlasting
Upon them that fear him, and his righteousness unto children's children;
To such as keep his covenant,
and to those that remember his commandments to do them.
Psalms 103:2-5, 8, 10-11, 13, 17-18

~~~~~

In the secular world, jobs are often chosen based on the ***benefits*** they have to offer. To receive those ***benefits***, the employee must perform in accordance with all the rules in the employee handbook. In the same way, living for God has tremendous ***benefits***, but God doesn't hand them out to just anyone who asks for them. To be eligible for His ***benefits***, one must reverence God, know what His Employee Handbook says, and obey its rules. I am thankful today that I was hired (Born Again) by the Master Employer, and that He gave me His Employee Handbook (The Holy Bible). I read it every day to guarantee that I can reap its ***benefits*** by being in compliance with its regulations.
~~~~~

Gem #15 **January 15**

Thou wilt shew me the path of life: in ***thy presence*** *is fulness of joy;*
at thy right hand there are pleasures for evermore.
Psalms 16:11

Let us come before ***his presence*** *with thanksgiving,*
and make a joyful noise unto him with psalms.
Psalms 95:2

Serve the LORD with gladness:
come before ***his presence*** *with singing.*
Psalms 100:2

Surely the righteous shall give thanks unto thy name:
the upright shall dwell in ***thy presence****.*
Psalms 140:13

Glory and honour are in ***his presence****;*
strength and gladness are in his place.
1 Chronicles 16:27

~~~~~

We Americans spend our lives working, shopping, traveling, making friends, eating, dieting, marrying, divorcing, starting families, building homes, or acquiring more things as we search for something to bring lasting joy, peace or pleasure. But when all is said and done, nothing thrills like being in the ***presence of God***. In His presence I receive strength and find joy, hope, renewal, direction, peace, pleasure, satisfaction and fulfillment.

Have you spent time in His presence today?
~~~~~

Gem #16 **January 16**

Put on the ***whole armour*** *of God,*
that ye may be able to stand against the wiles of the devil.
For we wrestle not against flesh and blood,
but against principalities, against powers, against the rulers of the darkness of this world, against spiritual wickedness in high places.
Wherefore take unto you the ***whole armour*** *of God,*
that ye may be able to withstand in the evil day,
and having done all, to stand. Stand therefore,
having your loins girt about with ***truth****,*
and having on the ***breastplate of righteousness****;*
And your feet shod with the preparation of the ***gospel of peace****;*
Above all, taking the ***shield of faith****,*
wherewith ye shall be able to quench all the fiery darts of the wicked.
And take the ***helmet of salvation****,*
and the ***sword of the Spirit****, which is the word of God:*
Praying *always with all prayer and supplication in the Spirit,*
and watching thereunto with all perseverance and
supplication for all saints;

Ephesians 6:11-18

~~~~~

The enemy knows that his time is short, and he is going about as a roaring lion to devour anyone who isn't properly armed to recognize him and his subtle tactics. Some people pick and choose which pieces of ***armor*** they want to wear, but only the ***whole armor*** will protect us from deception. I love those quiet moments at the beginning of each day when I can get into the Word and spend time in prayer to arm myself for whatever the day brings.

Have you armed yourself
with God's Whole Armor before facing your day?
~~~~~

Gem #17 **January 17**

The righteous shall ***flourish*** *like the palm tree:*
he shall grow like a cedar in Lebanon.
Those that be planted in the house of the Lord shall flourish
in the courts of our God. They shall still bring forth fruit in old age;
they shall be ***fat and flourishing;***
Psalms 92:12-14

The cedars of Lebanon are mentioned over 20 times in the Bible. These trees are evergreen and can grow up to 130 feet tall, with a trunk up to 8 feet in diameter. That is about as tall as a 9-story building.

Here are some of the reasons that the cedars of Lebanon have remained popular through the centuries. They have durable, decay-resistant, sweet-scented wood, which has been used as a building material and for constructing furniture. (My mother had a cedar chest when I was growing up, and I always loved opening it and smelling the scent of the wood.) The wood and oils of this tree are also naturally repellent to moths which made cedar-lined closets popular to protect clothing from getting moth holes eaten in them. Its seed oils have been used to control mosquito larvae. Extracts of its resin have antimicrobial properties which inhibit the growth of disease-producing micro-organisms, and its sap has been used to protect wooden structures against insects and fungi, as well as to treat various diseases.

Palm trees, on the other hand, grow straight up with their branches clustered in the top of the tree. Some of them even grow taller than the mighty cedars. Colombia's national tree is the tallest palm in the world, reaching up to 197 feet or comparable to a 14-story building. Palms have one deep tap root for nourishment purposes and smaller horizontal roots to keep the tree stable.

Consider these spiritual applications from the lessons of the palm and cedar trees.

- The sweet fragrance of our worship is pleasing to God and is a natural repellent to the attacks of the enemy.
- The strength of the mighty cedars is acquired through spending time in prayer and study of God's Word (1 Chronicles 16:28).
- The cedars grow in groups rather than in isolation. Assembling in God's house with other saints for worship and teaching of the Word strengthens and protects us from predators that prey on the isolated ones.
- Like the palm trees, Christians push their one tap root deeply into God's Word for nourishment and reach up toward God. Their shallow root system keeps them from getting too attached to the world, for they realize that this world is not their home.

Bible-teaching pastors and churches produce righteous saints who flourish and continue to produce fruit even in their old age. What a promise!

~~~~~

"Churches which do not manifest love become sickly and dwindle.
Churches which ***flourish*** in the love of God
are healthy and prolific."
Ken Raggio

~~~~~

Are you planted in a Church whose members are FAT and FLOURISHING?

Gem #18 **January 18**

There is a city, a place called **Heaven**.
God made it with His loving hands.
There flowers bloom, they bloom forever.
It's such a wonderful, beautiful land.
Wanda Phillips

~~~~~

These all died in faith, not having received the promises, but having seen them afar off, and were persuaded of them, and embraced them, and confessed that they were strangers and pilgrims on the earth. For they that say such things declare plainly that they seek a country. And truly, if they had been mindful of that country from whence they came out, they might have had opportunity to have returned. But now they desire a better country, that is, an heavenly: wherefore God is not ashamed to be called their God: for ***He hath prepared for them a city.***
Hebrews 11:13-16

In my Father's house are many mansions: if it were not so, I would have told you. ***I go to prepare a place for you.*** *And if I go and prepare a place for you, I will come again, and receive you unto myself; that where I am, there ye may be also.*
John 14:2-3

~~~~~

My thoughts this morning have been on ***Heaven,*** for it was on this day in 2001 that my husband left this world to join the ranks of those who have finished their earthly race and have arrived at their heavenly home to spend eternity with their Lord and Saviour, Jesus Christ. The song above is one I haven't heard since I was a teenager, but it expresses the longing that I have for a city called Heaven that has been prepared for the Church. I do not want to be so attached to the things of this life that I have no desire to leave them for the life to come.

I am dreaming today of that place of beauty, peace, safety and eternal fellowship with my Lord and His Saints.

Gem #19 **January 19**

And these words, which I command thee this day,
shall be in thine heart: And thou shalt ***teach*** *them diligently*
unto thy children, and shalt ***talk*** *of them when thou sittest*
in thine house, and when thou walkest by the way, and
when thou liest down, and when thou risest up.
Deuteronomy 6:6-7

Give thanks unto the Lord,
*...**make known** his deeds among the people.*
*Sing unto him, ...**talk** ye of all his wondrous works.*
*...**shew forth** from day to day his salvation. **Declare** his glory*
among the heathen; his marvellous works among all nations.
1 Chronicles 16:8-9, 23-24

I will sing of the mercies of the LORD for ever:
with my mouth will I make known
thy faithfulness to all generations.
Psalms 89:1

O give thanks unto the Lord;
*...**make known** his deeds among the people.*
*Sing unto him, ...**talk** ye of all his wondrous works.*
Psalms 105:1-2

~~~~~

So much of our talk is related to the daily events of life, yet Moses instructed the people to ***teach*** God's Words to their children and ***talk*** about them throughout the day. David continued that theme numerous times in the Psalms. God loves to hear His people brag on Him. There is power and energy in those conversations.

Do you need to be energized today? Start talking about the goodness of the Lord!
~~~~~

 **Gem #20** **January 20**

But it is good for me to ***draw near*** *to God: I have put my trust in the Lord GOD, that I may declare all thy works.*
Psalms 73:28

Draw nigh *to God, and he will draw nigh to you...*
James 4:8

Let us ***draw near*** *with a true heart in full assurance of faith...*
Hebrews 10:22

~~~~~

I am Thine, O Lord, I have heard Thy voice,
And it told Thy love to me;
But I long to rise in the arms of faith,
And be closer drawn to Thee.
Draw me nearer, nearer blessed Lord
To the cross where Thou hast died.
Draw me nearer, nearer, nearer blessed Lord
To Thy precious bleeding side.

~~~~~

Fanny Crosby wrote this hymn in 1875 while visiting in the home of William H. Doane in Cincinnati. During the family discussion of the blessedness of enjoying the nearness of God, sudden inspiration came to Fanny, and she dictated every line of the song "I Am Thine, O Lord." Shortly afterward, her friend, Mr. Doane composed the music for the song which has blessed many through the years.[4]

The scripture warning, *"Let him that thinketh he standeth, take heed lest he fall"* (1 Corinthians 10:12) requires me to make a fresh consecration to God every day.

I am hungry today to draw nearer to Jesus than to the things of life that pull so strongly on me.

---

[4] Kenneth W. Osbeck, *Amazing Grace: 366 Inspiring Hymn Stories for Daily Devotions* (Grand Rapids, MI: Kregel Publications, 1990) 232.

 **Gem #21** **January 21**

I was glad when they said unto me,
Let us go into the ***house of the Lord.***
Psalms 122:1

How amiable are thy ***tabernacles,*** *O Lord of hosts!*
My soul longeth, yea, even fainteth for the ***courts of the Lord:***
my heart and my flesh crieth out for the living God.
Psalms 84:1-2

I will declare thy name unto my brethren:
in the midst of the ***congregation*** *will I praise thee.*
Psalms 22:22

Not forsaking the assembling of ourselves together,
as the manner of some is; but exhorting one another:
and so much the more, as ye see the day approaching.
Hebrews 10:25

~~~~~

Sunday is the day that is typically set aside for worship in the United States. I love going to the house of God where I can worship with the family of God and hear words of instruction from my Pastor. My 4-year-old grandson loves Sundays because in his words, "I get to go and see Jesus." As long as we have the freedom to worship in this country, I will be in the house of God every time service is scheduled. These meetings are highlights in my week.

Are you glad when it is time to go into the House of the Lord?
~~~~~

Gem #22 **January 22**

I cried unto God with my voice,… and he gave ear unto me.
In the day of my trouble I sought the Lord...
*I **remembered** God, and was troubled:*
I complained, and my spirit was overwhelmed. Selah.
...I am so troubled that I cannot speak.
I have considered the days of old, the years of ancient times.
*I **call to remembrance** my song in the night:*
I commune with mine own heart: and my spirit made diligent search.
Will the Lord cast off for ever? and will he be favourable no more?
Is his mercy clean gone for ever? doth his promise fail for evermore?
Hath God forgotten to be gracious?
hath he in anger shut up his tender mercies? Selah.
And I said, This is my infirmity:
***But I will remember** the years of the right hand of the most High.*
***I will remember** the works of the Lord:*
*surely **I will remember** thy wonders of old.*
***I will meditate** also of all thy work, and **talk** of thy doings.*
Psalms 77:1-12

*My tongue also shall **talk of thy righteousness** all the day long…*
Psalms 71:24

~~~~~

In times of sickness, financial reversals, betrayal, losses or other overwhelming situations of life, it is easy to complain and ask God if He is aware of our troubles. Asaph found himself in this dilemma, but finally he ***remembered*** God's strength, His works, and His wonders in the past. He resolved to ***meditate*** on these things and ***talk*** about them to others. ***Remembering, meditating, and talking*** about God's goodness and mighty acts are indisputable remedies for the overwhelming stresses of life.

Are you in the mulligrubs today? Try remembering, meditating and talking about God's past goodness in your life. God loves that kind of talk, and He will lift you up.
~~~~~

Gem #23 **January 23**

Whatsoever thy hand findeth to do, do it with thy might;
for there is no work, nor device, nor knowledge, nor wisdom,
in the grave, whither thou goest.
Ecclesiastes 9:10

Wherefore do ye spend money for that which is not bread?
and your ***labour*** *for that which satisfieth not?*
hearken diligently unto me, and eat ye that which is good,
and let your soul delight itself in fatness.
Isaiah 55:2

Labour not for the meat which perisheth,
but for that meat which endureth unto everlasting life,
which the Son of man shall give unto you:
for him hath God the Father sealed.
John 6:27

~~~~~

We Americans are consumed with productivity, whether it is in our work or in our play. We work a job all day and come home exhausted. We go on vacation and try to cram every bit of sightseeing and entertainment we can into the time allotted and come home exhausted. We idolize our sports heroes and exhaust ourselves cheering for their success. The Bible does tell us to ***work with all our might,*** but Jesus very specifically taught that our priority in work should be toward accomplishing things that will have eternal value.

Does my daily to-do list include time for study of His Word, prayer for others, for direction and insight into His Word, or time to help others who are struggling? Do I spend my hard-earned money on things that will produce eternal rewards?

We will give account of our stewardship over the time, talents and treasures we have been given.
~~~~~

Gem #24 **January 24**

"He who runs from God in the morning
will scarcely find Him the rest of the day."
John Bunyan (1628-1688)

"Rose early to seek God and found Him whom my soul loveth.
Who would not rise early to meet such company?"
Robert Murray McCheyne (1813-1843)

~~~~~

O God, thou art my God; ***early will I seek thee:***
my soul thirsteth for thee, my flesh longeth for thee
in a dry and thirsty land, where no water is;
Psalms 63:1

I love them that love me;
and those that ***seek me early*** *shall find me.*
Proverbs 8:17

With my soul have I desired thee in the night;
yea, with my spirit within me will I ***seek thee early****...*
Isaiah 26:9

~~~~~

What is the first thing you do when you awake each day?

God is looking for those who have developed a daily habit of seeking Him early in their day.

I am starting my day by seeking for the "fountain of living water" to quench the thirst of my soul.

Gem #25 **January 25**

Blessed is the man whom thou choosest, *and causest to approach unto thee, that he may dwell in thy courts: we shall be satisfied with the goodness of thy house, even of thy holy temple.*

Psalms 65:4

For many are called, but ***few are chosen.***

Matthew 22:14

\~~~~~

I not only want to be called, but I also want to be one of the select few who experience the blessings of being ***chosen*** to approach God and linger in His presence while I learn the secrets of His nature that only intimacy can teach.

Have you been *chosen*?

Gem # 26 **January 26**

And ***ye are complete in him***,
which is the head of all principality and power:

Colossians 2:10

Epaphras, who is one of you, a servant of Christ, saluteth you, always labouring fervently for you in prayers, that ye may stand perfect and ***complete in all the will of God.***

Colossians 4:12

\~~~~~

Lord Jesus, when I reach out to people or things to find fulfillment, help me to remember that ***You are the one who completes me,*** and relationship with You brings true satisfaction and fulfillment. Let me also be an intercessor who prays for others to find their perfection and completion in You.

 **Gem #27** **January 27**

God be merciful unto us, and bless us;
and cause his face to shine upon us; Selah.
That thy way may be known upon earth,
thy saving health among all nations.
Let the people praise thee, O God;
let all the people praise thee.
O let the nations be glad and sing for joy:
for ***thou shalt judge the people righteously,***
and govern the nations upon earth. Selah.
Let the people praise thee, O God; let all the people praise thee.
Then shall the earth yield her increase; and God,
even our own God, shall bless us. God shall bless us;
and all the ends of the earth shall fear him.
Psalms 67:1-7

And ***the LORD shall be king over all the earth:***
in that day shall there be one LORD, and his name one.
Zechariah 14:9

~~~~~

I wonder what it would be like for all the earth to praise God and experience His ways, His saving health, bountiful crops, and righteous judgment instead of judgment based on who has the most money or the best attorney.

One day soon we will experience the blessings promised in this psalm when Jesus returns to rule this earth, and at that time, His true identity will be revealed for all the world to know. That will be a Happy Day!

Even so, COME LORD JESUS!!!
~~~~~

Gem #28 **January 28**

Praise ye the Lord. Praise, O ye servants of the Lord,
praise the name of the Lord. ***Blessed be the name of the Lord***
from this time forth and for evermore.
From the rising of the sun unto the going down of the same
the Lord's name is to be praised.
Psalms 113:1-3

I will extol thee, my God, O king; and ***I will bless thy name***
for ever and ever. Every day will I bless thee;
and I will praise thy name for ever and ever.
Psalms 145:1-2

~~~~~

How sweet the Name of Jesus sounds.
Blessed be the Name of the Lord.
It soothes my sorrows, heals my wounds.
Blessed be the Name of the Lord.

Cho. Blessed be the Name, blessed be the Name,
Blessed be the Name of the Lord. Blessed be the Name,
blessed be the Name, Blessed be the Name of the Lord.[5]

~~~~~

This little song is on my mind this morning. So much is going on in the world around me that could provoke fear, worry or anger, but today I choose to ***bless the name of Jesus*** rather than curse the darkness. My relationship with Jesus will guide me through the troubling times in which I live. ***Blessed be the name of the Lord.***

---

[5] There are various versions of the verses to the song *"Blessed Be The Name"* in modern hymnbooks. Some attribute the earliest words to Charles Wesley in 1739. Other hymnbooks credit the verses to W. H. Clark. All sources I consulted seem to credit the composition of the chorus to Ralph E. Hudson, 1843-1901.

Gem #29 **January 29**

*Let my prayer be set forth before thee as **incense**;*
and the lifting up of my hands as the evening sacrifice.
Psalms 141:2

For from the rising of the sun even unto the going down of the same my name shall be great among the Gentiles;
*and in every place **incense shall be offered unto my name**,*
and a pure offering: for my name shall be great among the heathen,
saith the Lord of hosts.
Malachi 1:11

*And the smoke of the **incense**, which came with the prayers of the saints,*
ascended up before God out of the angel's hand.
Revelation 8:4

~~~~~

Incense was an important component of the Tabernacle and Temple worship in Bible days. God gave Moses very specific instructions for the composition of the incense that was to be used on the Altar of Incense when the priests entered the Holy Place to worship. It could only be used for worshiping the one true God. Dozens of times the Old Testament talks about God's anger with Israel for offering incense to other gods. Then the prophet, Malachi prophesied of the day when God's name, JESUS, would be great among the Gentiles, and they would offer ***pure incense*** (worship) to Him.

I am thankful that I, as a Gentile, have the opportunity to personally know the name of the God of Israel. I pray today that my worship and praise to my King, JESUS will be pure and acceptable in His sight.
~~~~~

Gem #30 **January 30**

He is the ***rock****, His work is perfect: for all his ways are judgment: a God of truth and without iniquity, just and right is He.*
Deuteronomy 32:4

The Lord is my ***rock****, and my fortress, and my deliverer; my God, my strength, in whom I will trust…*
Psalms 18:2

...lay hold upon the hope set before us. Which hope we have as an ***anchor*** *of the soul, both sure and stedfast...*
Hebrews 6:18-19

~~~~~

In times like these, we need a Savior.
In times like these, we need an **anchor**.
Be very sure, Be very sure,
Your anchor holds and grips the solid **Rock**.

This **Rock** is Jesus, Yes He's the One.
This **Rock** is Jesus, The only One. Be very sure,
Be very sure, Your anchor holds and grips the solid **Rock**.[6]

~~~~~

The above little song is on my mind today. During my morning devotions and research through the Word, I discovered over 30 scriptures that referred to God as a Rock or an unmovable, unshakeable foundation. I am so thankful that in these disturbing times in which we live, I can place my confidence in the ***Rock, Christ Jesus,*** whose unchanging teachings have **anchored** me and given me hope that I can weather the storms of life and safely arrive at my eternal destination.

---

[6] "In Times Like These" was written in 1944 by Ruth Caye Jones, minister's wife and mother of five children as she read 2 Timothy 3:1 and prayed about the perilous times brought on the world by World War II.

Gem #31 **January 31**

Now I beseech you, brethren, by the name of our Lord Jesus Christ, that ye all speak the same thing, and that there be no divisions among you; but that ye be perfectly joined ***together*** *in the same mind and in the same judgment.*

1 Corinthians 1:10

For we are labourers ***together*** *with God: ye are God's husbandry, ye are God's building.*

1 Corinthians 3:9

Only let your conversation be as it becometh the gospel of Christ: ...that ye stand fast in one spirit, with one mind striving ***together*** *for the faith of the Gospel;*

Philippians 1:27

For the Lord himself shall descend from heaven with a shout, with the voice of the archangel, and with the trump of God: and the dead in Christ shall rise first: Then we which are alive and remain shall be caught up ***together*** *with them in the clouds, to meet the Lord in the air: and so shall we ever be with the Lord.*

1 Thessalonians 4:16-17

~~~~~

God didn't call us to work alone. We are part of a body of believers, and when every member knows its place, the body functions like a well-oiled machine, accomplishing God's will on earth.

It is time to forget our differences and unite into a powerful body of believers in one spirit, with one mind, working ***together*** to spread the faith of the Gospel to everyone, for after the work of the Church is accomplished, all the dead and the living will be caught up ***together*** to meet the Lord in the air, and they will forever be with Him.
~~~~~

Gem #32 **February 1**

Lord, who shall abide in thy tabernacle? who shall dwell in thy holy hill?
He that ***walketh uprightly****, and worketh righteousness,*
and speaketh the truth in his heart. He that backbiteth not with his tongue,
nor doeth evil to his neighbour, nor taketh up a reproach against
his neighbour. In whose eyes a vile person is contemned;
but he honoureth them that fear the Lord.
He that sweareth to his own hurt, and changeth not.
He that putteth not out his money to usury, nor taketh reward
against the innocent. He that doeth these things shall never be moved.
Psalms 15:1-5

For the Lord God is a sun and shield: the Lord will give grace and glory: no good thing will he withhold from them that ***walk uprightly****.*
Psalms 84:11

He layeth up sound wisdom for the righteous:
he is a buckler to them that ***walk uprightly.***
Proverbs 2:7

He that ***walketh uprightly*** *walketh surely:...*
Proverbs 10:9

~~~~~

The Bible speaks often of the benefits promised to those who ***walk uprightly***. Some of these benefits include the privilege of dwelling in God's Holy Hill, the gift of grace and glory, protection, and firm ground to prevent slipping off the path God has chosen for those privileged ones to walk upon. Every good thing in God's storehouse is available to those who walk uprightly, and He will not withhold good things from them. If I want to receive these benefits, I need to diligent in studying my Bible so I can learn the conditions I must obey in order to receive them.

Are you willing to *walk the walk* in order to receive the rewards?
~~~~~

Gem #33 **February 2**

Mine eyes shall be upon the faithful of the land,
that they may dwell with me: he that
***walketh in a perfect way**, he shall serve me.*
Psalms 101:6

Blessed are the undefiled in the way, who
***walk in the law of the Lord.** Blessed are they that keep*
his testimonies, and that seek him with the whole heart.
*They also do no iniquity: they **walk in his ways.***
Psalms 119:1-3

Blessed is every one that feareth the LORD;
*that **walketh in his ways**.*
Psalms 128:1

*He that **walketh in his uprightness** feareth the LORD:*
but he that is perverse in his ways despiseth him.
Proverbs 14:2

*...a man of understanding **walketh uprightly**.*
Proverbs 15:21

*Better is the poor that **walketh in his uprightness**,*
than he that is perverse in his ways…
*Whoso **walketh uprightly** shall be saved...*
Proverbs 28:6,18

~~~~~

God promises a blessing and salvation to those who ***walk in His laws*** and seek Him with their whole heart. This understanding of His ways doesn't come naturally. It requires spending time in His presence and disciplined and committed study of His Word. It's time to say no to things that distract us from knowing God and knowing His Word. Our eternal destiny is at stake.
~~~~~

Gem #34 **February 3**

Exalt ye the Lord our God, and worship at his footstool; for ***he is holy****.*
Exalt the Lord our God, and worship at his holy hill;
for ***the Lord our God is holy.***
Psalms 99:5, 9

\~\~\~\~\~

"The ugly reality of sin fades away when we lose our vision of the dazzling **holiness of God** (Isaiah 6). In our modern perception, the shed blood seems cannibalistic and barbaric, the price of forgiveness is cheapened, and the Good News is relegated to the 'religion' section of the local newspaper. Psalm 99 inspires us to recover the truth of God's character. He alone is **holy** – perfectly pure and worthy of profound reverence."
Don Wyrtzen[7]

Gem #35 **February 4**

And when they had ***prayed****, the place was shaken where they were assembled together; and they were all filled with the Holy Ghost, and they spake the word of God with boldness.*
Acts 4:31

...pray one for another, that ye may be healed.
The ***effectual fervent prayer*** *of a righteous man availeth much.*
James 5:16

\~\~\~\~\~

"Men may spurn our appeals, reject our message,
oppose our arguments, despise our persons,
but they are helpless against our **prayers**."
J. Sidlow Baxter

---

[7] Don Wyrtzen, *A Musician Looks at the Psalms* (Grand Rapids, MI: Daybreak Books, 1988) 267.

Gem #36 **February 5**

For in the time of trouble he shall ***hide me*** *in his pavilion:*
in the secret of his tabernacle shall he ***hide me****;*
he shall set me up upon a rock.
Psalms 27:5

Thou art my ***hiding place;*** *thou shalt preserve me from trouble;*
thou shalt compass me about with songs of deliverance. Selah.
Psalms 32:7

Thou art my ***hiding place*** *and my shield:*
I hope in thy word.
Psalms 119:114

~~~~~

I've found a hiding place, a blessed hiding place
I've found a hiding place, a blessed hiding place
There's glory in my soul, the hallelujahs roll
For since my Jesus came, I'm under His control
He keeps me night and day, He answers when I pray
And from the raging storms, to Him I steal away
I hear no tempter's knock, I feel no tempest shock
For in the solid Rock, I've found a hiding place.[8]

~~~~~

One of the timeless games that children love to play is "hide and seek." I played it as a child, and now my grandchildren enjoy playing it when they get together. As long as they are hiding, they are safe from the one who is trying to find them. Many times in life, we may feel like we are being chased by sickness, financial reverses, or heartaches and troubles of every description. It is in those times that God's Word promises the security of a hiding place in God. We can run straight to Him and find refuge and preservation from the disappointments and hurts of life as well as from attacks by the enemy of our soul.

---

[8] *"I've Found a Hiding Place"* from the Cathedrals' 1981 album, "Colors of His Love"

Gem #37 **February 6**

If we confess our sins, he is faithful and just to ***forgive*** *us our sins, and to cleanse us from all unrighteousness.*
1 John 1:9

Remember not the sins of my youth, nor my transgressions: according to thy ***mercy*** *remember thou me for thy goodness' sake, O LORD.*
Psalms 25:7

But thou, O Lord, art a God full of compassion, and gracious, long suffering, and plenteous in ***mercy*** *and truth.*
Psalms 86:5

For as the heaven is high above the earth, so ***great is his mercy*** *toward them that fear him.*
Psalms 103:11

It is of the Lord's ***mercies*** *that we are not consumed, because his compassions fail not. They are* ***new every morning****: great is thy faithfulness.*
Lamentations 3:22-23

~~~~~

If the Lord wanted to, He could snuff us out the moment we sin against His laws, but His ***mercy*** gives us a chance to repent, and once repentance takes place, He not only ***forgives***, but He also **cleanses** us from the sins. When we maintain a lifestyle of repentance after doing wrong, we can wake up every morning with a clean slate. I am thankful for His ***mercy*** and faithfulness to keep His Word IF I do my part.

~~~~~

"Prayer is the midwife of mercy, that helps to bring it forth."
Matthew Henry

Gem #38 **February 7**

The Lord is my shepherd; I shall not want.
***He maketh me to lie down** in green pastures:*
*he leadeth me beside the still waters. **He restoreth my soul**:*
he leadeth me in the paths of righteousness for his name's sake.
Psalms 23:1-3

It is vain for you to rise up early, to sit up late,
to eat the bread of sorrows:
*for so **he giveth his beloved sleep.***
Psalms 127:2

~~~~~

"Take rest: a field that has rested gives a bountiful crop."
Ovid

We Americans live our lives on the edge, cramming as much as we can into each day and neglecting the ***restorative power of rest***. Sometimes our bodies just can't go anymore, and we are forced to take time out and **rest**. I tend to work hard all day and burn the midnight oil when deadlines hang over my head; then eventually, exhaustion or sometimes sickness will force me to STOP and take care of myself. When I have one of those days, I've learned that if I can spend some time in prayer and rest during the day and also get a good night of sleep, I will wake up feeling refreshed. The first words out of my mouth when I open my eyes will be, "Thank you Jesus for the refreshing sense of your presence and the restoration I feel in my body."

Do not forget the importance of taking time out for rest and restoration. It will be time well-spent.
~~~~~

Gem #39 **February 8**

*Therefore was the **wrath of the Lord** kindled against his people,*
*insomuch that **he abhorred** [despised, rejected, hated] his own inheritance.*
And he gave them into the hand of the heathen;
and they that hated them ruled over them.
Psalms 106:40-41

And if some of the branches be broken off, and thou,
being a wild olive tree, wert grafted in among them,
and with them partakest of the root and fatness of the olive tree;
Boast not against the branches…
For if God spared not the natural branches,
***take heed** lest he also spare not thee.*
*Behold therefore the **goodness and severity** of God:*
*on them which fell, severity; but toward thee, goodness, **IF** thou continue*
in his goodness: otherwise thou also shalt be cut off.
Romans 11:17-18, 21-22

~~~~~

During a recent devotional reading in Psalms 106, I began to think about the fickle devotion of Israel toward God. Their relationship with Him was on again/off again throughout hundreds of years, and when God had had enough, He would reject them and deliver them into the hands of their enemies. Sometimes we Christians develop the same lackadaisical approach to our relationship with God. We may think that because God rejected natural Israel, we can live any way we please and remain in the Church. However, Paul taught the Romans that God will not show any favoritism to the Gentile branches that have been grafted in. We are still required to obey God's laws if we want to remain in His favor. I am eager to be one of God's favorites, so I am searching the Word daily to learn more of the things that make Him happy. Then I can continue being a recipient of God's goodness by applying the teachings I discover in His Word.
~~~~~

Gem #40 **February 9**

They soon forgat his works; they ***waited not*** *for his counsel:*
But lusted exceedingly in the wilderness,
and tempted God in the desert.
And he gave them their request; but sent leanness into their soul.
Psalms 106:13-15

Wait *on the Lord: be of good courage,*
and he shall strengthen thine heart:
Wait*, I say, on the Lord.*
Psalms 27:14

Truly my soul ***waiteth*** *upon God: from him cometh my salvation.*
Psalms 62:1

I ***wait*** *for the LORD, my soul doth* ***wait****,*
and in his word do I hope.
Psalms 130:5

But they that ***wait*** *upon the Lord shall renew their strength;*
they shall mount up with wings as eagles; they shall run, and not be weary; and they shall walk, and not faint.
Isaiah 40:31

~~~~~

I wonder how many times we badger God in prayer to give us something we desperately want, and He finally gives it to us even though it wasn't His best plan for us. Then later we say, If only I had ***waited***! I do not want God to send leanness into my soul and cause me to miss out on the abundance He would've given me to fulfill His divine destiny for my life if I had only ***waited***.

Teach me Lord to *wait*.
~~~~~

 **Gem #41** **February 10**

For [Abraham] looked for a city which hath foundations, whose builder and maker is God. These all died in faith, not having received the promises, but having seen them afar off, and were persuaded of them, and embraced them, and confessed that they were ***strangers and pilgrims on the earth****.*
But now they desire a better country, that is, an heavenly:
wherefore God is not ashamed to be called their God:
for he hath prepared for them a city.
Hebrews 11:10, 13, 16

~~~~~

I'm Longing For Home

I'm only a pilgrim and stranger in this unfriendly world that I roam
For Jesus who has brought me from darkness
Has promised me a heavenly home
In the Bible we read of a city whose builder and ruler is God
And someday when this life is over,
It's beautiful sights we'll behold.
I'm longing for home for the sun's going down
I want to go where sweet rest can be found
I'm just about through with this old house of clay
I'm leaving this world for glory someday.[9]

~~~~~

The old song above was sung by all my cousins and me at my grandmother's funeral. As I read the news and see things going on around me, I get very weary of the violence, increasing hostility against Christians and blatant disregard for the laws of God. I long for a world where I'm surrounded by the people of God and the glory of God. Someday soon, I will see God and many friends and family who have already arrived in His presence. O Happy day!

---

[9] "I'm Longing For Home," by O.S. Davis and Rupert Cravens, © Stamps Quartet Music, BMI.

Gem #42 **February 11**

*The **fear of the LORD** is the beginning of wisdom: and the knowledge of the holy is understanding.*
Proverbs 9:10

*The **fear of the Lord** tendeth to life: and he that hath it shall abide satisfied; he shall not be visited with evil.*
Proverbs 19:23

*The **fear of the Lord** is the beginning of wisdom: a good understanding have all they that do his commandments…*
Psalms 111:10

*The secret of the LORD is with them that **fear him**; and he will shew them his covenant.*
Psalms 25:14

*Come, ye children, hearken unto me: I will teach you the **fear of the Lord.***
Psalms 34:11

~~~~~

The *fear of the Lord* requires that I have a deep reverence for God and obey His commandments. It brings life, wisdom, satisfaction, and knowledge of holy things to me. God even shares His secrets with those who fear Him. I am compelled to teach these things to my children so that they too can be blessed with the good things of God.[10]

[10] Scriptures for further study of this topic: Deut. 6:2; 8:6; 10:12; 14:23; 17:19; 28:58-59; 31:12; Josh. 4:24; 24:14; 1 Sam. 11:7; 12:14; 1 Ki. 18:3, 12; 2 Ki. 4:1; 17:28-39; 2 Chron. 14:14; 17:10; 19:7-9; 20:29; Job 28:28; Psa. 19:9; 22:23; 33:8, 18; 34:7; 96:9; 102:15; 103:17; 135:20; Prov. 1:7, 29; 2:5; 8:13; 10:27; 14:26-27; 15:16, 33; 16:6; 22:4; 23:17; Isa. 2:10, 19, 21; 8:13; 11:2-3; 33:6; 59:19; Jer. 26:19; Hos. 3:5; Jonah 1:9, 16; Hag. 1:12; Mal. 3:16; Acts 9:31
~~~~~

Gem #43 **February 12**

And the L*ORD said unto Moses, ...I will give thee tables of stone,*
and a ***law, and commandments*** *which I have written;*
that thou mayest teach them.
Exodus 24:12

This ***book of the law*** *shall not depart out of thy mouth; but thou shalt* ***meditate therein*** *day and night, that thou mayest* ***observe to do*** *according to all that is written therein: for then thou shalt make thy way prosperous, and then* ***thou shalt have good success****.*
Joshua 1:8

The ***law of the Lord*** *is perfect, converting the soul:*
the ***testimony of the Lord*** *is sure, making wise the simple.*
The ***statutes of the Lord*** *are right, rejoicing the heart:*
the ***commandment of the Lord*** *is pure, enlightening the eyes.*
The ***fear of the Lord*** *is clean, enduring for ever:*
the ***judgments of the Lord*** *are true and righteous altogether.*
More to be desired are they than gold, yea, than much fine gold:
sweeter also than honey and the honeycomb.
Moreover by them is thy servant warned:
and ***in keeping of them there is great reward****.*
Psalms 19:7-11

~~~~~

Unlike man's laws, ***God's laws*** are true and perfect and have the authority and power to convert man from his sinful nature into a nature like God. Keeping God's laws should be our greatest desire, for they have more value than gold, and those who teach them and keep them will ultimately receive a great reward. I can't begin to count the number of times throughout my life when words from that Holy Book have popped into my mind and given me the answer I needed at just the right time.

O how love I thy law! it is my meditation all the day.
Psalms 119:97
~~~~~

Gem #44 **February 13**

And the king [Rehoboam] answered the people roughly,
and ***forsook the old men's counsel*** *that they gave him;*
And spake to them after the counsel of the young men, saying,
My father made your yoke heavy, and I will add to your yoke…
1 Kings 12:13-14

Whereupon the king [Jeroboam] ***took counsel****, and made two calves of gold, and said unto them, It is too much for you to go up to Jerusalem: behold thy gods, O Israel, which brought thee up out of the land of Egypt.*
1 Kings 12:28

Blessed is the man that walketh not
in the ***counsel of the ungodly****,*
nor standeth in the way of sinners,
nor sitteth in the seat of the scornful.
But his delight is in the law of the LORD;
and in his law doth he meditate day and night.
Psalms 1:1-2

~~~~~

While teaching a Bible lesson on the kings of Israel at our county jail, I discussed the power of ***influence***. Rehoboam forsook the wise counsel of his elders and ripped apart the kingdom that had been ruled by kings for 120 years. Jeroboam, who led the rebellion against Rehoboam, followed counsel to forsake the worship of Jehovah and led 10 of the tribes of Israel into idolatry. 23 times the Bible mentions kings who walked after the "sins of Jeroboam." **For 193 years, Jeroboam's sins influenced the Northern Kingdom** until the Assyrians finally conquered them and brought them into captivity.

HOW WILL YOU USE YOUR INFLUENCE IN THIS LIFE?
It could mean life or death to succeeding generations.
Choose wisely.
People are watching and following you.
~~~~~

Gem #45 **February 14**

Give ear, O my people, to my law: incline your ears to the words of my mouth. I will open my mouth in a parable: I will utter dark sayings of old: Which we have heard and known, and ***our fathers have told us****. We will not hide them from their children,* ***shewing to the generation to come*** *the praises of the LORD, and his strength, and his wonderful works that he hath done. For he established a testimony in Jacob, and appointed a law in Israel,* ***which he commanded our fathers, that they should make them known to their children: That the generation to come might know them, even the children which should be born;*** *who should arise and* ***declare them to their children****: That they might set their hope in God, and* ***not forget the works of God, but keep his commandments****:*
Psalms 78:1-7

~~~~~

If the Gospel message and miracle ministry of the Apostles is to survive until the end of this age, it is ***urgent*** that we who are parents and grandparents ***tell our children and grandchildren*** about the history of the Church. It is not enough to simply tell them. We must model the teachings of the Bible with such fire and passion that our children and grandchildren will want to experience the God and teachings of their parents more than the teachings of their worldly peers, school teachers, college professors, employers, or government officials. We have been silent too long while the very vocal atheists, agnostics, philosophers, and other ungodly voices of our culture have unashamedly proclaimed their heresies in the name of "science" and "tolerance" and have stolen our precious children from their heritage.

It is time to rise up and fight the lying voices of our culture and take back our children and grandchildren from the deceptive teachings of Satan and his agents.

It's time to weep and intercede for revival in our homes, our churches, our cities, our nation, and our world. Eternal destinies are at stake.
~~~~~

Gem #46 **February 15**

And Laban said unto [Jacob], …I have learned by experience that ***the Lord hath blessed me for thy sake****. And [Jacob] said unto him,*
…it was little which thou hadst before I came,
and it is now increased unto a multitude; and
the Lord hath blessed thee since my coming…
Genesis 30:27-30

And Joseph found grace in [Potiphar's] sight, and ...he made him overseer over his house, ... And it came to pass from the time that he had made him overseer in his house, and over all that he had, that ***the Lord blessed the Egyptian's house for Joseph's sake****; and the blessing of the LORD was upon all that he had...*
Genesis 39:4-5

And the Syrians …brought away captive out of the land of Israel a little maid… And she said unto her mistress, Would God my lord were with the prophet that is in Samaria! for he would ***recover him of his leprosy****. Then went [Naaman] down, and dipped himself seven times in Jordan, …and his flesh came again like unto the flesh of a little child, and he was clean. And he returned to the man of God, …and he said,*
… now I know that there is no God in all the earth, but in Israel:
2 Kings 5:2-3

~~~~~

The Bible and even history is full of stories of God's blessings upon the unrighteous because of the righteous people living in their midst. The judicial laws of Moses provided the foundation for the U.S. government. Many of today's advances in medicine, science, and technology were given to the world by Jews and Christians. The nations and leaders of this world are blessed, not because of their ingenuity or goodness, but because of the righteous people of God among them.

Are you living in such a way that those around you are blessed because you walked through their world??
~~~~~

Gem #47 **February 16**

I love the Lord, because
he hath heard my voice and my supplications.
Psalms 116:1

~~~~~

I LOVE THE LORD BECAUSE...

1. He first loved me. (1 John 4:19)
2. He took my place on Calvary and paid my sin debt. (Romans 5:8; Galatians 2:20)
3. He gave me His Word to light my path and direct my steps. (Psalms 119:105)
4. He shed His blood for the healing of my body and mind. (Isaiah 53:5; 1 Peter 2:24)
5. He filled me with His Holy Spirit and changed my sinful heart. (Ezekiel 36:26; Acts 1:8; 2:38)
6. He supplies ALL my needs. (Philippians 4:19)
7. He protects me from harm. (Psalms 91:10-11; Isaiah 54:17)
8. He gave me a beautiful family and church family. (1 Corinthians 12:13)
9. He gave me a Pastor to watch over me and teach me the ways of God. (Jeremiah 3:15; Ephesians 4:11-12)
10. I have a promise of eternal life after this earthly life is over. (John 3:16; Romans 8:11)

I could list hundreds of additional reasons why **I love the Lord.**

Why do you love the Lord?
Share your reasons with someone today.
~~~~~

Gem #48 **February 17**

What shall I render unto the LORD
for all his benefits toward me?
Psalms 116:12

~~~~~

How do I show my gratitude to God for all He has done for me?

1. I will pray daily. (Psalms 55:17; 1 Thessalonians 5:17)
2. I will offer my life as a living sacrifice. (Romans 12:1)
3. I will fear God and keep His commandments. (Ecclesiastes 12:13)
4. I will praise God publicly. (Psalms 22:22,25; 26:8; 35:18; 84:1-12; 107:32; 111:1; 116:14; 149:1; Hebrews 10:25)
5. I will share the Gospel with others who haven't heard it. (Mark 16:15)
6. I will serve others in love. (Galatians 5:13)
7. I will forgive others as I have been forgiven. (Luke 6:37)
8. I will give generously. (Proverbs 3:9-10; Luke 6:38)
9. I will study and memorize His Word. (Psalms 119:11; 2 Timothy 2:15)

There are many more things I could add to this list to show my appreciation for God's love and benefits in my life. My good works do not save me, but God has ordained that my salvation and change of heart should automatically produce good works. (Ephesians 2:8-10) Those good works will ultimately earn bonuses because God will reward each of us according to our works (Revelation 22:12).

What are you doing to show Him your gratitude
for all His benefits toward you?
~~~~~

Gem #49 **February 18**

With the ***merciful*** *thou wilt shew thyself* ***merciful;***
with an upright man thou wilt shew thyself upright;
Psalms 18:25

The LORD *is* ***merciful*** *and gracious, slow to anger,*
and plenteous in ***mercy.***
Psalms 103:8

And rend your heart, and not your garments,
and turn unto the LORD *your God:*
for he is gracious and ***merciful,*** *slow to anger,*
and of great kindness, and repenteth him of the evil.
Joel 2:13

Blessed are the ***merciful:*** *for they shall obtain* ***mercy.***
Matthew 5:7

Be ye therefore ***merciful,*** *as your Father also is* ***merciful.***
Luke 6:36

~~~~~

Over 70 times the Bible refers to the **mercy** of the Lord, and we are assured that His **mercy** has no end. It is tempting to think that God's **mercy** will cover all our transgressions and give us another chance to do right. However, David and Jesus taught that **God's mercy has conditions attached to it.** He is **merciful** to those who show **mercy** to others.

If you want to receive the blessings and divine favor of God on your life, then start showing compassion and kindness to others.

God will bless you for your acts of mercy.
~~~~~

Gem #50 **February 19**

Whosoever cometh to me, and ***heareth my sayings, and doeth them,***
...He is like a man which built an house, and digged deep,
and laid the foundation on a rock: and when the flood arose,
the stream beat vehemently upon that house,
and ***could not shake it****:*
for it was founded upon a rock*.*
But ***he that heareth, and doeth not****, is like a man*
that without a foundation built an house upon the earth;
against which the stream did beat vehemently,
and immediately ***it fell****;*
and the ruin of that house was great*.*
Luke 6:47-49

Wherefore ...receive with meekness ***the engrafted word,***
which is able to save your souls.
But ***be ye doers of the word, and not hearers only,***
deceiving your own selves. For if any be a ***hearer*** *of the word,*
and not a ***doer****, he is like unto a man beholding his natural face in a glass:*
For he beholdeth himself, and goeth his way,
and straightway forgetteth what manner of man he was.
But ***whoso looketh into the perfect law of liberty,***
and continueth therein*, he being not a forgetful* ***hearer****,*
but a ***doer*** *of the work, this man shall be blessed in his deed.*
James 1:21-25

~~~~~

As a Sunday School and Bible study teacher for many years, I find it alarming to see how many people go to church regularly and **hear** the Word taught, yet walk away and either do not remember, or else choose to disregard what they've heard. Jesus and James said it's not enough to only **hear** the Word. We must also be a **doer** of the Word. Those who **hear and obey** what they've **heard** are not only blessed, but they will also be saved by the Word.

Are you hearing and obeying the teachings in God's Word?
~~~~~

Gem #51 **February 20**

If ye walk in my statutes, and keep my commandments, and do them*; ...I will walk among you, and will be your God, and ye shall be my people.*

Leviticus 26:3, 12

Blessed are the undefiled in the way,
who ***walk in the law of the Lord.***
Blessed are they that ***keep his testimonies****,*
and that ***seek him with the whole heart.***
They also do no iniquity: they ***walk in his ways****.*
I will praise thee with uprightness of heart,
when I shall have learned thy righteous judgments*.*

Psalms 119:1-3, 7

And this is love, that we ***walk after his commandments****.*
This is the ***commandment****, That, as ye have heard*
from the beginning, ye should ***walk in it.***

2 John 1:6

~~~~~

Those who seek God with their whole heart will learn what God requires of them and will walk in His Laws. Knowledge of God's **Laws** enables a person to praise God more effectively. God loves those who keep His testimonies and pronounces a blessing on them. Do you need a blessing today? Study God's ways that are found in His Word and walk in them.

~~~~~

"The secular environment or worldly system we live in is diametrically opposed to the Word of God. Its philosophy and value system are poles apart from Christian beliefs, yet even believers are far more influenced by our materialistic culture than they realize. Am I more deeply affected by the World or by the Word?"

Don Wyrtzen

Gem #52 **February 21**

But ***his delight is in the law of the LORD;***
and in his law doth he meditate day and night.
Psalms 1:2

I have ***rejoiced in the way of thy testimonies,***
as much as in all riches. I will ***delight myself in thy statutes:***
I will not forget thy word. Thy ***testimonies also are my delight***
and my counselors. Let thy tender mercies come unto me,
that I may live: for ***thy law is my delight.***
I have longed for thy salvation, O LORD;
and ***thy law is my delight.***
Psalms 119:14, 16, 24, 77, 174

Thy ***words*** *were found, and I did eat them;*
and ***thy word was unto me the joy and rejoicing of mine heart:***
for I am called by thy name, O LORD God of hosts.
Jeremiah 15:16

~~~~~

What gives you **joy**?
What brings **delight** to your heart?
What causes you to **rejoice**?

Try reading and meditating on the laws of God. The more they get into your spirit, the more they will bring true **delight** and **fulfilment** to your life. Those words are alive and will energize your life. Pick up your Bible and spend some time absorbing its teachings. You will be forever changed.
~~~~~

Gem #53 **February 22**

Before I was ***afflicted*** *I went astray: but now have I kept thy word.*
It is good for me that I have been afflicted; that I might learn thy statutes.
Psalms 119:67, 71

Be sober, be vigilant; because your adversary the devil, as a roaring lion,
walketh about, seeking whom he may devour:
Whom resist stedfast in the faith, knowing that the same ***afflictions***
are accomplished in your brethren that are in the world.
But the God of all grace, who hath called us unto his eternal glory
by Christ Jesus, after that ye have ***suffered a while,***
make you perfect, stablish, strengthen, settle you*.*
1 Peter 5:8-10

~~~~~

Sometimes we get the mistaken idea that WE have got it all together and WE are responsible for all the successes WE have achieved in our life. It is in these times of success, prosperity, and good health that we can easily forget God. The Psalmist reminds us that ***affliction*** brought his wandering feet back to the Word of God. Peter tells us that the devil is on a rampage, seeking for those he can deceive and devour, but God uses ***affliction and suffering*** to remind us that He is our deliverer. Through life's adversities, God is strengthening and maturing us; and He is firmly grounding and establishing us in the Truth.

Is your little ship sailing smoothly on life's sea?

Get ready. The storms will come; but do not be dismayed. That is God's way of making you realize that He is your deliverer. Reach out in those times. He is as close as the mention of His name.
~~~~~

Gem #54 **February 23**

Blessed are they that keep his testimonies,
and that ***seek him with the whole heart****.*
With my ***whole heart*** *have I sought thee:*
O let me not wander from thy commandments.
I cried with my ***whole heart****; hear me, O LORD:*
I will keep thy statutes.
Psalms 119:2, 10, 145

Seek ye the LORD *while he may be found,*
call ye upon him while he is near:
Isaiah 55:6

And ye shall ***seek me****, and find me,*
when ye shall search for me with ***all your heart.***
Jeremiah 29:13

Ask, and it shall be given you; ***seek, and ye shall find****;*
knock, and it shall be opened unto you:
For every one that asketh receiveth; and ***he that seeketh findeth****;*
and to him that knocketh it shall be opened.
Matthew 7:7-8

~~~~~

Have you lost the wonder of reading God's Word, of going to Church, or of spending time in prayer?

God is not hanging out with people who are lackadaisical in their Christian lifestyle. It's time to step up your intensity levels and seek, praise, love, and live for God with your whole heart.

God's best blessings are waiting for those who wholeheartedly seek after Him.
~~~~~

Gem #55 **February 24**

Let my heart be sound in thy statutes; that I be not ***ashamed****.*
Then shall I not be ***ashamed****,*
when I have respect unto all thy commandments.
I will speak of thy testimonies also before kings,
and will not be ***ashamed****.*
Psalms 119:80, 6, 46

Study *to shew thyself approved unto God, a workman that needeth not to be* ***ashamed****, rightly dividing the word of Truth.*
2 Timothy 2:15

~~~~~

Have you ever been embarrassed because someone asked you a question about your beliefs, and you didn't have an answer for them? When I was a young mother, I was once challenged to prove my beliefs. My baby started crying, and my mind went totally blank. The challenger handed me a New Testament and dared me to prove what I believed. I, who had been a Bible quizzer and had memorized hundreds of scriptures during my life, could not think of one scripture to give this mocking woman. Meanwhile, my baby kept crying, and I finally handed the Bible back to the woman as she mockingly sneered at me and said, "I knew you couldn't prove it." I left that business establishment in embarrassment.

The Apostle Paul instructed Timothy that God's approval was on those whose diligent **study** produced the ability to correctly interpret the Word of Truth. The Psalmist says that if we have a sound knowledge of God's Word, we will not be **ashamed** or **embarrassed** to stand before kings and tell them what we believe.

Are you confident enough in your knowledge of the teachings of the Bible that you could explain them to kings and dignitaries? If not, it's time to lay aside other distractions and study God's Word until its teachings flow out of your mouth without hesitation.
~~~~~

 **Gem #56** **February 25**

My soul cleaveth unto the dust:
***quicken** thou me according to thy word.*
Behold, I have longed after thy precepts:
***Quicken** me in thy righteousness.*
This is my comfort in my affliction:
*for thy word hath **quickened** me.*
***Quicken** me after thy lovingkindness;*
so shall I keep the testimony of thy mouth.
I will never forget thy precepts:
*for with them thou hast **quickened** me.*
I am afflicted very much:
***quicken** me, O Lord, according unto thy word.*
Hear my voice according unto thy lovingkindness:
*O LORD, **quicken** me according to thy judgment.*
Plead my cause, and deliver me:
***quicken** me according to thy word.*
Great are thy tender mercies, O LORD:
***Quicken** me according to thy judgments.*
Consider how I love thy precepts:
***Quicken** me, O LORD, according to thy lovingkindness.*
Psalms 119:25, 40, 50, 88, 93, 107, 149, 154, 156, 159

~~~~~

The Psalmist uses the word, ***quicken*** 13 times in his writings to convey the idea of stirring up, reviving, restoring, preserving, saving or becoming more sensitive. When going through problems, the **Word of God** is our source for revival, restoration, preservation and salvation. Knowledge of the **Word** makes me more sensitive to God's heartbeat.

Are you experiencing afflictions, persecution, heartache, or dry places in your Christian walk?

Pick up your Bible and allow those life-giving words to ***quicken*** your spirit and restore your joy.
~~~~~

Gem #57 **February 26**

I have ***more understanding than all my teachers****:*
for thy testimonies are my meditation.
Psalms 119:99

But the Comforter, which is the ***Holy Ghost****, whom the Father*
will send in my name, he ***shall teach you all things****,*
and bring all things to your remembrance,
whatsoever I have said unto you.
John 14:26

Howbeit when he, the ***Spirit of truth****, is come,*
he ***will guide you into all truth****…*
John 16:13

But the natural man receiveth not ***the things of the Spirit of God****:*
for they are foolishness unto him: neither can he know them,
because they ***are spiritually discerned****.*
1 Corinthians 2:14

~~~~~

Today's world puts a high premium on education. Students are advised to go to college so they can get better jobs. While secular education may improve our employment options, it does little to improve our spiritual understanding. The Psalmist said that meditation on God's Word gave him more understanding than all his teachers. How can this be? The Bible is a spiritual book and cannot be accurately understood by human intellect. Jesus gave the ***Holy Ghost to the Church to teach them all things***. When the supreme Teacher resides in our hearts, we have a learning advantage over any instructor, government official or religious leader who has not been filled with the Holy Spirit.

Are you struggling to understand the Bible?
Be filled with the Spirit, and your comprehension will soar.
~~~~~

Gem #58 **February 27**

Preparing To Worship

And it was so, that when they that bare the ark of the Lord had gone six paces, he ***sacrificed*** *oxen and fatlings. And David danced before the Lord with all his might; and David was girded with a linen ephod. So David and all the house of Israel brought up the ark of the Lord with shouting, and with the sound of the trumpet.*

2 Samuel 6:13-15

~~~~~

Sunday is the day usually set aside to go to God's house and worship. The above scripture describes David's sacrificial and exuberant worship when the Ark was returned to Jerusalem, but 1 Chronicles 15 tells us of his extensive **preparations before** he entered into worship. Let's take a look at them.

- First of all, he called a meeting of 862 Levites and descendants of Aaron. He **outlined a plan for praising God** with songs and musical instruments as they moved the Ark.
- He selected 2 priests and 6 other Levite leaders and commanded them to **sanctify themselves before** they attempted to carry the Ark on their shoulders.
- He **appointed 3 Levite song leaders** and instructed them to play brass cymbals as they led in worship.
- **Many other Levite musicians were appointed** to play cornets, trumpets, psalteries and harps to accompany the singers.
- He also **prepared numerous unblemished animals to be offered as sacrifices** at the beginning and end of the march.

What preparations have you made in advance before you enter into God's house to worship? Did these preparations take time and cost you something? God is not honoured with our duty-driven efforts of dragging out of bed, dressing carelessly, dragging into church late and by-passing the prayer room. He deserves our best preparation to enter into His Holy Presence,

for when we've prepared our hearts to seek Him,
He will surely prepare a blessing for us.
~~~~~

Gem #59 **February 28**

***It is time for thee, Lord, to work**:*
for they have made void thy law.
Psalms 119:126

***Give me understanding**, and I shall keep thy law;*
yea, I shall observe it with my whole heart.
Thy hands have made me and fashioned me:
***give me understanding**, that I may learn thy commandments.*
*I am thy servant; **give me understanding**,*
that I may know thy testimonies.
The righteousness of thy testimonies is everlasting:
***give me understanding**, and I shall live.*
Let my cry come near before thee, O Lord:
***give me understanding** according to thy word.*
Psalms 119:34, 73, 125, 144, 169

~~~~~

It is alarming to witness the relentless war against Christianity and the WORD of God in our government and halls of education. Five times the Psalmist asked for God to ***give him understanding*** of His Word in the 119th chapter. As more and more of God's Laws get struck down by ungodly men and women in positions of authority, it is imperative that God's people know and understand His Word so they will not fall into the trap of following any law or teaching that opposes God's Word. The Apostles told their rulers, *"We ought to obey God rather than men"* (Acts 5:29). It is impossible for us to obey something we are unfamiliar with.

It is time to immerse ourselves in the Word and let God give us understanding and courage to obey God rather than men.
~~~~~

Gem #60 **February 29**

For ever, O LORD, ***thy word is settled*** *in heaven.*
Psalms 119:89

For verily I say unto you, Till heaven and earth pass,
one jot or *one* ***tittle shall in no wise pass from the law,***
till all be fulfilled.
Matthew 5:18

The grass withereth, the flower fadeth:
but the ***word of our God shall stand for ever.***
Isaiah 40:8

Heaven and earth shall pass away,
but my ***words shall not pass away.***
Matthew 24:35; Mark 13:31; Luke 21:33

~~~~~

"The Bible is called the Word of God because the whole transcript is an inspired, faithful, and infallible record of what God determined essential for us to know about Himself, the cosmos in which we live, our spiritual allies and adversaries, and our fellow man."
Walter Martin

~~~~~

God's Word has outlasted any words written by man throughout human history. It continues to be the bestselling book of all times. Many have tried to destroy it over and over again, yet it continues to stand. Earthly kingdoms and leaders rise and fall and eventually are forgotten, but God's Word never fails. It will continue to give direction to anyone who will pick up that Holy Book and follow its teachings.

Will you accept the challenge today to fully embrace its teachings? If you do, you will be forever changed.

Gem #61 **March 1**

__The way of life is above__ to the wise,
that he may depart from hell beneath.
Proverbs 15:24

Know therefore this day, and consider it in thine heart,
that __the LORD he is God in heaven above__,
and upon the earth beneath: there is none else.
Deuteronomy 4:39

~~~~~

The scripture in Proverbs 15 reminds me of the old hymn, ***"I Have Found The Way,"*** so I spent part of my devotion time today by sitting at the piano and singing its encouraging words.

1. I have found ***the way*** that leads to endless day,
   Yonder in the Gloryland;
   And the road is bright for Jesus is the Light,
   And I'll hold His guiding hand.
2. I will never fear while Jesus is so near
   I will bravely meet the foe.
   Happy songs I'll sing in honor to the King,
   And to Glory onward go.
3. To the journey's end, led by a Faithful Friend
   Never more in sin to roam;
   By the way called Straight, I'll reach the golden gate,
   Of the soul's eternal home.[11]

Everything I achieve in this life should be done with the purpose of inheriting the life above this earthly life. Jesus is the way, the Truth and the life. When His way of living becomes my way, I don't have to worry about Hell. The way of life will never intersect with the way beneath. I am thankful today that ***"I Have Found The Way."***

---

[11] Words by Rev. L.E. Green and Music by Adger M. Pace.
~~~~~

Gem #62  **March 2**

*Hear my cry, O God; attend unto my prayer. ...**when my heart is overwhelmed:** lead me to the rock that is higher than I. For thou hast been a shelter for me...*

Psalm 61:1-3

*I cried unto the LORD with my voice; with my voice unto the LORD did I make my supplication. I poured out my complaint before him; I shewed before him my trouble. **When my spirit was overwhelmed** within me, then thou knewest my path…*

Psalms 142:1-3

\~~~~~

Sometimes life gets too ***overwhelming***. I am thankful that during those times, I can go to the Rock, Christ Jesus and find comfort.

Gem #63 **March 3**

***Fight the good fight of faith, lay hold on eternal life,** whereunto thou art also called, and hast professed a good profession before many witnesses.*

1 Timothy 6:12

\~~~~~

I intend to ***fight and hold on*** to the precious Truths that have been handed to me by others who have gone before me so that when my race is run, I can say with the Apostle Paul:

> ***I have fought a good fight**, I have finished my course, I have kept the faith: Henceforth there is laid up for me a crown of righteousness, which the Lord, the righteous judge, shall give me at that day:*
>
> **2 Timothy 4:7-8**

Gem #64 **March 4**

JESUS - The most precious, powerful name in all the earth.

Salvation is in that Name.

Neither is there salvation in any other: for there is ***none other name*** *under heaven given among men, whereby we must be saved.*

Acts 4:12

Healing is in that Name.

...In my name...they shall lay hands on the sick, and they shall recover.

Mark 16:17-18

Baptism is in that Name.

Then Peter said... Repent, and be ***baptized every one of you in the name of Jesus Christ****...and ye shall receive the gift of the Holy Ghost.*

Acts 2:38

...they were baptized in the **name of the Lord Jesus**.

Acts 8:16

Do Everything in that Name.

And whatsoever ye do in word or deed, ***do all in the name of the Lord Jesus,*** *giving thanks to God and the Father by him.*

Colossians 3:17

Devils are subject to that Name.

*...****In my name*** *shall they cast out devils...*

Mark 16:17

Paul, ...said to the spirit, I command thee ***in the name of Jesus Christ*** *to come out of her. And he came out the same hour.*

Acts 16:18

~~~~~

I am thankful today that I have Jesus' name covering my life and have experienced many times over the power of praying in **Jesus' name** and calling on **His name** in a crisis.
~~~~~

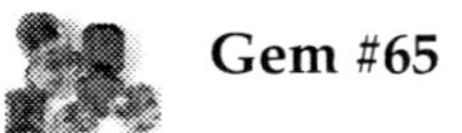

Gem #65 **March 5**

Rivers of waters run down my eyes*, because they keep not thy law.*
I beheld the transgressors, and was ***grieved****;*
because they kept not thy word.
Psalms 119:136, 158

And the LORD said unto him, Go through the midst of the city, through the midst of Jerusalem, and ***set a mark*** *upon the foreheads of the men that* ***sigh and that cry*** *for all the abominations that be done in the midst thereof.*
Ezekiel 9:4

And I sought for a man among them, that should make up the hedge, and ***stand in the gap*** *before me for the land, that I should not destroy it: but I found none.*
Ezekiel 22:30

If my people, which are called by my name, shall humble themselves, and ***pray****, and* ***seek*** *my face, and* ***turn*** *from their wicked ways; then will I* ***hear*** *from heaven, and will* ***forgive*** *their sin, and will* ***heal*** *their land.*
2 Chronicles 7:14

~~~~~

I awoke before daylight this morning feeling a strong burden to pray. I got up and walked the floor in intense **intercession** for a while. The more that evil abounds, the more God is searching for intercessors who will **weep** for the sins of our nation. It's easy to just drift with the current and ignore the extreme danger we are in, thinking things will turn around and get better soon. I admit that I am not as consistent as I should be in interceding for my country. God wants to work, but He is waiting for His people to pray.

Will you lay aside your busyness or leave your comfortable bed to accept the call? Our nation's destiny is at stake.
~~~~~

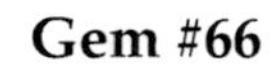

Gem #66 **March 6**

Therefore as by the offence of one judgment came upon all men
to condemnation; even so by the righteousness of one
the free gift came upon all men unto justification of life.
For as by one man's ***disobedience*** *many were made sinners,*
so by the ***obedience*** *of one shall many be made righteous.*
Romans 5:18-19

[Jesus] hath God exalted with his right hand to be a Prince and a Saviour,
for to give repentance to Israel, and forgiveness of sins. And we are his
witnesses of these things; and so is also the ***Holy Ghost,***
whom God hath given to them that obey him*.*
Acts 5:31-32

~~~~~

Disobedience versus Obedience. Ever since Adam and Eve's disobedient act in the Garden of Eden, there has been a major tug-of-war between good and evil. Satan tempts humanity to become lawless and disobedient, while God reaches out in mercy to those who submit to His laws and obey them. Because sin brings separation from God, judgment, and ultimately death, Jesus came in flesh to provide atonement for our sin nature through His death at Calvary. His obedient act provided the free gift of the Holy Ghost for everyone who would obey His plan of salvation.

I'm thankful for that obedient act which paved the way for my unrighteousness to become righteousness in Him.

Have you received the free gift of the Holy Ghost? The price for this gift has already been paid, and it is available to all who obey His commandments.
~~~~~

Gem #67 **March 7**

*My soul **thirsteth** for God, for the living God:*
when shall I come and appear before God?
Psalms 42:2

O God, thou art my God; early will I seek thee:
*my soul **thirsteth** for thee, my flesh longeth for thee*
in a dry and thirsty land, where no water is;
Psalms 63:1

I stretch forth my hands unto thee:
*my soul **thirsteth** after thee, as a thirsty land. Selah.*
Psalms 143:6

*Blessed are they which do **hunger and thirst** after*
righteousness: for they shall be filled.
Matthew 5:6

~~~~~

The Psalmist acknowledged his thirst and longing for God. He recognized that the world could not quench the thirst that was in his soul. Often we try to satisfy our hunger and thirst with money, possessions, relationships, travel, sports, etc. when in reality our soul is thirsting for God. Jesus invited those who were thirsty to come to Him for living water (John 4:14; 6:35; 7:37), and He promised to bless and satisfy those who hungered and thirsted after Him.

Do you have unfulfilled longings and can't put your finger on what you're longing for? Try seeking more diligently after God and spending more time in His Word. Then and only then will your thirst be quenched.
~~~~~

Gem #68 **March 8**

*My **help** cometh from the LORD, which **made heaven and earth**.*
Psalms 121:2

*Our **help** is in the name of the LORD, who **made heaven and earth**.*
Psalms 124:8

*And Hezekiah prayed before the LORD, and said, O LORD God of Israel, ...thou art the God, even thou alone, of all the kingdoms of the earth; thou hast **made heaven and earth**. LORD, bow down thine ear, and hear: open, LORD, thine eyes, and see: and hear the words of Sennacherib, which hath sent him to reproach the living God. Now therefore, O LORD our God, I beseech thee, save thou us out of his hand, that all the kingdoms of the earth may know that thou art the Lord God, even thou only.*
2 Kings 19:15-16, 19

~~~~~

When Hezekiah was threatened by Sennacherib, he took the threatening letter and laid it on the altar and reminded God that because He had ***made heaven and earth***, it was a simple matter for Him to save Judah from the threats of a pagan king. The Psalmist also reminds us that our help comes from the Lord who ***made heaven and earth.***

What is threatening you today? What situations are overwhelming you? What do you need? The Maker of heaven and earth is waiting for you to call on Him. He has the help and the answers that you need. Reach out to Him today.

~~~~~

"Many times I'm unaware that I need help until some crisis or tragedy sharply reminds me that I am very human and needy! Even then I often go to the wrong sources of help. Experts have their place, but they can never substitute for trust in the Lord who is our ultimate help."
Don Wyrtzen

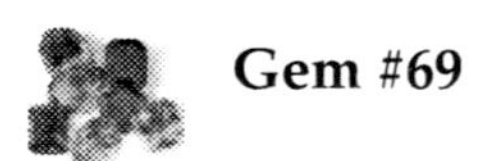

Gem #69 **March 9**

Ah Lord GOD! behold, ***thou hast made the heaven and the earth*** *by thy great power and stretched out arm, and there is nothing too hard for thee: Thou shewest lovingkindness unto thousands, and recompensest the iniquity of the fathers into the bosom of their children after them: the Great, the Mighty God, the LORD of hosts, is his name, Great in counsel, and mighty in work: for thine eyes are open upon all the ways of the sons of men: to give every one according to his ways, and according to the fruit of his doings:*

Jeremiah 32:17-19

And when they heard that, they lifted up their voice to God with one accord, and said, Lord, thou art God, which hast ***made heaven, and earth****, and the sea, and all that in them is: And now, Lord, behold their threatenings: and grant unto thy servants, that with all boldness they may speak thy word, By stretching forth thine hand to heal; and that signs and wonders may be done by the* ***name of thy holy child Jesus.*** *And when they had prayed, the place was shaken where they were assembled together…*

Acts 4:24, 29-31

~~~~~

During my devotion time in the past two days, I discovered that a common prayer of God's people was to mention the fact that **God had made the heaven and the earth,** and consequently, no request that a person could make was too hard for God to fulfil.

Are you facing situations that seem impossible to resolve?

The eyes of the **Maker of heaven and earth** are watching, and He will give answers to those whose ways are pleasing to Him.
~~~~~

Gem #70 **March 10**

Sanctify them through thy ***truth: thy word is truth****.*
John 17:17

And he shall ***judge*** *the world in* ***righteousness****,*
he shall minister ***judgment*** *to the people in* ***uprightness****.*
Psalms 9:8

Say among the heathen that the LORD reigneth: ...he shall ***judge*** *the people* ***righteously****. ...for he cometh to judge the earth: he shall judge the world with righteousness, and the people with his* ***truth****.*
Psalms 96:10, 13

And I saw the dead, small and great, stand before God; and the books were opened: and another book was opened, which is the book of life: and the dead were ***judged*** *out of those things which were written in the books,* ***according to their works****. And whosoever was not found written in the book of life was cast into the lake of fire.*
Revelation 20:12, 15

~~~~~

Man's judgment is often based on false information, plea bargaining or bribes. In many areas of the world, Christians have a very small chance of getting honest and fair treatment with earthly judges; but the day is soon coming when the God who created everything will come and **judge** the people of this world with righteous judgment. The basis for His verdicts will be the words that are written in the Holy Bible. We'd better know that book and live it, for there will be no plea bargaining when we stand before this Judge. He is keeping very good records, and our record will determine our eternal destiny.

It is urgent that we study and obey the Bible while we have a chance.
~~~~~

Gem #71 **March 11**

Fear thou not; for I am with thee: be not dismayed; for I am thy God: I will strengthen thee; yea, ***I will help thee****; yea, I will uphold thee with the right hand of my righteousness. For I the LORD thy God will hold thy right hand, saying unto thee, Fear not;* ***I will help thee.*** *Fear not, thou worm Jacob, and ye men of Israel;* ***I will help thee,*** *saith the LORD, and thy redeemer, the Holy One of Israel.*

Isaiah 41:10, 13-14

Thus saith the LORD, In an acceptable time have I heard thee, and in a day of salvation have ***I helped thee****: and I will preserve thee, and give thee for a covenant of the people, to establish the earth, to cause to inherit the desolate heritages;*

Isaiah 49:8

Our soul waiteth for the LORD: ***he is our help*** *and our shield.*

Psalms 33:20

Because ***thou hast been my help,*** *therefore in the shadow of thy wings will I rejoice.*

Psalms 63:7

~~~~~

Today's culture promotes the concept of the "self-made man," and much attention is given to "self-improvement" through seminars, books, and paying for the services of some self-proclaimed "life coach." While these means of helping us grow may have a very limited place in our life, the most important helper for our spiritual and natural growth is God and His Word, and His services are free. Be filled with the Spirit, and He will lead you and guide you into all Truth (John 16:13). For further instruction and perfection, attach yourself to a body of believers and submit to the teaching of a pastor (Hebrews 13:17). Then you will receive the total package of **help** to become the person God ordained you to be.
~~~~~

Gem #72 **March 12**

And the L*ORD God formed man of the dust of the ground,*
and ***breathed into his nostrils the breath of life;***
and man became a living soul.
Genesis 2:7

The spirit of God hath made me,
and ***the breath of the Almighty hath given me life.***
Job 33:4

O God, thou art terrible out of thy holy places:
the God of Israel is he that ***giveth strength and power***
unto his people. Blessed be God.
Psalms 68:35

He ***giveth power to the faint;***
and to them that have no might he ***increaseth strength.***
Isaiah 40:29

Come unto me, all ye that labour and are heavy laden,
and ***I will give you rest.***
Matthew 11:28

~~~~~

We humans are prone to take life by the tail and plan our days, our education, our careers, our families, our vacations, and even our funerals without consulting God to determine if He is pleased with those decisions. God is the giver of life. If we'll let Him, He will give strength, power, and rest to those who come to Him.

Are you weary, overwhelmed, and frustrated with the incessant demands of life?

Slow down and spend some time in the presence of the ***Life-Giver.*** He has whatever you need.
~~~~~

Gem #73 **March 13**

*Lo, **children are an heritage of the Lord**: and the fruit of the womb is his reward. As arrows are in the hand of a mighty man; so are children of the youth. Happy is the man that hath his quiver full of them: they shall not be ashamed, but they shall speak with the enemies in the gate.*

Psalms 127:3-5

~~~~~

"**Children** are our most valuable resource."

Herbert Hoover

"If I could relive my life, I would devote my entire ministry to reaching **children** for God!"

Dwight L. Moody

~~~~~

In our materialistic society, ***children*** are often undervalued. Couples remain childless so they can have careers and travel without the "burden" of caring for ***children***. The American culture and lifestyle often requires both parents to work, thus leaving the influencing and training of ***children*** in the hands of day care personnel. Promiscuous lifestyles have resulted in the abortion of millions of babies. Even many babies conceived between legally married couples are aborted because they are an inconvenience to the mother or couple. Mistreatment of thousands of ***children*** has resulted in their removal from their families and placement into foster families. The Psalmist doesn't condone such selfish disregard for ***children***. He says they are a ***heritage from the Lord***. Proper nurturing and training of ***children*** will produce adults who will become strong Christians and will build dynamic churches and Christian communities.

If you have been blessed with children, you have been given a great reward from the Lord.

Gem #74

March 14

Praise ye the L*ORD.* ***Blessed*** *is the man that feareth the Lord,*
that delighteth greatly in his commandments.
His seed shall be mighty upon earth: the generation of the upright
shall be blessed. *Wealth and riches shall be in his house:*
and his righteousness endureth for ever.
Psalms 112:1-3

Blessed *is every one that feareth the Lord; that walketh*
in his ways. For thou shalt eat the labour of thine hands:
happy shalt thou be, and it shall be well with thee.
Thy wife shall be as a fruitful vine by the sides of thine house:
thy children like olive plants round about thy table.
Behold, that thus shall the man be ***blessed*** *that feareth the* L*ORD.*
Psalms 128:1-4

~~~~~

Sometimes we tend to equate ***blessings*** with the acquisition of material possessions, i.e. homes, cars, labor-saving appliances, technology gadgets, etc. However, the Psalmist reminds us that the man who fears the Lord and finds delight in walking in His ways is blessed of the Lord. This blessing extends to his wife and children. Often, men and women look to their job as the avenue for acquiring wealth and possessions. However, the Psalmist reminds us that:

True wealth and riches are composed of those who are already in our house.

Things may lose their value or be taken from us, but the man who by example and teaching has created a Godly family, is wealthy beyond imagination. His legacy will be passed to future generations.
~~~~~

Gem #75 **March 15**

My heart is fixed, O God, my heart is fixed:
I will sing and give praise.
Psalms 57:7

O God, ***my heart is fixed****; I will sing and give praise,*
even with my glory.
Psalms 108:1

Ye shall observe to do therefore as the LORD your God
hath commanded you: ***ye shall not turn aside***
to the right hand or to the left.
Deuteronomy 5:32

Enter ye in at the ***strait gate****: for wide is the gate,*
and broad is the way, that leadeth to destruction,
and many there be which go in thereat:
Because ***strait is the gate, and narrow is the way,***
which leadeth unto life, and few there be that find it.
Matthew 7:13-14

~~~~~

Today, **my heart is fixed** on the prize of spending eternity with the Lover of my soul. I have had many opportunities throughout my life to forsake the teachings of my elders, but my love for God and the Word has held me steadfast to the old paths that I've been taught. Many around me have forsaken the narrow way in favour of the bright lights of worldliness, but the Bible teaches that God expects His people to be peculiar and separated from the culture of this world (Titus 2:4; 1 Peter 2:9). The way into His Kingdom is restricted and narrow, and I have no desire to taste of the pleasures of the broad way that leads to destruction. Although I find great delight in His presence, ***my heart is fixed*** on the teachings and treasures I've found in His Word, for it is the Word that will judge me.
~~~~~

Gem #76 **March 16**

But he knoweth the way that I take:
***when he hath tried me**, I shall come forth as gold.*
Job 23:10

***Thou hast proved mine heart**; thou hast visited me in the night;*
***thou hast tried me**, and shalt find nothing;*
I am purposed that my mouth shall not transgress.
Psalms 17:3

O bless our God, ye people, and make the voice of his praise to be heard:
***Which holdeth our soul in life**, and suffereth not our feet to be moved.*
*For thou, O **God, hast proved us: thou hast tried us**,*
as silver is tried. Thou broughtest us into the net; thou laidst
affliction upon our loins. Thou hast caused men to ride over
our heads; we went through fire and through water:
but thou broughtest us out into a wealthy place.
Psalms 66:8-12

~~~~~

God purposefully brings me into traps and afflictions, and allows Satan and people and to take advantage of me. He even sends me through fire and water, but after the difficulties are past, He brings me into a place of abundance and refreshing. The key to victory in Psalms 66:8-9 is to bless God and praise Him during the difficult moments because He has a firm hold on my soul and will not allow my feet to be moved from my foundation of Truth.

I wonder if lack of praise during tough times would permit God to release me!!

Lord, deliver me from grumbling and complaining during hard times, and let grateful praises to You flow from my heart and out of my lips so that others will hear and be encouraged to praise You during their hard trials.
~~~~~

Gem #77

March 17

Say not ye, There are yet four months, and then cometh ***harvest****?*
behold, I say unto you, Lift up your eyes, and look on the fields;
for they are white already to ***harvest****.*

John 4:35

Therefore said he unto them, The ***harvest*** *truly is great,*
but the ***labourers are few****: pray ye therefore the Lord of the harvest,*
that he would send forth ***labourers*** *into his* ***harvest****.*

Luke 10:2

The fruit of the righteous is a tree of life;
and he that ***winneth souls*** *is wise.*

Proverbs 11:30

~~~~~

"The Church was born in a blaze of personal soulwinning;
it was a house-to-house, faith-to-faith operation."

John Arcovio

"How much precious time is wasted in watching useless things,
not necessarily evil things, but things that have nothing to do with
the spiritual advancement of our own lives or the lives of those
around us? We've wasted so much time on the unprofitable;
and as a steward, we shall give an account
to Him whose time it is."

B.H. Clendennen

"I have one desire now – to live a life of reckless abandon for the
Lord, putting all my energy and strength into it."

Elisabeth Elliot

~~~~~

Lord, help me to be about my Father's business of sowing seed, watering it with intercessory prayers, winning souls, teaching, encouraging, loving, giving, and serving. There are millions of people to reach with the Gospel and not much time to do it.

Gem #78 **March 18**

*For as the **rain cometh down**, and …**watereth the earth**,*
*and **maketh it bring forth and bud**, that it may give seed to the sower,*
and bread to the eater: So shall my word be that goeth forth
out of my mouth: …it shall accomplish that which I please…
Isaiah 55:10-11

*Judah mourneth… And their nobles have sent their little ones to the waters: they came to the pits, and **found no water**; they returned with their vessels empty; they were ashamed and… covered their heads.*
Because the ground is chapt, for there was no rain in the earth,
the plowmen were ashamed, they covered their heads.
Jeremiah 14:2-3

~~~~~

The early morning rain during my devotion time today sent me on a search through the Bible to discover what it had to say about rain. I chose two passages to illustrate the benefits received when rain comes and the hardships experienced when the rain is withheld. I was also reminded of an entry I had made in my prayer journal on 6/29/05. I conclude this lesson with those thoughts.

~~~~~

"We enjoy life without problems, but trouble-free living is like blue skies and sunshine without rain. The ground gets hard, and the plants dry up and wither. In the Spirit, troubles are the refreshing rain that brings moisture to my dry, barren spirit. Even though problems and troubles don't feel good, they help me grow.
As plants turn green and bloom with the moisture, so my spirit becomes tender and gentle and attracts others who are going through barren times in their lives. We think it is in our sunshiny, worry-free moments that we have it all together and are making progress, but the opposite is really true. If we go too long between clouds and rain, we become hard in attitude and critical. David said, *'Before I was afflicted, I went astray.'* (Psalms 119:67) So don't complain about the problems. Wrap them with praise so that you can be refreshed and grow in God." ~ PE

Gem #79 **March 19**

But when Peter was come to Antioch, I withstood him to the face, because he was to be blamed. For before that certain came from James, he did eat with the Gentiles: but when they were come, he withdrew and separated himself, fearing them which were of the circumcision. And the ***other Jews dissembled*** *likewise with him; insomuch that* ***Barnabas also was carried away with their dissimulation****.*

Galatians 2:11-13

Let love be without ***dissimulation****. Abhor that which is evil; cleave to that which is good.*

Romans 12:9

~~~~~

My morning reading and research led me on a quest to discover what the Bible had to say about those who ***dissimulate*** or do things with an ulterior or hypocritical motive. Peter tried to "buddy up" to the Gentiles by eating with them when no Jews were around, but when other Jewish Christians were with him, he ignored the Gentile Christians and ate only with the Jews, so they wouldn't be offended with him. These acts of hypocrisy were noted by other Jews, and soon, even Paul's ministry companion, Barnabas, was caught up in the hypocrisy. That's when Paul had had enough. He confronted Peter with his ***dissimulation*** and rebuked him for living like the Gentiles when he was with them, but pretending to the Jews that he was living according to Jewish law when he was with them. Paul expanded the teaching of ***dissembling*** to the Romans when he instructed them to love others without ***dissimulation***. If love for one another is one of the identifying marks of a Christian (John 13:35), then we cannot afford to be hypocritical in any area of our life.

One little seed of dissimulation can spread and infect a whole church. Be careful!
~~~~~

Gem #80 **March 20**

*And I will make my **covenant** between me and thee,*
*and will multiply thee exceedingly. And I will establish my **covenant***
between me and thee and thy seed after thee in their generations
*for an everlasting **covenant**, to be a God unto thee,*
and to thy seed after thee. And God said unto Abraham,
*Thou shalt keep my **covenant** therefore, thou, and*
thy seed after thee in their generations.
Genesis 17:2, 7, 9

*This is the **covenant** that I will make with them after those days,*
saith the Lord, I will put my laws into their hearts,
and in their minds will I write them;
And their sins and iniquities
will I remember no more.
Hebrews 10:16-17

~~~~~

COVENANT - **the conditional promises** made to humanity by God, as revealed in Scripture.

The Old Testament **Covenant** between God and man only dealt with the sins rather than the heart which caused man to commit the sins. Thankfully, the New Testament **Covenant** changes our heart when we are filled with the Holy Ghost. God's laws are still in force, but they are written in our heart, and that love relationship we have with God motivates us to keep His commandments. This new Covenant is still conditional. God loves those who keep His commandments (John 15:10). I want to study and know His Word so well that His commandments are embedded deeply in my heart.

Then my obedience to His commandments will ensure
that my Covenant relationship with my God
will never be broken.
~~~~~

Gem #81 **March 21**

I will bless the LORD*, who hath given me counsel:*
my reins also instruct me in the night seasons.
Psalms 16:7

My foot standeth ***in*** *an even place:*
in *the congregations* ***will I bless the LORD****.*
Psalms 26:12

I will bless the Lord *at all times:*
his praise shall continually be in my mouth.
Psalms 34:1

Bless the Lord, *O my soul: and all that is within me,*
bless his holy name.
Psalms 103:1

Blessed be the LORD God *of Israel from everlasting to everlasting:*
and let all the people say, Amen. Praise ye the LORD.
Psalms 106:48

Lift up your hands in the sanctuary, and ***bless the Lord.***
Psalms 134:2

~~~~~

How many times do we come to the Lord in prayer and ask Him to bless us? Often the Bible instructs us to ***Bless the Lord***. He cannot bless Himself, so He relies on His creation to bless Him. As we compliment Him for His goodness, holiness, mercy, love, faithfulness, etc., He will in turn leave a blessing behind for us.

How about changing your prayer today from "Bless Me" to "I Will Bless You, O Lord"?
~~~~~

Gem #82 **March 22**

Sing praises to the L*ORD, which dwelleth in Zion:*
***declare** among the people his doings.*
Psalms 9:11

Make me to understand the way of thy precepts:
*so shall **I talk** of thy wondrous works.*
Psalms 119:27

And when they were come to Jerusalem, they were received
of the church, and of the apostles and elders,
*and **they declared** all things that God had done with them.*
Acts 15:4

*Moreover, brethren, **I declare** unto you the Gospel*
which I preached unto you, which also ye have received,
and wherein ye stand;
By which also ye are saved,...
1 Corinthians 15:1-2

But ye are a chosen generation, a royal priesthood,
an holy nation, a peculiar people;
that ye should shew forth the praises of him
who hath called you out of darkness into his marvellous light;
1 Peter 2:9

~~~~~

I have spent considerable time researching Bible teachings on talking, declaring, shewing forth and making known the good things God has done. Over 60 times we are instructed to talk about these things.

I wonder what would happen in our world if the Church would talk more about the things of God rather than the ordinary stuff of life??
~~~~~

Gem #83 **March 23**

Thy ***word is a lamp*** *unto my feet, and a* ***light*** *unto my path.*
The entrance of thy ***words giveth light****;*
it giveth understanding unto the simple.
Psalms 119:105, 130

We have also a more sure word of prophecy;
whereunto ye do well that ye take heed,
as unto a ***light*** *that shineth in a dark place,*
until the day dawn, and the ***day star*** *arise in your hearts:*
2 Peter 1:19

~~~~~

"Without the searchlight of God's Word,
we'd be left to flounder in the dark, looking for the way.
But His Law points out the snares of the wicked,
and we can avoid stumbling into their traps."
Don Wyrtzen[12]

~~~~~

The more of **God's Word** that we absorb into our heart, the brighter our life becomes to the world. Jesus said, *"Ye are the* ***light*** *of the world"* (Matthew 5:14). Rampant sin has made the world very dark, but those who have applied themselves to study and memorize God's Word become little patches of light in the darkness, showing the way to sinners who are looking for a way out of the darkness.

Increase your knowledge of the Word
so your light will show someone the way.

[12] Don Wyrtzen, A Musician Looks at the Psalms (Grand Rapids, MI: Daybreak Books, 1988) 326.

Gem #84 **March 24**

I will both lay me down in peace, and sleep:
for thou, Lord, only makest me dwell in ***safety****.*
Psalms 4:8

Hold thou me up, and I shall be ***safe****:*
and I will have respect unto thy statutes continually.
Psalms 119:17

But whoso hearkeneth unto me shall dwell ***safely****,*
and shall be quiet from fear of evil.
Proverbs 1:33

The name of the Lord is a strong tower*:*
the righteous runneth into it, and is ***safe****.*
Proverbs 18:10

The fear of man bringeth a snare:
but whoso putteth his trust in the Lord shall be ***safe****.*
Proverbs 29:25

~~~~~

If our only hope was in this life, we would be very fearful because of the lawlessness, corruption, violence and total disregard of God's laws among those who do not fear God. But the Word promises safety to those who listen to His commands and obey them. Those who are called by His name and trust in Him can find protection in Him and sleep peacefully at night. As the old song says,

"The tempest may sweep o'er the wild stormy deep;
In Jesus I'm safe evermore."[13]

---

[13] *"The Haven of Rest"* was written by Henry Gilmour, a dentist who became a Gospel musician, soloist and choir director during the last 25 years of his life. This song first appeared in *Sunlight Songs* in 1890. (From *"Amazing Grace: 366 Inspiring Hymn Stories for Daily Devotions"* by Kenneth W. Osbeck; pg. 195).
~~~~~

Gem #85 **March 25**

But the hour cometh, and now is,
when the true worshippers shall worship
the Father in spirit and in truth:
for ***the Father seeketh*** *such to worship him.*
John 4:23

Be sober, be vigilant; because your adversary ***the devil,***
as a roaring lion, ***walketh about,***
seeking *whom he may devour:*
Whom ***resist*** *stedfast in the faith…*
1 Peter 5:8-9

Submit *yourselves therefore* ***to God.***
Resist the devil*, and he will flee from you.*
Draw nigh to God, and he will draw nigh to you.
Cleanse your hands, ye sinners; and purify your hearts…
James 4:7-8

~~~~~

There are two spiritual forces in the world today. **The devil, as a roaring lion, seeks to destroy** everyone so they will not inherit eternal life. Meanwhile, **Jesus, as the true lion** of the tribe of Judah, (Revelation 5:5) **is seeking true worshipers** who will study and obey His Laws so He can give them eternal life.

Don't be a victim of the false roaring lion.
Resist him today and submit to the true lion, Jesus Christ.
~~~~~

Gem #86 **March 26**

The fear of the LORD is the instruction of wisdom;
*and **before honour is humility.***
Proverbs 15:33

Before destruction the heart of man is haughty,
*and **before honour is humility.***
Proverbs 18:12

*By **humility** and the fear of the LORD*
*are riches, and **honour**, and life.*
Proverbs 22:4

And I will punish the world for their evil,
and the wicked for their iniquity;
*and I will cause the **arrogancy of the proud** to cease,*
*and will lay low the **haughtiness** of the terrible.*
Isaiah 13:11

~~~~~

Do you sometimes feel as though you get no respect from your spouse, children, co-workers, Sunday School students, etc.? Proverbs tells us that the fear of the Lord teaches us wisdom, and the wisdom of God through His Word instructs us in the ways to acquire many character virtues, one of which is humility. Not only does God hate arrogance and pride, but people are also offended by those who are smart-aleck and think they know it all.

If you want to be honored by those you love,
honor is preceded by a spirit of humility.
~~~~~

Gem #87 **March 27**

Continue in prayer, and watch in the same with thanksgiving;
Withal ***praying also for us****, that God would open unto us a door of utterance, to speak the mystery of Christ, for which I am also in bonds:*
That I may make it manifest, as I ought to speak.
Colossians 4:2-4

Brethren, ***pray for us****.*
1 Thessalonians 5:25

Finally, brethren, ***pray for us****, that the word of the Lord may have free course, and be glorified, even as it is with you:*
2 Thessalonians 3:1

In weariness and painfulness, in watchings often, in hunger and thirst, in fastings often, in cold and nakedness.
Beside those things that are without, that which cometh upon me daily, ***the care of all the churches.***
2 Corinthians 11:27-28

For after that in the wisdom of God the world by wisdom knew not God, ***it pleased God by the foolishness of preaching to save them that believe.***
1 Corinthians 1:21

~~~~~

Unless a person has pastored a group of believers, they have no idea of the huge weight of responsibility involved in that ministry. Paul mentioned some of the perils of being a minister of the Gospel, not the least of which was the daily care of all the churches he had established. He requested that the Church pray for its leaders to have open doors to freely speak of the mystery of Christ. Since God has ordained that we cannot be saved without preaching in our lives, it is imperative that the saints pray for their leaders, for without their preaching, we cannot be saved.
~~~~~

Gem #88 **March 28**

I will ***praise thee,*** *O* LORD, ***with my whole heart…***
Psalms 9:1

For Moses had said, ***Consecrate yourselves*** *today to the* LORD,
…that he may ***bestow upon you a blessing*** *this day.*
Exodus 32:29

Notwithstanding no ***devoted thing,*** *that a man shall* ***devote unto the* LORD** *of all that he hath, …shall be sold or redeemed:*
***every devoted thing is most holy unto the* LORD.**
Leviticus 27:28

…vessels of silver, and vessels of gold, and vessels of brass: Which also king ***David did dedicate unto the* LORD,** *with the silver and gold that he had* ***dedicated of all nations which he subdued;***
2 Samuel 8:10-11

Commit thy works *unto the* LORD,
and thy thoughts shall be established.
Proverbs 16:3

~~~~~

It is easy to praise God with my lips, but is my lifestyle one of praise to Him? David was one of the greatest praisers recorded in the Bible, but he also dedicated the spoils of war to the Lord and gave huge amounts of gold, silver and valuables to Solomon for use in the Temple when it was built. Moses told Israel that consecrating themselves to God would bring God's blessings on them. God isn't interested in praise that comes only from the lips.

He is looking for a lifestyle of wholehearted devotion, desire, commitment, consecration and dedication, not only of ourselves, but also of the possessions He allows us to acquire.
~~~~~

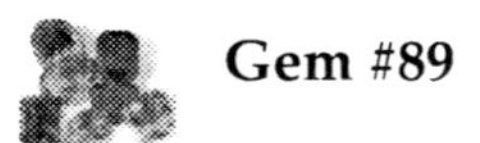

Gem #89 **March 29**

Deliverance from enemies and troubles is a huge theme of the Bible. There are numerous ***prayers for deliverance*** as well as ***testimonies of God's deliverance***. Many testimonies were set to music and used as praises to God. There are ***promises from God for deliverance.*** I also found occasions where people testified of God's past deliverance and used that testimony as a ***statement of faith*** to God or others ***for future deliverance***. Often, we try to figure our own way out of life's dilemmas and only cry out to God for help as a last resort, but the scriptural pattern shows us that Bible characters regularly prayed for deliverance from life's struggles as well as from their enemies. Then when God delivered, they ***testified*** about it to others.

Prayer to God

Return, O LORD, ***Deliver my soul****:*
oh save me for thy mercies' sake.
Psalms 6:4

God's Promise

And call upon me in the day of trouble:
I will deliver thee*, and thou shalt glorify me.*
Psalms 50:15

Faith Statement

Thou art my hiding place; ***thou shalt preserve me*** *from trouble;*
thou shalt compass me about with songs of deliverance*. Selah.*
Psalms 32:7

Testimony

Blessed be the Lord *my strength… My goodness, and my fortress;*
my high tower, and ***my deliverer****; my shield, and he in whom*
I trust; who subdueth my people under me.
Psalms 144:1-2

~~~~~
~~~~~

Are you overwhelmed with the stresses and problems of life?

Instead of looking to psychiatrists, tranquilizers, alcohol, drugs, gym memberships, vacations, illicit relationships, acquiring more possessions or whatever else you seek in your attempts to find deliverance from life's dilemmas, look to Jesus. He is the **Master Deliverer,** and He has solutions you never dreamed of. Call on Him. He'll deliver, if you will call.

Gem #90 **March 30**

I have no greater joy than to hear that my children walk in truth.
3 John 1:4

~~~~~

Many things in life bring me joy, such as doing something nice for others who can't repay me, spending time with my children, grandchildren and others who are important to me, working hard to accomplish a goal, spending time in the mountains and basking in the wonders of God's handiwork, cooking a nutritious meal for myself and others, preparing a Bible lesson and sharing it with others, spending time in prayer and study of the Word, or relaxing with an inspirational book while listening to soft music.

But I can't think of anything that would bring me greater joy than to know that the values and love for Truth that my husband and I tried to instill in our children while they were growing up has taken root and produced the same love for Truth in their lives, so that one day we will all stand before God and hear Him say,

"Well done thou good and faithful servant.
Enter into the joys of the Lord."
~~~~~

Gem #91 **March 31**

The law of the Lord *is perfect, converting the soul:* ***the testimony of the Lord*** *is sure, making wise the simple.* ***The statutes of the Lord*** *are right, rejoicing the heart:* ***the commandment the Lord*** *is pure, enlightening the eyes.* ***The fear of the Lord*** *is clean, enduring for ever:* ***the judgments of the Lord*** *are true and righteous altogether. More to be desired are they than gold, yea, than much fine gold:* ***sweeter also than honey and the honeycomb.***
Psalms 19:7-10

O taste and see that the Lord is good:
blessed is the man that trusteth in him.
Psalms 34:8

I will sing unto the LORD as long as I live:
I will sing praise to my God while I have my being.
My meditation of him shall be sweet: *I will be glad in the LORD.*
Psalms 104:33-34

How sweet are thy words unto my taste!
yea, sweeter than honey to my mouth!
Psalms 119:103

*...Son of man, ...**eat this roll**, and go speak unto the house of Israel. So I opened my mouth, and **he caused me to eat that roll**. ...**Then did I eat it; and it was in my mouth as honey for sweetness.***
Ezekiel 3:1-3

~~~~~

The Word of God contains more sweet treats than any candy store you could visit. In addition, nothing we eat can taste as sweet as time spent in God's presence. Just give God and His Word the "taste test" and you will discover so many delicious sensations to please your taste buds.

Have you had your sweet tooth satisfied today?
~~~~~

Gem #92 **April 1**

For the preaching of the ***cross*** *is to them that perish foolishness;*
but unto us which are saved it is the power of God.
1 Corinthians 1:18

Then said Jesus unto his disciples, If any man will come after me,
let him deny himself, and take up his ***cross****, and follow me.*
For whosoever will save his life shall lose it:
and whosoever will lose his life for my sake shall find it.
Matthew 16:24-25

And, having made peace through the ***blood of his cross****, by him to*
reconcile all things unto himself… And you, that were sometime alienated
and enemies in your mind by wicked works, yet now hath he reconciled
In the body of his flesh through death, to present you holy and
unblameable and unreproveable in his sight:
Colossians 1:20-22

Jesus keep me near the Cross, There a precious fountain.
Free to all a healing stream, Flows from Calvary's mountain.
In the Cross, In the Cross. Be my glory ever
Till my raptured soul shall find rest beyond the river.[14]

~~~~~

The ***Cross*** is a key component of the Christian teachings. Our sins were atoned for on Jesus' ***cross***. We take up our cross and follow Jesus. That cross cannot fit through just any door. The way of the ***cross*** is one of sanctification, separation, consecration, and identification. Although many people in modern Christianity would take away the teachings and songs about the ***cross and the blood*** of Jesus, I value them and hold them close. They are part of my identification with Jesus.

Does your lifestyle identify you with the cross of Jesus?

---

[14] Lyrics to "Near The Cross" were written by Fanny J. Crosby and published in 1869. Music was written by William Doane.
~~~~~

Gem #93 **April 2**

Surely he shall deliver thee from the snare of the fowler,
and from the noisome pestilence. He shall ***cover*** *thee with*
his feathers, and under his wings shalt thou trust:
his truth shall be thy shield and buckler.
Psalms 91:3-4

Blessed is he whose transgression is forgiven, whose ***sin is covered.***
Psalms 32:1

Thou hast forgiven the iniquity of thy people,
thou hast ***covered all their sin****. Selah.*
Psalms 85:2

I will greatly rejoice in the LORD, my soul shall be joyful in my God;
for he hath clothed me with the garments of salvation,
he hath ***covered me with the robe of righteousness****,*
as a bridegroom decketh himself with ornaments,
and as a bride adorneth herself with her jewels.
Isaiah 61:10

~~~~~

While reading in Psalms this morning my attention was drawn to the word ***covered.*** We often think of insurance when the word ***covered*** is discussed, and we research what things are covered before we invest in a policy. No earthly policy can compare with God's insurance policy. As I read through the Bible and made notes of things that God covers in our lives, three specific coverings attracted my attention. God's wings and feathers ***cover*** and hide us from the enemy of our soul. Through baptism, His blood is applied to ***cover*** our sins, and finally He ***covers*** us with a robe of righteousness in preparation for the long-anticipated wedding of the Church with her Heavenly Bridegroom.

Are you in the select group whose policy
includes this type of coverage?
~~~~~

Gem #94 **April 3**

For it became him, for whom are all things, …to make the captain of their salvation perfect through ***sufferings****. For in that he himself hath* ***suffered*** *being tempted, he is able to succour them that are tempted. Though he were a Son, yet learned he obedience by the things which he* ***suffered;***

Hebrews 2:10, 18; 5:8

Blessed be …the God of all comfort; Who comforteth us in all our ***tribulation****, that we may be able to comfort them which are in any* ***trouble****, by the comfort wherewith we ourselves are comforted of God. For as the* ***sufferings*** *of Christ abound in us, so our consolation also aboundeth by Christ. And whether we be* ***afflicted****, it is for your consolation and salvation, which is effectual in the enduring of the same* ***sufferings*** *which we also* ***suffer…*** *And our hope of you is stedfast, knowing, that as ye are partakers of the* ***sufferings****, so shall ye be also of the consolation.*

2 Corinthians 1:3-7

But the God of all grace, who hath called us unto his eternal glory by Christ Jesus, after that ye have ***suffered*** *a while, make you perfect, stablish, strengthen, settle you.*

1 Peter 5:10

~~~~~

Jesus gave us several examples of the purpose for ***suffering***. He was perfected and learned obedience through ***suffering***. He also gained understanding of the human perspective on temptation, and because He overcame, He can help us overcome. In addition, Paul taught that the God who comforts and sustains us in our ***afflictions and sufferings*** has ordained that we share those experiences with others who are ***suffering*** so they too can be comforted. Peter adds more insight into the subject with his teaching that ***suffering*** serves the purpose of maturing and establishing us in the faith. So even though I don't enjoy the ***suffering*** part of the growth process, it is very necessary for the overall stability of the Church.
~~~~~

Gem #95 **April 4**

The LORD *is nigh unto them that are of a broken heart;*
and saveth such as be of a ***contrite*** *spirit.*
Psalms 34:18

For thus saith the high and lofty One that inhabiteth eternity,
whose name is Holy; I dwell in the high and holy place, with him also
that is of a ***contrite and humble****, to revive the spirit of the* ***humble****,*
and to revive the heart of the ***contrite*** *ones.*
Isaiah 57:15

Thus saith the LORD*, The heaven is my throne, and the earth*
is my footstool: where is the house that ye build unto me?
and where is the place of my rest? For all those things
hath mine hand made, and all those things have been,
saith the LORD*: but to this man will I look, even to him that*
is poor and of a ***contrite*** *spirit, and trembleth at my word.*
Isaiah 66:1-2

~~~~~

"**Humility** is perfect quietness of heart. It is to expect nothing, to wonder at nothing that is done to me, to feel nothing done against me. It is to be at rest when nobody praises me, and when I am blamed or despised. It is to have a blessed home in the Lord, where I can go in and shut the door, and kneel to my Father in secret, and am at peace as in a deep sea of calmness, when all around and above is trouble."
Andrew Murray

~~~~~

God is looking for those who recognize their insufficiency without Him. A spirit of ***humility and contrition*** will bring Him near. Are you feeling burned out, frustrated, or hopeless due to all the bad news and stresses of life? He is eager to revive the ***humble*** and ***contrite*** ones and to spend time with them. Bring your needs to Him today. He has answers, and He cares!

Gen #96 **April 5**

But rather seek ye the kingdom of God; and all these things shall be added unto you. Fear not, little flock; for it is your Father's good ***pleasure*** *to give you the kingdom.*
Luke 12:31-32

For the LORD taketh ***pleasure*** *in his people: he will beautify the meek with salvation.*
Psalms 149:4

The LORD taketh ***pleasure*** *in them that fear him, in those that hope in his mercy.*
Psalms 147:11

...let them say continually, Let the LORD be magnified, which hath ***pleasure*** *in the prosperity of his servant.*
Psalms 35:27

For it is God which worketh in you both to will and to do of his good ***pleasure****.*
Philippians 2:13

Have I any ***pleasure*** *at all that the wicked should die? saith the Lord GOD: and not that he should return from his ways, and live?*
Ezekiel 18:23

~~~~~

Revelation 4:11 tells us that the entire universe and everything in it was created for ***God's pleasure***. Because everything in nature and especially the body systems of humans were created with such precision, no doubt God put much thought, time and effort into creating all these things that we take for granted. In addition to the pleasure God receives from creating things, what else brings Him pleasure?
~~~~~

A journey through the Word reveals considerable information about ***God's pleasure***, but it seems that ***God's greatest pleasure*** can be found in the people who seek Him and strive to follow His commandments. He takes great delight in birthing them into His Kingdom and revealing its wonders to them. He also loves to provide for their everyday needs, beautify them with salvation, prosper them spiritually, and equip them to fulfill His will. He grieves deeply when a wicked person dies.

What about your life?
Is it bringing pleasure or grief to God?

Gem #97 **April 6**

*As the hart **panteth** after the water brooks,*
*so **panteth** my soul after thee, O God.*
Psalms 42:1

*I opened my mouth, and **panted**:*
for I longed for thy commandments.
Psalms 119:131

~~~~~

Pant – to long for something or someone with breathless or intense eagerness; to yearn, thirst, or hunger.

Just as our natural body longs for water in order for all systems to function efficiently, so our spiritual body longs for God and His Word. Without sufficient water, our bodies become dehydrated. In like manner, without sufficient time spent in God's presence and in the study of His Word, our spiritual nature becomes dehydrated. **Have you lost that feeling of breathless or intense eagerness to spend time in prayer and Bible study?** You may be spiritually dehydrated. Schedule some time to pray and study the Bible, and that breathless expectation for the things of God will return.
~~~~~

Gem #98 **April 7**

...These that have turned the world ***upside down*** *are come hither also;*
Acts 17:6

...the righteous are ***bold*** *as a lion.*
Proverbs 28:1

Now when they saw the ***boldness of Peter and John****, and perceived that they were unlearned and ignorant men, they marvelled; and they took knowledge of them, that they had been with Jesus.*
Acts 4:13

And now, Lord, behold their threatenings: and grant unto thy servants, that ***with all boldness they may speak thy word,*** *And when they had prayed, the place was shaken where they were assembled together; and they were all filled with the Holy Ghost, and they* ***spake the word of God with boldness.***
Acts 4:29, 31

But Barnabas took [Paul], and brought him to the apostles, and declared unto them how he had seen the Lord in the way, ...and how he had ***preached boldly*** *at Damascus in the name of Jesus. And he* ***spake boldly*** *in the name of the Lord Jesus, and disputed against the Grecians: but they went about to slay him.*
Acts 9:27, 29

And he went into the synagogue, and spake ***boldly*** *for the space of three months, disputing and persuading the things concerning the kingdom of God.*
Acts 19:8

And many of the brethren in the Lord, waxing confident by my bonds, are much more ***bold to speak the word without fear****.*
Philippians 1:14

~~~~~
~~~~~

The Christians of the early Church were so convinced that the Gospel message was the only way to salvation that they ***boldly*** proclaimed the Gospel everywhere they went and turned their world upside down. During the two years Paul spent in Asia, everyone heard the Word of the Lord. Those early disciples were fearless before kings and magistrates, religious leaders, and pagans. They even fearlessly disciplined those in the church who sinned, and excommunicated those who tried to slip in and change the Gospel message.

Many of the modern churches have lost the spirit of ***holy boldness.*** They tiptoe around sin and even tolerate carnality and worldliness lest someone be offended. Our government has tried to intimidate the Church and silence their bold proclamations against sin by passing laws against "hate speech."

Where are the John the Baptists who fearlessly tell Herod that it is unlawful for him to take his brother's wife?

Where are the Peters who boldly tell Ananias and Sapphira that they have lied to the Holy Ghost?

Where are the Pauls who refuse to allow deceivers to prevent others from hearing and obeying the Gospel?
He even dared to call Elymas a child of the devil and an enemy of righteousness.

If we truly believe that the Gospel message is the ***power of God unto salvation*** (Romans 1:16), then it is time to quit trying to blend in with the world.

May God help us to fearlessly proclaim the Gospel and make no compromises with sin.
The world needs our bold witness.

Gem #99 **April 8**

I will praise thee;
*for **I am fearfully and wonderfully made:***
marvellous are thy works;
and that my soul knoweth right well.
Psalms 139:14

***Thine hands have made me** and fashioned **me** together round about…*
Job 10:8

The spirit of God hath made me,
and the breath of the Almighty hath given me life.
Job 33:4

***Thy hands have made me** and fashioned me:*
give me understanding, that I may learn thy commandments.
Psalms 119:73

~~~~~

The human body is a marvelous creation. Every system and organ and physical feature is so detailed and intricately designed. Today I praise God for life and the fact that He knows me inside and out. People may mistake my motives or misunderstand my words and actions, but He knows my heart.

~~~~~

"The human embryo is not the result of a biological accident, no matter what the circumstances. Rather, it embraces the image of God and is not to be equated with junk or trash to be discarded! God presides over the mysteries of human reproduction and because He does, all life has meaning and eternal significance."
Don Wyrtzen[15]

---

[15] Don, Wyrtzen, *A Musician Looks At The Psalms* (Grand Rapids, MI: Daybreak Books, 1988) 377.

Gem #100 **April 9**

How precious also are thy thoughts unto me, O God!
how great is the sum of them! If I should count them,
they are more in number than the sand:
when I awake, I am still with thee.
Psalms 139:17-18

For I know the thoughts that I think toward you,
saith the LORD, *thoughts of peace, and not of evil,*
to give you an expected end.
Jeremiah 29:11

Many, O LORD my God, are thy wonderful works which thou
hast done, ***and thy thoughts which are to us-ward:***
they cannot be reckoned up in order unto thee:
if I would declare and speak of them,
they are more than can be numbered.
Psalms 40:5

I love them that love me;
and those that ***seek me*** *early shall find me.*
Proverbs 8:17

~~~~~

I love the quiet of early mornings when my mind is clear, and I can meditate on the scriptures. It is in these quiet moments with the Lord that I remember how often He thinks peaceful thoughts about my life. He loves for me to seek Him and take delight in His presence and His Word. As the Psalmist says, it is a comfort to know that when I awake, He is still with me and is eager to share new treasures with me and give me direction for my day.

Have you spent time seeking Him today?
~~~~~

Gem #101 **April 10**

Behold, happy is the man whom ***God correcteth****:*
therefore despise not thou the ***chastening of the Almighty****:*
Job 5:17

My son, despise not the ***chastening of the LORD****;*
neither be weary of ***his correction****:*
Proverbs 3:11

But when we are judged, ***we are chastened of the Lord,***
that we should not be condemned with the world.
1 Corinthians 11:32

Now no ***chastening*** *for the present seemeth to be joyous, but grievous:*
nevertheless afterward it yieldeth the peaceable fruit of righteousness
unto them which are exercised thereby.
Hebrews 12:11

As many as I love, I rebuke and chasten:
be zealous therefore, and repent.
Revelation 3:19

~~~~~

I never have enjoyed getting in trouble, so for most of my life, I've tried to abide by the rules to avoid getting punished. However, I realize that correction is a necessary part of learning to be obedient and responsible. Paul taught that chastening of the Lord in this life will prevent condemnation with the world when we stand before God after this life. So even though I don't like the chastening that results from wrongdoing, it will produce righteousness in me…

…if I receive it humbly and make the necessary adjustments in my attitude and actions.
~~~~~

Gem #102 **April 11**

Jesus answered, Verily, verily, I say unto thee,
Except a man be born of water and of the Spirit,
he cannot enter *into the kingdom of God.*
John 3:5

Now when they heard this, they... said unto Peter and to the rest of the apostles, Men and brethren, What shall we do?
Then Peter said unto them, Repent, and ***be baptized every one of you in the name of Jesus Christ for the remission of sins,*** *and ye shall receive the gift of the Holy Ghost.*
Acts 2:37-38

~~~~~

I am feeling so thankful this morning as I remember the night of April 11, 1965 when as a 9-year old girl in DeRidder, Louisiana, I was ***born again of the water*** when my Pastor, Rev. V. A. Guidroz baptized me in the name of Jesus Christ for the remission of my sins. Then on August 8, 1965 as a 9-year old girl at the Apostolic Temple in Houston, Texas, I was ***born again of the Spirit***[16] when I was filled with the Holy Ghost and spoke in tongues for the very first time. Since then, I've been on a journey to develop maturity in my Christian walk. Although I've had many ups and downs and twists and bends in this road of life, I wouldn't trade these Biblical experiences for anything else this world has to offer.

[16] Although many people are born again of water and Spirit at the same time, the Bible pattern shows that sometimes the two events occur at different times. In Acts 8:15-17, the Samaritans were baptized in Jesus' name by Philip, but later were filled with the Holy Ghost when Peter and John prayed for them. In Acts 10:44-48, the Gentiles received the Holy Ghost while Peter was preaching, and afterward, Peter commanded them to be baptized in the name of Jesus. In Acts 19:1-6, the Ephesians believers had been baptized according to John the Baptist's teaching, but were rebaptized in Jesus' name after receiving Paul's teaching. Then Paul laid his hands on them, and they were all filled with the Holy Ghost.
~~~~~

Gem #103 **April 12**

And Jabez called on the God of Israel, saying,
Oh that thou wouldest bless me indeed, and enlarge my coast,
and that thine hand might be with me, and that thou wouldest
***keep me from evil,** that it may not grieve me!*
And God granted him that which he requested.
1 Chronicles 4:10

Keep me as the apple of the eye,
hide me under the shadow of thy wings,
Psalms 17:8

Keep back thy servant also from presumptuous sins;
let them not have dominion over me: then shall I be upright,
and I shall be innocent from the great transgression.
Psalms 19:13

***O keep my soul,** and deliver me: let me not be ashamed;*
for I put my trust in thee.
Psalms 25:20

Keep me, O LORD, from the hands of the wicked;
preserve me from the violent man; who have purposed
to overthrow my goings.
Psalms 140:4

Keep me from the snares which they have laid for me,
and the gins of the workers of iniquity.
Psalms 141:9

~~~~~

The enemy of our soul would love nothing better than to trip us up and destroy our relationship with God and everything that is righteous and holy. But if our constant prayer to God is, ***"Keep me from evil and all its influences,"*** He will hear and protect us, and we will be safe.
~~~~~

Gem #104 **April 13**

The God of my rock; in him will I trust:
he is my shield, and the horn of my salvation,
my high tower, and ***my refuge****, my saviour;*
thou savest me from violence.
2 Samuel 22:3

The LORD *also will be* ***a refuge*** *for the oppressed,*
a refuge *in times of trouble.*
Psalms 9:9

God is our ***refuge*** *and strength,*
a very present help in trouble.
Psalms 46:1

But I will sing of thy power; yea, I will sing aloud
of thy mercy in the morning: for thou hast been my defence and
refuge *in the day of my trouble.*
Psalms 59:16

Trust in him at all times; ye people, pour out your heart before him:
God is a ***refuge*** *for us. Selah.*
Psalms 62:8

~~~~~

When I read the news, I find many reasons to feel distressed and overwhelmed. Prices for goods and services continue to rise, yet income doesn't keep pace with the cost of living increases. Wars and acts of terror are constant threats. Weather disasters interrupt our daily routines. In spite of our best attempts to stay healthy, sickness and diseases abound. Where do we run to find hope and relief from all the dangers and distresses around us? The Bible reminds us over and over that God is our ***refuge*** from all the troubles that surround us. If we can just find a hiding place in the shadow of His wings, we can safely weather the storms of life.
~~~~~

Gem #105 **April 14**

...ye also are full of goodness, filled with all knowledge,
able also to admonish one another.
Romans 15:14

And to know the love of Christ, which passeth knowledge,
that ye might be ***filled with all the fulness of God****.*
Ephesians 3:19

And be not drunk with wine, ...but ***be filled with the Spirit;***
Ephesians 5:18

Being ***filled with the fruits of righteousness****, which are by*
Jesus Christ, unto the glory and praise of God.
Philippians 1:11

...we ...do not cease to pray for you, and to desire that ye
might be ***filled with the knowledge of his will***
in all wisdom and spiritual understanding;
Colossians 1:9

~~~~~

Many Christians have developed spiritual anorexia. They think they are full, yet in reality their spirit is starving. What are you filling your spirit with? God's Word has the answers to every question and every situation we face in this life. We can't expect to flourish in the things of God if our Bible is left untouched for days, or if we only read it for the sake of checking the box that we have completed our daily Bible reading. Knowledge of the Word will teach us God's will; we will learn the fruits of righteousness and will be able to produce those fruits in our life. The knowledge we have acquired through study of the Word will enable us to admonish and encourage others.

Are you spiritually anorexic? Open God's Word and fill yourself with the proper nutrients you need to flourish in God.
~~~~~

Gem #106 **April 15**

Thy word is a ***lamp*** *unto my feet, and a* ***light*** *unto my path.*
The entrance of thy words giveth ***light****;*
it giveth understanding unto the simple.
Psalms 119:105, 130

Then spake Jesus… I am the ***light*** *of the world: he that followeth me shall not walk in darkness, but shall have the* ***light*** *of life.*
John 8:12

Ye are the ***light*** *of the world… Let your* ***light*** *so shine before men, that they may see your good works, and glorify your Father which is in heaven.*
Matthew 5:14, 16

…the god of this world hath blinded the minds of them which believe not, lest the ***light of the glorious gospel of Christ****… should shine unto them.*
2 Corinthians 4:4

~~~~~

This world is a very dark place because of the huge amount of evil that surrounds us, yet the hope of the world lies in the Word of God, the Spirit of God, and the people of God who are Spirit-filled. The Old Testament speaks often about the Light of God and the Light of His Word. The New Testament especially likens God's people to lights in a dark, evil world. Every time God's Word is preached, darkness is pushed back. Everywhere God's Spirit-filled people go, darkness is dispelled. When we are filled with God's Spirit and His Word, we have essentially armed ourselves with the armor of Light (Romans 13:12) and are equipped to bring that light to a world that is perishing in darkness. Every week I go to a very dark place in our city, and I bring God's Spirit and the Light of His Word into the darkness of our county jail.

Make a difference in your world today by letting your light shine upon someone who is in darkness.
~~~~~

Gem #107 **April 16**

Fight the good fight of faith*, lay hold on eternal life,*
whereunto thou art also called, and hast professed
a good profession before many witnesses.
1 Timothy 6:12

Put on the whole armour of God*, that ye may be able*
to stand against the wiles of the devil. For we wrestle
not against flesh and blood, but against principalities,
against powers, against the rulers of the darkness of this world,
against spiritual wickedness in high places.
Ephesians 6:11-12

For though we walk in the flesh, ***we do not war after the flesh****:*
(For the weapons of our warfare are not carnal, but mighty
through God to the pulling down of strong holds;)
Casting down imaginations, and every high thing that
exalteth itself against the knowledge of God, and bringing
into captivity every thought to the obedience of Christ;
2 Corinthians 10:3-5

Thou therefore ***endure hardness, as a good soldier of Jesus Christ****.*
No man that warreth entangleth himself with the affairs of this life;
that he may please him who hath chosen him to be a ***soldier****.*
2 Timothy 2:3-4

But thanks be to God, which ***giveth us the victory***
through our Lord Jesus Christ.
1 Corinthians 15:57

~~~~~

The Old Testament tells many stories about fighting between the Jews and their enemies. It seems that war was a way of life to defend home and family. However, when Jesus came to earth, He specifically said that His followers were not to fight in His defense because His Kingdom was a spiritual one (John 18:36). One of Jesus' greatest followers, the Apostle Paul, taught that we were not to
~~~~~

concern ourselves with fighting against flesh and blood. Instead, we are to ***arm ourselves with the armour of God and fight the good fight of faith*** which involves fighting against the powers of darkness, spiritual wickedness, and anything that tries to exalt itself against the knowledge of the things of God. American Christians have not had to defend their faith like millions of Christians through the centuries have done, but the Devil is ruthless, and his modus operandi is to destroy anyone who will not proclaim him as lord of their lives. It's time for us to re-learn the art of spiritual warfare, for the evil around us will only continue to worsen (2 Timothy 3:13).

American Christians may one day face some tough times, but if we are a soldier in the army of Jesus Christ, we are assured of victory in the end.

Gem #108 **April 17**

*For the **eyes of the LORD** run to and fro throughout the whole earth, to shew himself strong in the behalf of them whose heart is perfect toward him…*
2 Chronicles 16:9

*…**for ye are the temple of the living God**; as God hath said, **I will dwell in them**, and walk in them; …and they shall be my people.*
2 Corinthians 6:16

~~~~~

God is searching for people who will consecrate themselves to be His Holy Temple. He longs to fill that person with His Spirit and be their Strength and Guide through all the complexities and adversities of life.

Are you lacking in strength and direction for your life?
Run to God. He is the answer for every longing of your heart.
~~~~~

Gem #109 **April 18**

*Now **faith** is the substance of things hoped for,*
the evidence of things not seen.
Hebrews 11:1

*By faith Noah, being warned of God of things **not seen as yet,** moved with fear, prepared an ark to the saving of his house; by the which he condemned the world, and became heir of the righteousness which is by faith.*
Hebrews 11:7

~~~~~

It is easy to praise God ***after*** our prayers are answered, but God is looking for those who will demonstrate great faith by worshiping and praising Him ***before*** they see the answer. The Bible gives examples of Abraham and Isaac, Daniel, Shadrach, Meshach and Abednego, who when faced with life-threatening situations, worshipped God ***first,*** and they were delivered. Noah built the ark ***before*** he even knew what rain was. The Israelites shouted and praised God ***before*** the walls of Jericho fell. Jehoshaphat appointed singers to go into battle ***before*** the army, and as they sang and praised, God smote the enemy. A Canaanite woman came to Jesus, asking for healing for her daughter, and Jesus said He was only sent to the children of Israel. But her worship ***before*** receiving any hope of an answer pleased Jesus, and she received her answer. A leper came to Jesus and worshipped ***before*** asking Jesus for healing, and Jesus healed him.[17]

What answers do you need from God today?
Worship and praise Him ***before*** you see the answer to your need.
God loves to respond to those who demonstrate "Great Faith."

---

[17] Scriptures for further study on the power of exhibiting faith BEFORE the answer comes. Genesis 22:1-19; Hebrews 11:17-19; Joshua 6:20; 2 Chronicles 20:21-22; Daniel 3:18; Daniel 6:10-28; Matthew 8:2-3; 5:22-28.
~~~~~

Gem #110 **April 19**

...**Happy** is that people, whose God is the LORD.
Psalms 144:15

~~~~~

Our secular and even church culture puts significant emphasis on the pursuit of happiness. In fact, the framers of our American Declaration of Independence inserted a line stating that all citizens had the God-given rights of "life, liberty and the pursuit of happiness."

What does the Bible have to say about pursuing happiness? Actually, the word is not even in the King James Version of the Bible. According to the dictionary, "happiness" is a noun which indicates having a source for joy or contentment, whereas the word ***"happy"*** is an adjective simply indicating an emotional state of being. So, what reasons does the Bible give for being happy? There are 7 of them.

1. The gift of having God as our Lord and being obedient to His laws (Deuteronomy 33:29; Psalms 144:15; 146:5; Proverbs 16:20; 28:14; 29:18; John 13:17; Romans 14:22)
2. The gift of correction when we do wrong (Job 5:17)
3. The gift of children (Genesis 30:13; Psalms 127:5)
4. The gift of wisdom from God (1 Kings 10:8; 2 Chronicles 9:7; Proverbs 3:13, 18)
5. The gift of showing kindness to the poor (Proverbs 14:21)
6. The gift of hard work and the ability to provide for our family (Psalms 128:2)
7. The gift of suffering for the name of Jesus (Acts 26:2; James 5:11; 1 Peter 3:14; 4:14)

If we have these 7 gifts in our life,
we are indeed "happy people."
~~~~~

Gem #111 **April 20**

I will ***extol*** *thee, O LORD; for thou hast lifted me up,*
and hast not made my foes to rejoice over me.
Psalms 30:1

Sing unto God, sing praises to his name: ***extol*** *him that rideth upon*
the heavens by his name JAH, and rejoice before him.
Psalms 68:4

I will ***extol*** *thee, my God, O king; and I will bless thy name for ever and*
ever. Every day will I bless thee; and I will praise thy name for ever and
ever. Great is the LORD, and greatly to be praised;
and his greatness is unsearchable.
Psalms 145:1-3

Let the ***high praises*** *of God be in their mouth,*
and a two-edged sword[18] *in their hand;*
Psalms 149:6

~~~~~

Praising God should be a part of the Christian's daily lifestyle. The Bible talks about praise over 250 times. However, the word ***extol*** is only used a handful of times. According to the dictionary, ***extol*** is lavish praise, exalted praise, or high praise.

God is worthy of being ***extolled***, and He will love the extra effort you put into praising Him.

How about stepping up your praise to God today from simple praise to *high praise*?

[18] Note: The two-edged sword in our hand is the Word of God according to Hebrews. 4:12.
~~~~~

Gem #112

April 21

...the children of men put their trust under the shadow of thy wings. They shall be ***abundantly satisfied*** *with the fatness of thy house; and thou shalt make them drink of the river of thy pleasures.*

Psalms 36:7-8

Thou visitest the earth, and waterest it: thou ***greatly enrichest*** *it with the river of God, which is full of water: thou preparest them corn, when thou hast so provided for it. Thou waterest the ridges thereof* ***abundantly****: thou settlest the furrows thereof: thou makest it soft with showers: thou blessest the springing thereof. Thou crownest the year with thy goodness; and thy paths drop* ***fatness****.*

Psalms 65:9-11

Let the wicked forsake his way, and the unrighteous man his thoughts: and let him return unto the LORD, and he will have mercy upon him; and to our God, for he will ***abundantly pardon.***

Isaiah 55:7

...I am come that they might have life, and that they might have it ***more abundantly.***

John 10:10

And to know the love of Christ, which passeth knowledge, that ye might be ***filled with all the fulness of God****. Now unto him that is able to do exceeding* ***abundantly above*** *all that we ask or think, according to the power that worketh in us, Unto him be glory...*

Ephesians 3:19-21

~~~~~

God is not stingy in sharing His wealth and goodness with His people. When He gives, He gives abundantly, whether it is in the natural provision of food, shelter and clothing, or in the spiritual provision of life, mercy, grace and pardon of our sins. What do you need today? Ask, and expect to receive an ***abundant answer***.
~~~~~

Gem #113 **April 22**

For the arms of the wicked shall be broken: but ***the LORD upholdeth the righteous.*** *The steps of a good man are ordered by the LORD: and he delighteth in his way. Though he* ***fall****, he shall not be utterly cast down: for* ***the LORD upholdeth him*** *with his hand.*

Psalms 37:17, 23-24

And as for me, ***thou upholdest me*** *in mine integrity, and settest me before thy face for ever.*

Psalms 41:12

The LORD upholdeth all that fall, *and raiseth up all those that be bowed down.*

Psalms 145:14

Fear thou not; for I am with thee: be not dismayed; for I am thy God: I will strengthen thee; yea, I will help thee; yea, ***I will uphold thee*** *with the right hand of my righteousness.*

Isaiah 41:10

The eternal God is thy refuge*, and underneath are the everlasting arms: and he shall thrust out the enemy from before thee; and shall say, Destroy them.*

Deuteronomy 33:27

~~~~~

The dictionary says that ***"uphold"*** means to support, defend or lift up. When you feel like you are falling into despair due to the severe pressures of life, look to God. His everlasting arms are under the righteous, holding them, supporting them, and defending them from the accusations of the enemy. I am thankful today for the refuge and arms of love that hold me during my times of sickness, disappointment and frustration.
~~~~~

Gem #114 **April 23**

***Thy words have upholden him** that was falling,*
and thou hast strengthened the feeble knees.
Job 4:4

***Uphold me according unto thy word**, that I may live: and let me not be ashamed of my hope. **Hold** thou me up, and I shall be safe: and I will have respect unto **thy statutes** continually.*
Psalms 119:116-117

*Thou hast proved mine heart; thou hast visited me in the night; thou hast tried me, and shalt find nothing; I am purposed that my mouth shall not transgress. ...by the **word of thy lips** I have kept me from the paths of the destroyer. **Hold up my goings** in thy paths, that my footsteps slip not.*
Psalms 17:3-5

***My people are destroyed for lack of knowledge**: because thou hast rejected **knowledge**, I will also reject thee, that thou shalt be no priest to me: seeing thou hast forgotten the law of thy God, I will also forget thy children.*
Hosea 4:6

~~~~~

Not only does God uphold the righteous, but His Word also upholds those who know it. People backslide because they do not know the Word well enough to use it as a weapon against the accusations of the enemy. Jesus told the Devil, *"It is written."* We are living in perilous, deceptive times, and our knowledge of the Word and of the Author of the Word will keep us from being deceived by the gifted orators and smooth talkers of the day. *"Thy word have I hid in mine heart, that I might not sin against thee."* (Psalms 119:11)

Will your knowledge of the Word uphold you when deceivers try to trip you up?
~~~~~

Gem #115 **April 24**

[Jesus said,] If ye love me, ***keep my commandments****.*
John 14:15

Know therefore that the LORD thy God, he is God, the faithful God, which keepeth covenant and mercy with them that love him and ***keep his commandments*** *to a thousand generations;*
Deuteronomy 7:9

Ye shall diligently ***keep the commandments*** *of the LORD your God, and his testimonies, and his statutes, which he hath commanded thee.*
Deuteronomy 6:17

Now therefore, if ye will ***obey my voice indeed, and keep my covenant****, then ye shall be a peculiar treasure unto me above all people: for all the earth is mine:*
Exodus 19:5

~~~~~

God is serious about His laws. Over 500 times we are commanded to ***obey and keep*** His commandments, laws, statutes, ordinances and covenants. Moses pronounces blessings on those who obey and curses on those who disobey. Jesus said if we loved Him, we would ***keep His commandments***.

Do you know what His commandments are?

Study the Word. There are hundreds of guidelines that make up the Christian lifestyle. **Keeping His commandments is not legalism**; it is the process of learning what pleases God and doing those things that bring Him pleasure.

Do you really love Jesus?
If you do, you will find delight in
learning and keeping His commandments.
~~~~~

Gem #116 **April 25**

There is a ***way*** *which seemeth right unto a man,*
but the end thereof are the ways of death.
Proverbs 14:12; 16:25

As for God, ***his way is perfect****: the word of the LORD is tried:*
he is a buckler to all those that trust in him.
Psalms 18:30

Blessed is every one that feareth the LORD; that walketh in ***his ways****.*
Psalms 128:1

The ***way of the Lord*** *is strength to the upright:*
but destruction shall be to the workers of iniquity.
Proverbs 10:29

In the ***way of righteousness*** *is life:*
and in the pathway thereof there is no death.
Proverbs 12:28

Righteousness keepeth him that is upright ***in the way****:*
but wickedness overthroweth the sinner.
Proverbs 13:6

~~~~~

God has given humanity the freedom to decide which ***way*** they want to live. The god of this world has so blinded men's eyes that they often choose the ***way*** that seems right to them, yet it ends in death. However, ***God's ways*** are perfect and right, and they are spelled out in His Word. His Word has stood the test of time and has been proven to be right over and over again.

If you want to learn the way of righteousness, study God's book, The Holy Bible, for in that way only, life can be found.
~~~~~

Gem #117 **April 26**

*Jesus saith unto him, I am **the way, the truth, and the life**: no man cometh unto the Father, but by me.*
John 14:6

*[Paul] desired of him letters to Damascus to the synagogues, that if he found any of **this way...** he might bring them bound unto Jerusalem.*
Acts 9:2

*And the same time there arose no small stir about **that way.***
Acts 19:23

*[Paul said,] And I persecuted **this way** unto the death, binding and delivering into prisons both men and women.*
Acts 22:4

*And when Felix heard these things, having more perfect knowledge of **that way**, he deferred them, and said, When Lysias the chief captain shall come down, I will know the uttermost of your matter.*
Acts 24:22

~~~~~

Much is written in the Old Testament about the blessings and favor on those who walk in the righteous ways of the Lord. When Jesus began His public ministry, He boldly proclaimed that He was the Way, the Truth, and the Life. Everything that a person needed could be found in Him. The teachings of the early Church focused on Jesus, and those teachings were often called "The Way." Unbelievers felt threatened by any mention of the name of Jesus or of His teachings, and the early Church followers were fiercely persecuted for their bold stand for Jesus. Things have not changed. Unbelievers still hate the name of Jesus and anything that has to do with His ways, but if we expect to spend eternity in Heaven with Him, then we must live our life according to ***His way*** that is very specifically defined in His Word, for ***His way is the only way.***
~~~~~

Gem #118 **April 27**

Be strong and of a good courage, fear not, nor be afraid of them:
for the LORD thy God, he it is that doth go with thee;
he will not fail thee, nor forsake thee.
Deuteronomy 31:6

And they that know thy name will put their trust in thee:
for thou, ***LORD, hast not forsaken them that seek thee.***
Psalms 9:10

Let your conversation be without covetousness;
and be content with such things as ye have: for he hath said,
I will never leave thee, nor forsake thee.
Hebrews 13:5

~~~~~

Jesus has never failed nor forsaken me. I must not fail Him.
This beautiful old song by Doris Akers is my prayer.

~~~~~

I Cannot Fail The Lord

The Lord of my life He has never failed.
On my own I could never succeed.
This One I came to know,
There's so much I owe
And I cannot fail the Lord.
And things when done
In His Name are won
In the past I didn't trust God
I trusted in myself,
Now, thank God, I have His help
And I cannot fail the Lord.
I cannot fail the Lord,
I cannot fail the Lord
He has never failed me yet
Every problem He has met
And I cannot fail the Lord.

Gem #119 **April 28**

And [Jesus] answered and said unto them, ***My mother and my brethren are these which hear the word of God, and do it.***
Luke 8:21

He that is of God heareth God's words*: ye therefore hear them not, because ye are not of God.*
John 8:47

And hereby we do know that ***we know him, if we keep his commandments.*** *He that saith, I know him, and keepeth not his commandments, is a liar, and the truth is not in him. But* ***whoso keepeth his word, in him verily is the love of God perfected****: hereby know we that we are in him.*
1 John 2:3-5

But be ye doers of the word, and not hearers only, *deceiving your own selves.*
James 1:22

~~~~~

Here is the litmus test for determining if I belong to God's family:

Am I obeying all of God's Word? I don't want to stand in judgment and hear God say He never knew me because I failed to obey His Words.

~~~~~

"Christian, there are times when we've got to step out from the crowd and take a solitary stand for the Truth of God. Everybody else may be doing it; everybody else may be saying it; everybody else (even other Christians) may be calling it right, but if the word of God says otherwise, you must not be swayed by the foolishness of this world."
Leroy Elms

Gem #120 **April 29**

And David ***danced before the LORD*** *with all his might;*
and David was girded with a linen ephod.
2 Samuel 6:14

Let them ***praise his name in the dance:***
let them sing praises unto him with the timbrel and harp.
Psalms 149:3

Praise him with the timbrel and dance:
praise him with stringed instruments and organs.
Psalms 150:4

O ***clap your hands****, all ye people;*
shout unto God *with the voice of triumph.*
Psalms 47:1

Make a joyful noise unto the LORD*, all the earth:*
make a loud noise, *and rejoice, and sing praise.*
Psalms 98:4

~~~~~

The Bible gives many examples of people praising God exuberantly. He expects more than just half-hearted worship or singing from us. He wants our whole bodies to be involved in praising Him. We are instructed to praise Him with musical instruments and loud, joyful singing accompanied by clapping of hands and dancing. The loud prayers and praises of the Early Church shook buildings and opened prison doors (Acts 4:31; 12:5-11; 16:25-26).

Do you want to make God happy?
Get your body in motion and praise Him loudly,
joyfully, fervently and enthusiastically.
~~~~~

 **Gem #121** **April 30**

For I am the LORD your ***God****: ye shall therefore sanctify yourselves,*
and ye shall be ***holy****; for I am* ***holy...***
Leviticus 11:44

Follow peace with all men,
and ***holiness****, without which no man shall see the Lord:*
Hebrews 12:14

But ye are a chosen generation, a royal priesthood, an ***holy*** *nation,*
a ***peculiar*** *people; that ye should shew forth the praises of him who*
hath called you out of darkness into his marvellous light;
1 Peter 2:9

~~~~~

Dozens of references in scripture instruct God's people to be ***holy*** because He is ***holy***. Additional scriptures describe God's people as ***peculiar***. Today's modern church often rejects the idea of being peculiar, holy or different. After all, how can we win the world if we don't look like them and act like them?? Where is that idea found in scripture?? God has always expected His people to stand out, be lights in the midst of darkness, and be sanctified, set apart, and holy. For some reason, the Church submits to rules of conduct and dress codes in the work place, but struggles with the fact that God also has rules of conduct and dress. It's time to stop trying to fit in with the world and find delight in being God's different, set-apart, peculiar, and holy people. The benefits of being holy unto God far outweigh any benefits the world has to offer, for...

Without holiness, no man shall see the Lord.

~~~~~

"The greatest miracle that God can do today is to take an unholy
man out of an unholy world and make him ***holy***,
then put him back into that unholy world and keep him ***holy*** in it."
Leonard Ravenhill

Gem #122 **May 1**

I …beseech you that ye walk worthy of the vocation wherewith ye are called, With all lowliness and meekness, with longsuffering, forbearing one another in love; ***Endeavouring to keep the unity of the Spirit*** *in the bond of peace.* ***There is one body, and one Spirit,*** *even as ye are called in one hope of your calling;*

Ephesians 4:1-4

~~~~~

One of the oldest bridges in Rome, the Ponte Fabricio, also earned the nickname of "The Bridge of Four Heads" in the sixteenth century. Because the bridge had fallen into disrepair, Pope Sixtus V hired four renowned architects to work together to repair the bridge. They couldn't agree on how the work should be done and even came to blows many times during the project. The Pope was grieved at their feuding, but he let them finish the task before he announced their punishment. He had all four of them beheaded on the bridge; then on the very spot of their execution, he erected a monument to them consisting of four heads carved into one block of stone. "Now," he said, "for the rest of eternity, they are committed to a peaceful and quiet unity."[19]

God is the head of one body, the Church, to whom the task has been given to preach the Gospel to every creature. Paul taught that the members of the body were to work together with humility while making every effort to maintain peace and preserve the unity of the Spirit. Jesus said that a divided kingdom could not stand (Matthew 12:25). Although Pope Sixtus V's punishment of the quarreling architects may seem a bit extreme, the consequences for being contentious in God's Kingdom are far worse. Eternal separation from God and His people in the lake of fire is not worth the temporary satisfaction we may gain from fussing and trying to get our way. Let's "endeavor to keep the unity of the Spirit in the bond of peace" as we labor together to build the Kingdom of God.

---

[19] Nino Lo Bello, *The Incredible Book of Vatican Facts and Papal Curiosities* (Liguori, MO: Liguori Publications, 1998) 108-109
~~~~~

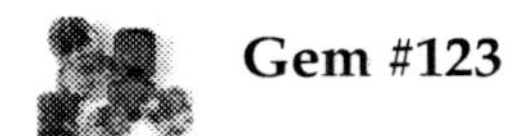

Gem #123 **May 2**

*He shall pray unto God, and he will be **favourable** unto him: and he shall see his face with joy: for he will render unto man his righteousness.*
Job 33:26

*For thou, LORD, wilt bless the righteous; with **favour** wilt thou compass him as with a shield.*
Psalms 5:12

*Fools make a mock at sin: but among the righteous there is **favour.***
Proverbs 14:9

*Sow to yourselves in **righteousness**, reap in mercy; break up your fallow ground: for it is time to **seek the Lord, till he come and rain righteousness upon you**.*
Hosea 10:12

~~~~~

As a young girl, I remember the desire I had to please my school teachers and find favor with them. Often other students called those favored ones the *"teacher's pet."* I achieved that status one year with my 7th grade home room teacher. She often had me grading papers for her and recording the grades in her grade book. She even had me put my desk up front next to hers where I could face the class. If she had to leave the room, I was the designated monitor to take note of anyone who misbehaved while she was out. God has favorites also. When we pray to Him, He renders or rewards us with His righteousness. It is the righteous who are surrounded with God's favor and blessings.

Do you want to be God's "pet"?

Seek Him today until He comes and rains righteousness on you. Then and only then, will you be one of His favorites.
~~~~~

Gem #124 **May 3**

Make a joyful noise unto the Lord, all the earth:
make a loud noise, and rejoice, and sing praise.
Sing unto the Lord with the harp;
with the harp, and the voice of a psalm.
With trumpets and sound of cornet make a
joyful noise before the Lord, the King.
*...for **He cometh to judge the earth**:*
with righteousness shall he judge the world,
and the people with equity [impartiality].
Psalms 98:4-6, 9

*...the day of wrath and revelation of the righteous **judgment** of God;*
Who will render to every man according to his deeds:
For there is no respect of persons with God.
Romans 2:5-6, 11

And if ye call on the Father, who without respect of persons
***judgeth** according to every man's work,*
pass the time of your sojourning here in fear:
1 Peter 1:17

~~~~~

Soon and very soon, my King will come to judge the earth. I may experience the biased, unfair judgment of men at times, but when Jesus comes, His judgment will be fair and impartial based on my obedience to His laws. We should sing and rejoice with exuberance as we anticipate that soon-coming day.
~~~~~

Gem #125 **May 4**

Give unto the Lord the ***glory*** *due unto his name: bring an offering, and come before him: worship the Lord in the* ***beauty of holiness****.*
1 Chronicles 16:29

Give unto the Lord the ***glory*** *due unto his name;*
worship the Lord in the ***beauty of holiness****.*
Psalms 29:2

Give unto the LORD the ***glory*** *due unto his name: bring an offering, and come into his courts. O worship the LORD in the*
beauty of holiness: *fear before him, all the earth.*
Psalms 96:8-9

And when [Jehoshaphat] had consulted with the people, he appointed singers unto the Lord, and that should ***praise the beauty of holiness,*** *as they went out before the army, and to say, Praise the Lord; for his mercy endureth for ever.*
2 Chronicles 20:21

~~~~~

HOLINESS applies to Christians who are ***consecrated*** [set apart] to God's service and ***conformed*** [in compliance] in all things to the will of God. ~ Eaton's 1897 Bible Dictionary

~~~~~

Three times the Bible instructs us to worship the Lord in the ***beauty of Holiness****,* and one time the phrase is used as a method for winning a battle against Israel's enemies. The ***beauty of holiness*** that brings glory to God is the worship that comes from those who have set a standard of separation from the world and live a lifestyle of obedience to the commands of the Bible.

May my worship today be done in the ***beauty of holiness*** which glorifies the Lord.

Gem #126 **May 5**

Neither have I gone back from the commandment of his lips;
I have ***esteemed the words of his mouth*** *more*
than my necessary food.
Job 23:12

O how ***love I thy law****! it is my meditation all the day.*
Psalms 119:97

Thy word *is very pure: therefore thy servant* ***loveth it.***
Psalms 119:140

~~~~~

The story is told of a blind French girl who was given a copy of the gospel of Mark in Braille. As she read and reread the book, she came to have faith in Christ, and the book became more precious with each reading. She read it so much that she developed calluses on her fingers that eventually prevented her from feeling the raised dots. She was so determined to read God's word that she peeled the skin off the tips of her fingers to make them more sensitive, but in doing so she permanently damaged the nerves. Devastated, she picked up the book to kiss it farewell, only to discover that her lips were even more sensitive than her fingers. And she spent the rest of her days reading God's word with her lips.

How much do you love God's Word? It is more necessary and valuable than the daily food with which you feed your body. Pick up the Word today and feast on its contents. Your spirit will be renewed.

~~~~~

"It is impossible to estimate the full influence of the reading of the Word in a home day after day and year after year. It filters into the hearts of the young. It is absorbed into their souls. Its holy teachings become the principles of their lives, which rule their conduct and shape all their actions."
James Russell Miller

Gem #127 **May 6**

And he shall speak great words against the most High,
and shall ***wear out the saints of the most High,***
and think to change times and laws…
Daniel 7:25

For with stammering lips and another tongue will he speak to this people.
To whom he said, ***This is the rest*** *wherewith ye may*
cause the weary to rest; and ***this is the refreshing…***
Isaiah 28:11-12

[Jesus said,] Come unto me, all ye that labour and are heavy laden,
and ***I will give you rest.*** *Take my yoke upon you, and learn of me;*
for I am meek and lowly in heart: and ***ye shall find rest*** *unto your souls.*
For my yoke is easy, and my burden is light.
Matthew 11:28-30

~~~~~

Modern life puts many demands upon our time. In spite of the availability of more labor-saving devices, we are busier than ever, and many of us live in a state of constant exhaustion. The prophet Daniel warned us that in the last days, one of Hell's primary agendas would be to wear out the saints of the Most High so they would be too busy or too tired to wage warfare against his evil schemes. It is time for the Church to wake up and shake herself. Although it is very important to get sufficient sleep every night to refresh our body, it is equally important to spend time in God's presence and in His Word so we can receive the spiritual rest and the strength we need to fight our adversary and take a bold stand against his evil agenda. Are you searching for a solution to your continual weariness?? Come to Jesus and soak up the life-giving strength and restoration that can only be found in His presence and in His Word. Then go out and…

Fight for what is right;
for Greater is He that is in you than he that is in the world.
~~~~~

Gem #128 **May 7**

***This is my comfort** in my affliction:*
*for **thy word** hath quickened me.*
Psalms 119:50

For whatsoever things were written aforetime were written
for our learning, that we through patience and
***comfort of the scriptures** might have hope.*
Romans 15:4

~~~~~

Life is not always a bed of roses or smooth sailing on the sea of life. Many of our days are filled with hurt, sickness, misunderstandings, losses, sorrow or grief. Often people try to comfort us in those times of pain, but sometimes their attempts at comfort only make the pain worse. Shortly after the death of my husband, I remember some well-meaning people who attempted to comfort me by quoting a scripture. A frequently quoted scripture was, *"Precious in the sight of the Lord is the death of his saints"* (Psalms 116:15). One time I was hurting so badly that I just blurted out to one well-meaning, but ignorant person, "Well, it may be precious to God, but it isn't precious to me." Yet in spite of the pain that some scriptures inflicted on me in those dark days right after Ron's death, the Word was my comfort and my hope. I found so many passages that soothed my wounded, broken spirit, and over the past 14 years, the Word has been the anchor that has held me fast.

Are you depressed, lonely, sick, or forsaken by those you love?

Look to the Word. It will comfort you, revive and encourage you, and restore hope that God knows where you are and will see you safely through.
~~~~~

Gem #129 **May 8**

And [Hannah] was in bitterness of soul, and prayed unto the LORD,
and wept sore. And she vowed a vow, and said, O LORD of hosts,
if thou wilt indeed look on the affliction of thine handmaid,
and remember me, … but wilt give unto thine handmaid a man child,
then I will give him unto the Lord all the days of his life…
And ***Samuel judged Israel all the days of his life.***
1 Samuel 1:10-11; 7:15

By faith Moses, when he was born, was hid three months of his parents,
because they saw he was a proper child;
and ***they were not afraid of the king's commandment.***
Hebrews 11:23

~~~~~

In America, the second Sunday of May is set aside to give honor to Mothers everywhere, so in today's lesson, I share a story about Jochebed and Hannah, mothers of Moses and Samuel, two of Israel's greatest leaders. No doubt these two men were deeply influenced by the faith and prayers of their mothers. Jochebed believed God had a purpose for her son, Moses and hid him from the king and his spies. Then when he was adopted by the king's daughter, Jochebed was allowed to nurse him for several years. She was so successful in teaching him the ways of God during those early years, that all the wealth and education of Egypt were unable to sway him from his roots. Many years later, Hannah's desperate prayer to have a child caused her to vow to give him back to God all of his life. I can't imagine the sacrifice involved in keeping that promise. Israel's destiny was radically changed because of Moses' and Samuel's influence during their lifetimes. Today God is looking for dedicated, faithful mothers who will weep and train their children to be great men and women of God. A mother's prayers are powerful and can change the course of history.

Mothers, accept the challenge today and let your prayers and teaching produce great men and women in God's Kingdom!
~~~~~

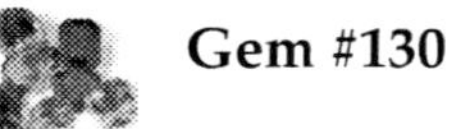

Gem #130 **May 9**

So was ended all the work that king Solomon made for the house of the LORD. And Solomon brought in the things which David his father had dedicated; even the silver, and the gold, and the vessels, did he put among the ***treasures of the house of the Lord.***
1 Kings 7:51

And of the Levites, Ahijah was over the ***treasures of the house of God,*** *and over the treasures of the dedicated things. The sons of Jehieli; Zetham, and Joel his brother, which were over* ***the treasures of the house of the Lord.***
1 Chronicles 26:20, 22

~~~~~

The Bible describes in vivid detail the treasures contained in the Tabernacle, and later in the Temple of God. Men were even assigned the task of guarding those treasures. Heathen nations coveted the rich treasures of God's house, and on many occasions, the Bible tells of heathen kings making war against Israel and carrying away the treasures of the house of God.

What kind of treasures can we find in modern-day houses of God? What about pastors who teach the Word of God and lead the people into deeper understanding of God's ways? What about the elders who possess a lifetime of rich experiences to teach the younger people how to live an overcoming life? What about the power of corporate worship and the joy of basking in God's presence with the family of God? What about the living Word of God that contains unlimited amounts of inspiration and building blocks upon which to build a Godly and holy, Christian lifestyle? If you are not connected to a Bible-based pastor and family of God, you are missing out on one of the greatest treasures that you can possess in this life. Find a place to worship and plant yourself there. Then you will possess treasures that money cannot buy.
~~~~~

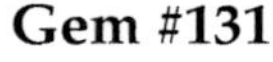

Gem #131 **May 10**

For ***the ways of man*** *are before the eyes of the* LORD*,*
and he pondereth all his goings.
Proverbs 5:21

O lord, ***thou hast searched me, and known me****. Thou knowest my downsitting and mine uprising, thou understandest my thought afar off. Thou compassest my path and my lying down, and art acquainted with all my ways. Search me, O God, and know my heart: try me, and know my thoughts: And see if there be any wicked way in me, and lead me in the way everlasting.*
Psalms 139:1-3, 23-24

\~\~\~\~\~

We often wear a mask when we are in public to prevent people from knowing the ***"real me."*** But God knows the very thoughts of my heart and even the motives behind all my actions. Nothing is hidden from Him. If we have secret sins in our life, it is time to repent and allow God's searchlight to point out our wickedness and lead us into His everlasting ways of truth, holiness and purity.

Gem #132 **May 11**

I remember the days of old; I meditate on all thy works;
I muse on the work of thy hands. I stretch forth my hands unto thee:
my soul thirsteth after thee, as a thirsty land. Selah.
Psalms 143:5-6

\~\~\~\~\~

As I read of the wars and calamity in our world, there is much reason to fear, but this morning I am remembering times of God's provision in my past, times of healing and miraculous intervention in times of danger. My eyes are on Him instead of the troubles around me. Today I am thirsting for more of Him and I am reaching out my hands to Him for assurance that in His arms, I am safe.

Gem #133 **May 12**

Nebuchadnezzar the king made an image of gold, ... he set it upin the plain of Dura, in the province of Babylon. Then an herald cried aloud, To you it is commanded... That at what time ye hear the sound of ...all kinds of musick, ye fall down and worship the golden image that ...the king hath set up: And whoso falleth not down and worshippeth shall the same hour be cast into the midst of a burning fiery furnace... Then Nebuchadnezzar spake, and said, Blessed be the God of Shadrach, Meshach, and Abednego, who hath sent his angel, and delivered his servants that trusted in him... that they might not serve nor worship any god, except their own. Therefore I make a decree, That every people, nation, and language, which speak any thing amiss against the God of Shadrach, Meshach, and Abednego, shall be cut in pieces, ...because there is no other God that can deliver after this sort.

Daniel 3:1, 4-6, 28-29

The same hour was the thing fulfilled upon Nebuchadnezzar: and he was driven from men, and did eat grass as oxen, and his body was wet with the dew of heaven, till his hairs were grown like eagles' feathers, and his nails like birds' claws. And at the end of the days I Nebuchadnezzar lifted up mine eyes unto heaven, and mine understanding returned unto me, and I blessed the most High, and I praised and honoured him that liveth for ever, whose dominion is an everlasting dominion, and his kingdom is from generation to generation:

Daniel 4:33-34

~~~~~

King Nebuchadnezzar was consumed with his agenda to force his subjects to honor and bow down to him. He was stopped in his tracks when God delivered the three Hebrew boys from the fiery furnace and made a decree that everyone must worship the Hebrews' God. But his memory of God's mighty power forsook him the very next chapter, and he again proclaimed himself as the great king of Babylon who had done so many mighty works. God again cut him down to size and sent him out to live like an animal for
~~~~~

seven years. Then he recognized God's sovereignty and control over all the affairs of men.

Fast forward to the twenty-first century, and it looks like our government officials have forsaken everything that is righteous and Godly and are getting by with it. But don't be dismayed, for there is coming a day when *"every knee shall bow…and every tongue shall confess to God"* (Romans 14:11). **God will have the last say.**

Gem #134 **May 13**

Therefore take no thought, saying, What shall we eat? or, What shall we drink? or, Wherewithal shall we be clothed? (For after all these things do the Gentiles seek:) for your heavenly Father knoweth that ye have need of all these things. But seek ye first the kingdom of God, and his righteousness; ***and all these things shall be added unto you.***
Matthew 6:31-33

But my God shall ***supply all your need*** *according to his riches in glory by Christ Jesus.*
Philippians 4:19

~~~~~

There's no need to get in a panic about how to pay the bills, put food on the table, clothes on your back or provide a place to live. God has promised His children that if they would take care of Kingdom business first, He would see to it that their basic needs were supplied.

So if you are struggling to make ends meet, try changing priorities and put God's business first. He will keep His promise to take care of those who belong to Him.
~~~~~

Gem #135 **May 14**

Honour the LORD with thy substance*, and with the firstfruits of all thine increase: So shall thy barns be filled with plenty, and thy presses shall burst out with new wine.*

Proverbs 3:9-10

Give, and it shall be given unto you*; good measure, pressed down, and shaken together, and running over, shall men give into your bosom. For with the same measure that ye mete withal it shall be measured to you again.*

Luke 6:38

Every man according as he purposeth in his heart, so ***let him give****; not grudgingly, or of necessity: for* ***God loveth a cheerful giver****.*

2 Corinthians 9:7

~~~~~

Giving is a major doctrine of the Bible and is mentioned almost 1,400 times. This doctrine encompasses so many areas. Normally we tend to think of giving in terms of giving money, and that is mentioned numerous times. However, we are instructed to ***give thanks, give praise, and give ear to teaching.*** Then there are hundreds of scriptures that tell of the things ***God gives to His people*** such as peace, strength, land, provision, the Holy Ghost, and the list goes on. It is the nature of God to give, and He loves and blesses those who demonstrate cheerful, generous giving. If you feel lonely, financially strapped, or frustrated over things you do not understand, try exercising the doctrine of giving. Give time to children, the elderly or shut-ins. Give friendship to those who are alone and misunderstood. Give money to God, to the poor, to someone who has lost their job or their home to a natural disaster. Give of your knowledge to those who are asking questions. Give ear to instruction from pastors, elders, parents, teachers, and authorities. If we can learn to give generously, cheerfully, and faithfully, our lives will be greatly enriched and blessed. Try it. You will not be disappointed.
~~~~~

Gem #136

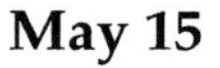
May 15

Let the priests, the ministers of the LORD, ***Weep between the porch and the altar,*** *and let them say, spare thy people, O LORD, and give not thine heritage to reproach, that the heathen should rule over them: wherefore should they say among the people, Where is their God?*

Joel 2:17

They that sow in tears shall reap in joy. He that goeth forth and ***weepeth,*** *bearing precious seed, shall doubtless come again with rejoicing, bringing his sheaves with him.*

Psalms 126:5-6

~~~~~

Our nation is in trouble because it has forsaken its moral and Biblical foundations. Our churches are in trouble because the spirit of tolerance has crept in and persuaded them to tolerate sin and worldliness. Our families are in trouble because couples have forsaken the vow of commitment to each other. Evil men and women have ignored God's laws of marriage between a man and a woman and have perverted marriage by men marrying men and women marrying women (Leviticus 18:22; 20:13; Romans 1:21-28). Babies are undervalued, and 40-50 million are aborted worldwide every year. Confusion abounds because God's laws are ignored!

GOD IS VERY ANGRY!!

Where are the weepers who are weeping for the sins of God's people? Where are the sowers who sow God's laws into the hearts of the wayward? If we will weep as we sow, God promises a joyful harvest.
~~~~~

Gem #137 **May 16**

Thou hast forgiven the iniquity of thy people,
thou hast ***covered all their sin****.*
Psalms 85:2

As far as the east is from the west, so far hath he
removed our transgressions from us*.*
Psalms 103:12

...thou hast in love to my soul delivered it from the pit of corruption:
for thou hast ***cast all my sins behind thy back****.*
Isaiah 38:17

He will turn again, he will have compassion upon us;
he will subdue our iniquities; and thou wilt ***cast all***
their sins into the depths of the sea.
Micah 7:19

And you, being dead in your sins and the uncircumcision of
your flesh, hath he quickened together with him,
having ***forgiven you all trespasses;***
Colossians 2:13

But if we walk in the light, as he is in the light,
we have fellowship one with another, and the ***blood*** *of*
Jesus Christ his Son ***cleanseth us from all sin.***
1 John 1:7

~~~~~

When the devil comes knocking on your door and reminding you of the sins in your past, speak the Word to him and let him know that God has removed *ALL* your sins from your record and through His blood, those sins are covered, and your record is clean. The devil is subject to the Word. Know it and speak it, and he will flee.
~~~~~

Gem #138 **May 17**

And when they had prayed, the place was shaken where they were assembled together; and they were ***all filled with the Holy Ghost,*** *and they spake the word of God with boldness. And with* ***great power*** *gave the apostles witness of the resurrection of the Lord Jesus…*

Acts 4:31, 33

And when they were come, and had gathered the church together, they rehearsed ***all that God had done with them****, and how he had opened the door of faith unto the Gentiles.*

Acts 14:27

~~~~~

Before Jesus ascended into Heaven, He instructed His disciples to be filled with the Holy Ghost (Luke 24:49; John 20:22; Acts 1:8) so they would be empowered to preach the Gospel. After being filled with the Holy Ghost, the formerly timid disciples were changed into fearless, bold, and powerful ambassadors of the Gospel. God worked through them to perform miraculous healings and deliverances in the lives of those who heard their message.

If we want to be effective today in ministry, the pattern for the Church has not changed. We must be filled with the Spirit so that God can work through us to convert and meet the needs of the hungry, hurting people who cross our path.

~~~~~

"The world has yet to see what God will do with, and for, and through, and in, and by, the man who is fully consecrated to Him,"

John Knox

Gem #139 **May 18**

It came even to pass, as the trumpeters and ***singers*** *were as one,*
to make one sound to be heard in praising and thanking the LORD…
that then the house was filled with a cloud,
even the house of the LORD;
2 Chronicles 5:13

And when they began to ***sing and to praise****,*
the LORD set ambushments against the children of
Ammon, Moab, and mount Seir,
which were come against Judah;
and they were smitten.
2 Chronicles 20:22

And at midnight Paul and Silas prayed,
and ***sang praises*** *unto God: and the prisoners heard them.*
And suddenly there was a great earthquake, so that the foundations
of the prison were shaken: and immediately all the doors were opened,
and every one's bands were loosed.
Acts 16:25-26

~~~~~

There is power in a song that is sung as praise and worship to God. Israel's songs of worship in the Temple brought the glory of God into the house. Their songs of praise in battle brought deliverance from their enemies. Paul and Silas' songs of praise in the prison brought an earthquake that freed them and all the prisoners, and ultimately resulted in the salvation of the jailer and his family.

Are you feeling down in your spirit? Begin to sing, and you will witness the hand of God as He turns your sorrow into joy.
~~~~~

 **Gem #140** **May 19**

And being not weak in faith, [Abraham] considered not his own body now dead, when he was about an hundred years old, neither yet the deadness of Sarah's womb:
He staggered not at the promise of God through unbelief; but was strong in faith*, giving glory to God;*
And being fully persuaded that,
what he had promised,
he was able also to perform.
Romans 4:19-21

Jesus said unto him, ***If thou canst believe, all things are possible*** *to him that believeth.*
Mark 9:23

~~~~~

Even though Abraham and Sarah had long passed the age of physically being able to produce children, Abraham believed God's promise that they would have a son. Jesus said that all things were possible to those who believe. Think about the promises that God has made to the Church: forgiveness of sins to those who are baptized in His name; salvation and eternal life to those who obey His commandments; provision for all their needs; healing for their sick bodies; He will never leave or forsake them.

Are you staggering at God's promises through unbelief? If so, then pray the prayer of Mark 9:24:

"Lord, I believe; help thou mine unbelief."

God has great and powerful things in store for those who will simply ***believe*** His Word and act on it.
~~~~~

Gem #141 **May 20**

Now the L*ORD had said unto Abram, Get thee out of thy country, and from thy kindred, and from thy father's house, unto a land that I will shew thee: And I will make of thee a great nation, and I will bless thee, and make thy name great; and thou shalt be a blessing: And* ***I will bless them that bless thee****, and curse him that curseth thee: and in thee shall all families of the earth be blessed. And the* L*ORD appeared unto Abram, and said, unto they seed will I give this land: and there builded he an altar unto the* L*ORD, who appeared unto him.*

Genesis 12:1-3, 7

Pray for the peace of Jerusalem: ***they shall prosper that love thee.***

Psalms 122:6

...I will gather you from all the nations, and from all the places whither I have driven you, saith the L*ORD; and* ***I will bring you again*** *into the place whence I caused you to be carried away captive.*

Jeremiah 29:14

~~~~~

The fact that Israel has survived against all odds for thousands of years is overwhelming evidence of the Truth of God's Word. The land that makes up modern-day Israel was promised to Abraham and his seed. Even though the nation was destroyed by Assyria, Babylon, and Rome, God raised it again in 1948. No other nation in the world has maintained such a distinct identity in culture, language and geography as have the Jews. God's Word promises a blessing on those who will bless the Jews and pray for the peace of that hotly-contested land. If you want to be blessed of God, then...

PRAY FOR THE PEACE OF JERUSALEM.
~~~~~

Gem #142 **May 21**

*Be **kindly affectioned** one to another with brotherly love;*
in honour preferring one another;
Romans 12:10

*And **be ye kind** one to another, tenderhearted, forgiving one another,*
even as God for Christ's sake hath forgiven you.
Ephesians 4:32

Put on therefore, as the elect of God, holy and beloved,
***bowels of mercies, kindness,** humbleness of mind, meekness,*
longsuffering; Forbearing one another, and forgiving one another,
if any man have a quarrel against any: even as Christ forgave you,
so also do ye. And above all these things put on charity,
which is the bond of perfectness.
Colossians 3:12-14

~~~~~

"Kindness is a language which
the deaf can hear and the blind can see."
Mark Twain

~~~~~

It is so easy to get caught up in our own little world and ignore others who are struggling. Sometimes just a simple word or act of kindness to someone will lift them out of despair and hopelessness. The character traits of kindness, mercy, humility, longsuffering, tenderheartedness, and forgiveness are sometimes lacking in the people of God. Life can be tough, but if we would observe the trials of others and show kindness, compassion, and tenderness, their hard trials would be easier to manage.

Gem #143 **May 22**

Labour *not to be rich: cease from thine own wisdom.*
Proverbs 23:4

Wherefore do ye spend money for that which is not bread? and your ***labour*** *for that which satisfieth not? hearken diligently unto me, and eat ye that which is good, and let your soul delight itself in fatness.*
Isaiah 55:2

And [Jesus] said unto them, Take heed, and beware of covetousness: for a man's life consisteth not in the abundance of the things which he possesseth.
Luke 12:15

Labour *not for the meat which perisheth, but for that meat which endureth unto everlasting life, which the Son of man shall give unto you…*
John 6:27

Then saith he unto his disciples, The harvest truly is plenteous, but the ***labourers*** *are few; Pray ye therefore the Lord of the harvest, that he will send forth* ***labourers*** *into his harvest.*
Matthew 9:37-38

~~~~~

We ***labor*** to provide food, clothing and shelter which are necessary for sustaining life. However, after the essentials are provided, we spend additional time laboring to provide for entertainment, recreation, and acquisition of "stuff." Jesus warned against spending inordinate amounts of time acquiring possessions. His approval of our lives depends, not on our labors to accumulate "stuff," but rather on our labors to spread the Gospel and bring men and women into His Kingdom. It's time to perform an evaluation and make whatever adjustments are required to ensure that Kingdom matters receive higher priority than our desire to amass wealth and possessions.
~~~~~

Gem #144 **May 23**

Then Job arose, …and fell down upon the ground, and worshipped,
And said, …the LORD gave, and the LORD hath taken away;
Blessed be the name of the Lord. In all this Job sinned not,
nor charged God foolishly.

Job 1:20-22

Though he slay me, yet will I trust in him…
He also shall be my salvation…

Job 13:15-16

For I know that my redeemer liveth, and that he shall stand at the latter day upon the earth: And though after my skin worms destroy this body, yet in my flesh shall I see God: Whom I shall see for myself, and mine eyes shall behold, and not another…

Job 19:25-27

But he knoweth the way that I take: when he hath tried me,
I shall come forth as gold.

Job 23:10

~~~~~

Job experienced loss like few people on earth ever have, yet in the face of every loss, he continued to voice his faith that God would work everything out for his ultimate good. God gets no glory out of your whining and complaining during your hard trials. When you are going through tough times, remember Job and speak words of faith.

God responds to faith, and in His timing, He will deliver you.
~~~~~

Gem #145 **May 24**

Remember that ***thou magnify his work, which men behold.***
Every man may see it; man may behold it afar off.
Job 36:24-25

***O magnify the* LORD** *with me, and let us exalt his name together.*
Psalms 34:3

I will praise the name of God with a song,
and will ***magnify him*** *with thanksgiving.*
Psalms 69:30

~~~~~

When I was a little girl, I remember receiving a small magnifying glass as the prize in my box of Cracker Jacks. I was so intrigued with this little toy. I can remember the amazement I experienced when I would hold the little glass in front of many objects and see them appear larger under the glass. Many years later, my husband bought a small set of binoculars that we could use when we attended large meetings so that we could see the speakers on the platform or scan the crowd in search of someone we knew. (That was long before the days of projection systems which put the speakers on a screen for all to see more clearly.) Although the magnifying glass and the binoculars made objects appear larger, the truth of the matter is that these two items were merely tools to help me see things more clearly. The objects never changed size; only my perception was changed with the aid of the tools.

In a similar way we can apply the same concept to our view of God. He fills the universe, and there is no magnifying glass that can make Him larger than He is. However, Job said that ***we are the tools*** which magnify God's work which others behold. The Psalmist said that God was magnified through our praise, singing and thanksgiving. Acts 19:11-17 shows that Paul's lifestyle of performing miracles and casting out evil spirits caused the name of the Lord Jesus to be magnified. Therefore, when I magnify the Lord through
~~~~~

my worship and lifestyle of manifesting Godly attributes and power, not only do I see God more clearly, but I also become the tool by which others can see Him more clearly.

Is your life a magnification tool that allows others to see God more clearly?

Gem #146 **May 25**

O clap your hands, all ye people;
shout** unto God with the **voice of triumph.
Psalms 47:1

But thanks be to God, which giveth us
*the **victory through our Lord Jesus Christ.***
1 Corinthians 15:57

*For whatsoever is born of God overcometh the world: and this is the **victory that overcometh** the world, even our faith.*
1 John 5:4

~~~~~

The Israelites marched once around Jericho for six days in absolute silence, but on the seventh day, after marching seven times around the city in total silence, the command came from Joshua for everyone to ***shout for victory***. When God heard the people shout, He brought down the walls and gave His people the victory over the city (Joshua 6). Sometimes our hard trials make us weep in silence before God because we can't see any solutions to our problems. But if we can pray in the Spirit and build our faith (Jude 1:20), then by faith, we can…

Shout with a voice of triumph and thanksgiving as we watch God bring victory to our situation.
~~~~~

Gem #147 **May 26**

And he said to them all, If any man will come after me,
let him ***deny himself, and take up his cross*** *daily, and follow me.*
Luke 9:23

And whosoever doth not ***bear his cross,***
and come after me, cannot be my disciple.
Luke 14:27

Henceforth there is laid up for me a ***crown of righteousness****, which the Lord, the righteous judge, shall give me at that day: and not to me only, but unto all them also that love his appearing.*
2 Timothy 4:8

Blessed is the man that endureth temptation: for when he is tried, he shall receive the ***crown of life****, which the Lord hath promised to them that love him.*
James 1:12

And when the chief Shepherd shall appear, ye shall receive a ***crown of glory*** *that fadeth not away.*
1 Peter 5:4

~~~~~

Jesus taught that the sorrow, rejection, betrayal, and persecution He experienced would also be part of the experiences of His followers. He didn't promise wealth, fame, success and earthly crowns. He taught submission, surrender, sacrifice, self-denial and service to others. Today's church culture has forsaken the teaching of the cross with its message of denial and sacrifice in favor of the more pleasing message of prosperity and popularity. It's time to get back to the teachings of the Book.

Only those who have borne the Cross in this life will wear the Crown in the next one.
~~~~~

Gem #148 **May 27**

Master, which is the great commandment in the law?
Jesus said unto him, Thou shalt ***love the Lord thy God***
with all thy heart, and with all thy soul, and with all thy mind.
This is the first and great commandment. And the second
is like unto it, Thou shalt ***love thy neighbour*** *as thyself.*
On these two commandments hang all the law and the prophets.
Matthew 22:36-40

Owe no man any thing, but to ***love one another****: for he that loveth*
another hath fulfilled the law. For this, Thou shalt not commit adultery,
Thou shalt not kill, Thou shalt not steal,
Thou shalt not bear false witness, Thou shalt not covet;
and if there be any other commandment,
it is briefly comprehended in this saying, namely,
Thou shalt ***love thy neighbour*** *as thyself.*
Love worketh no ill to his neighbour:
therefore ***love is the fulfilling of the law****.*
Romans 13:8-10

For all ***the law*** *is* ***fulfill****ed in one word, even in this;*
Thou shalt ***love thy neighbour*** *as thyself.*
Galatians 5:14

~~~~~

Jesus' teaching in Matthew 22 is one of the most important scriptures in the New Testament. He said every law and prophecy hinges on the commandments to ***love God and love others***. If I love God, I won't offend Him by disregarding His commandments. If I love others, I won't steal from them, gossip about them, or harm them in any way. Concerning the importance of love (charity), Paul said it like this: *"And now abideth faith, hope, charity, these three; but the greatest of these is charity"* (1 Corinthians 13:13).
~~~~~

Gem #149 **May 28**

O lord, thou hast searched me, and known me. Thou knowest my downsitting and mine uprising, thou ***understandest my thought*** *afar off. Thou compassest my path and my lying down, and art acquainted with all my ways.*

Psalms 139:1-3

Talk no more so exceeding proudly; let not arrogancy come out of your mouth: for the LORD is a God of knowledge, and by him ***actions are weighed****.*

1 Samuel 2:3

And thou, Solomon my son, know thou the God of thy father, and serve him with a perfect heart and with a willing mind: for the LORD searcheth all hearts, and ***understandeth all the imaginations of the thoughts:*** *if thou seek him, he will be found of thee; but if thou forsake him, he will cast thee off for ever.*

1 Chronicles 28:9

The LORD knoweth the ***thoughts of man****, that they are vanity.*

Psalms 94:11

~~~~~

Often, in spite our best efforts to communicate with others, our motives, actions and words are questioned and misunderstood. But the God who made us, knows everything about us. He knows when we lie down and when we get up. He understands our thoughts and is acquainted with all our ways.

So the next time you feel misunderstood, just take those feelings to Jesus. ***He truly knows and understands.***
~~~~~

Gem #150 **May 29**

And [the Lord] said unto me, My grace is sufficient for thee: for my strength is made perfect in weakness… Therefore ***I take pleasure*** *in infirmities, in reproaches, in necessities, in persecutions, in distresses for Christ's sake: for when I am weak, then am I strong.*

2 Corinthians 12:9-10

Beloved, think it not strange concerning the fiery trial which is to try you… But ***rejoice,*** *inasmuch as ye are partakers of Christ's sufferings… If ye be reproached for the name of Christ,* ***happy are ye;*** *for the spirit of glory and of God resteth upon you: on their part he is evil spoken of, but on your part he is glorified.*

1 Peter 4:12-14

~~~~~

When we think of the words "pleasure" or "happy," we think of pleasant things such as beautiful flowers and things in nature, spending time with friends, family and grandchildren, taking vacations, listening to beautiful music and spending time in God's presence. But taking pleasure in infirmity, in being reproached, being in need, being persecuted, or in distress for Christ's sake? Or being happy and rejoicing in the fiery trials that come my way? How many times do I complain about my struggles and about being misunderstood? It's time to take a fresh look at our hard trials in life and remember that God gets the most glory out of our life when we are weak and unable to solve our problems. It is through life's distresses that He can come to our rescue and show the world His power.

~~~~~

"It was strictly forbidden to preach to other prisoners. It was understood that whoever was caught doing this received a severe beating. A number of us decided to pay the price for the privilege of preaching, so we accepted their [the communists'] terms. It was a deal; we preached and they beat us. We were happy preaching. They were happy beating us, so everyone was happy."

Richard Wurmbrand

Gem #151 **May 30**

But whoso hearkeneth unto me shall dwell ***safely****,*
and shall be quiet from fear of evil.
Proverbs 1:33

The name of the LORD is a strong tower:
the righteous runneth into it, and is ***safe****.*
Proverbs 18:10

The fear of man bringeth a snare:
but whoso putteth his trust in the LORD shall be ***safe****.*
Proverbs 29:25

And ***fear not*** *them which kill the body,*
but are not able to kill the soul: but rather fear him
which is able to destroy both soul and body in hell.
Matthew 10:28

~~~~~

Two major concerns of today's world are ***peace and safety***. The Bible declares that those who cry peace and safety in the last days will be met with sudden destruction (1 Thessalonians 5:3). But those who are righteous have no need to fear the perilous days of the end of this age, for the Word has promised safety to those who put their trust in the Lord. Safety doesn't necessarily mean protection from persecution or even death at the hands of evil men, for Jesus warned His followers to expect persecution (Matthew 10:22). Our consolation during perilous times is the fact that our soul is in safe-keeping with Jesus, and nothing that evil men can do to us will destroy that safe place we have in Him.

Are you fearful of the dangers of our world?
Run to Jesus, and put your trust in Him.
Only in Him will you find safety.
~~~~~

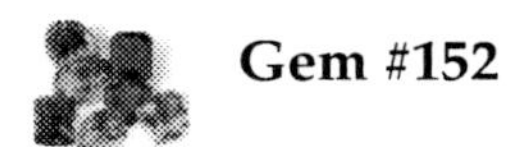

Gem #152 **May 31**

If ye then be risen with Christ, seek those things which are above,
where Christ sitteth on the right hand of God.
Set your affection on things above, *not on things on the earth.*
For ye are dead, and your life is hid with Christ in God.
Colossians 3:1-3

~~~~~

"I can safely say, on the authority of all that is revealed in the Word of God, that any man or woman on this earth who is bored and turned off by worship is not ready for heaven."
A. W. Tozer

"Following Jesus isn't something you can do at night where no one notices. It's a twenty-four-hour-a-day commitment that will interfere with your life. That's not the small print – that's a guarantee."
Kyle Idleman

~~~~~

Romans 6 teaches us that after we have died to sin, been buried in the waters of baptism, and risen again through Spirit infilling, we become a servant of righteousness rather than of sin. That resurrection to a new life should cause us to desire and seek for things that have eternal value and will expand God's Kingdom rather than pursuing temporal things that only satisfy for a moment. After God redeems us from a life of sin, He jealously guards His property and doesn't take kindly to us trying to combine the best of both worlds into our lifestyle. Following Him requires a daily decision to take up our cross and die to the fleshly nature. (Luke 9:23-24; 14:27) He demands wholehearted love and obedience to His commandments.

What is distracting you from wholeheartedly following Jesus?

Gem #153 **June 1**

And these signs shall follow them that believe; in my name shall they cast out devils; ***they shall speak with new tongues;***
Mark 16:17

But ye shall receive power, after that the Holy Ghost is come upon you…
Acts 1:8

And when the ***day of Pentecost*** *was fully come, they were all with one accord in one place. And suddenly there came a sound from heaven as of a rushing mighty wind, and it filled all the house where they were sitting. And there appeared unto them cloven tongues like as of fire, and it sat upon each of them.* ***And they were all filled with the Holy Ghost, and began to speak with other tongues, as the Spirit gave them utterance.*** *Then they that gladly received his word were baptized: and the same day there were added unto them about three thousand souls.*
Acts 2:1-4, 41

~~~~~

The Feast of Pentecost – Pentecost was an annual Jewish celebration that took place fifty days after the Passover. On the first day of Pentecost after Jesus' resurrection, 120 of Jesus' followers (including his mother, brothers, and disciples) were assembled in the Upper Room in Jerusalem to await the promised coming of the Holy Ghost. When it came with fire and speaking in tongues, the excited group hastened into the streets to spread this new experience. Peter's sermon that day resulted in an increase of 3,000 believers added to the church. The book of Acts records that multitudes of believers were added to the Church as the Pentecostal experience was spread around the globe. God has continued to pour out His Spirit on believers for almost two thousand years.

If you have not yet experienced your personal Pentecost, today is a good day to receive the Holy Ghost. *"For the promise is unto you, and to your children, and to all that are afar off, even as many as the LORD our God shall call."* (Acts 2:39) Will you answer His call?
~~~~~

Gem #154 **June 2**

But as truly as I live, all the earth shall be
filled with the glory of the Lord.
Numbers 14:21

And blessed be his glorious name for ever:
and let the whole earth ***be filled with his glory;***
Amen, and Amen.
Psalms 72:19

For the earth shall be filled with the ***knowledge of the glory of the Lord,*** *as the waters cover the sea.*
Habakkuk 2:14

~~~~~

God's glory surrounds the earth, but it has become obscured by the gods of this world which have successfully convinced masses of humanity that temporary things which bring satisfaction to the flesh are of more value than eternal things which feed the soul. Words like sacrifice, submission, obedience, death to self-will, commitment, and consecration are frowned upon, and words like happiness, fulfillment, positive mental attitude, self-esteem and grace are substituted. Although it may seem like evil is winning, there will soon come a day when Jesus will set up His throne on earth, and with His saints, He will rule and reign for 1,000 years. Then the whole earth will be filled with the glory of the Lord. I long for that day.

~~~~~

"The deepest passion of the heart of Jesus was not the saving of men, but the glory of God; and then the saving of men, because that is for the glory of God."
G. Campbell Morgan

Gem #155 **June 3**

But Barnabas took [Saul], and brought him to the apostles, and declared unto them how he had seen the Lord in the way, and that he had spoken to him, and how he had preached boldly at Damascus in the name of Jesus.

Acts 9:27

And Barnabas determined to take with them John, whose surname was Mark. But Paul thought not good to take him with them, who departed from them from Pamphylia, and went not with them to the work. And the contention was so sharp between them, that they departed asunder one from the other: and so Barnabas took Mark, and sailed unto Cyprus;

Acts 15:37-39

~~~~~

Barnabas was known as one who encouraged others. He had the unique ability of seeing potential in people who were often overlooked by others. He was possibly the one most responsible for overlooking Saul's past and supporting his conversion; later, he also promoted Paul's ministry to the Gentiles. He saw potential in young Mark and overlooked his youthful immaturity by giving him opportunities to become involved in ministry. Later Mark wrote the Gospel of Mark, and even Paul eventually recognized Mark as a valuable asset to his ministry (2 Timothy 4:11).

How many potential Pauls and Marks do we throw away because they haven't reached maturity in their Christian walk? God needs more people with a "Barnabas" spirit who will see potential in others and nurture them to become great men and women of God.
~~~~~

Gem #156 **June 4**

Buy the truth, and sell it not;
*also **wisdom**, and instruction, and understanding.*
Proverbs 23:23

*And **wisdom** and knowledge shall be the stability of thy times,*
and strength of salvation: the fear of the LORD is his treasure.
Isaiah 33:6

*But the **wisdom** that is from above is first pure, then peaceable, gentle,*
and easy to be intreated, full of mercy and good fruits, without partiality,
and without hypocrisy.
James 3:17

~~~~~

"**Wisdom** is the right use of knowledge. To know is not to be wise. Many men know a great deal, and are all the greater fools for it. There is no fool so great a fool as a knowing fool. But to know how to use knowledge is to have wisdom."
Charles Spurgeon

~~~~~

Wisdom by definition is the application of knowledge. When the two women stood before Solomon, arguing over which one was the mother of the baby, he listened to their stories, but it was his wisdom in handling the matter that revealed the true mother. We can fill our heads with knowledge, but without the wisdom required to apply that knowledge, we can make decisions that could bring unintended harm or loss to ourselves or others.

God desperately needs men and women who not only have knowledge, but like the Old Testament men of Issachar (1 Chronicles 12:32), they also understand how to apply that knowledge and gently instruct the Church in what they need to do.

Gem #157 **June 5**

Again, the kingdom of heaven is like unto ***treasure*** *hid in a field; the which when a man hath found, he hideth, and for joy thereof goeth and selleth all that he hath, and buyeth that field. Again, the kingdom of heaven is like unto a merchant man, seeking goodly pearls: Who, when he had found* ***one pearl of great price,*** *went and sold all that he had, and bought it.*

Matthew 13:44-46

~~~~~

"As the mine has rich veins of gold and silver hidden beneath the surface, so that all must dig who would discover its precious stores, so **the Holy Scriptures have treasures of truth** that are revealed only to the earnest, humble, prayerful seeker. God designed the Bible to be a lesson book to all mankind, in childhood, youth, and manhood, and to be studied through all time. He gave His word to men as a revelation of himself. Every new truth discerned is a fresh disclosure of the character of its Author. The study of the Scriptures is the means divinely ordained to bring men into closer connection with their Creator and to give them a clearer knowledge of His will. It is the medium of communication between God and man."

Ellen White

~~~~~

Jesus likened the Kingdom of Heaven to hidden treasure and merchants looking for treasure. He created every human with a longing in their heart that only He could fill; however, the gods of this world have blinded the eyes of humanity to the treasure that God offers, and have substituted treasures that glitter for a moment, but have no lasting ability to satisfy the need for God in our heart. God is looking for those who can distinguish between genuine Kingdom treasures and imitation worldly treasures. May God give me a discerning heart to dig deeply into His Word and find the hidden treasures He has to offer and forsake the imitation treasures offered by the world.

Gem #158 **June 6**

And [Rehoboam] did evil,
because ***he prepared not his heart to seek the LORD.***
2 Chronicles 12:14

So Jotham became mighty,
because ***he prepared his ways before the LORD his God.***
2 Chronicles 27:6

For Ezra had ***prepared his heart to seek the law of the LORD,***
and to do it, and to teach in Israel statutes and judgments.
Ezra 7:10

~~~~~

I'm not one to do things on the spur-of-the-moment. I like to have time to think things out and make preparations for them. When Ron and I were raising our family, we took yearly family vacations. For months before our trip, I would collect travel information and maps, and we would discuss and plan every detail. Likewise, when guests would come to visit, I would prepare my home for their comfort, plan menus, shop for groceries and prepare food for them.

On a spiritual note, God responds when we call on Him in a crisis, but He gives His best to those who ***prepare their hearts*** to seek Him. Rehoboam's story reminds us that lack of preparation in our search for God opens our heart to evil and deception, whereas Jotham and Ezra's preparations to serve God brought God's blessings to them.

Do you want God's best for your life?
If so, time and preparation are prerequisites.
~~~~~

 **Gem #159** **June 7**

And when he had sent the multitudes away, he went up into a mountain
apart *to pray: and when the evening was come,*
he was there alone.

Matthew 14:23

And he said unto them, Come ye yourselves ***apart*** *into a desert place,*
and rest a while: for there were many coming and going,
and they had no leisure so much as to eat.

Mark 6:31

And after six days Jesus taketh with him Peter, and James, and John,
and leadeth them up into an high mountain ***apart*** *by themselves:*
and he was transfigured before them.

Mark 9:2

~~~~~

On seven occasions, the Bible mentions the need for setting apart some time and space from the unceasing demands of ministry. Not only did Jesus take time out for prayer, but He also took His disciples apart from the crowds so they could have time to receive rest and nourishment for their bodies, as well as instruction for more effective ministry. Because our culture is so driven by time-management and production quotas, we sometimes fall into the trap of believing that more time spent ministering to those who need our message equals more effectiveness. Unfortunately, that mind-set simply is not true. We do not have endless amounts of energy and virtue to give away unless we discipline ourselves to spend sufficient time maintaining our body through rest and nourishment and maintaining our spirit through prayer, Bible study and fellowship of others who can encourage our weary spirits.

Are you feeling overwhelmed by the unending demands of the needy people all around you? Step back, and spend some time apart to reflect and restock your physical and spiritual reservoir. You will be less frustrated and more effective.
~~~~~

Gem #160

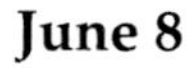

June 8

The world measures the status of individuals by their job, where they live, what kind of vehicle they drive, or the name brand on their clothes. Most Christians will never attain the riches of a Bill Gates or an Oprah Winfrey, but the Bible contains numerous references to the riches of God, and it tells us that His people are the beneficiaries of everything God has. The fact that our Heavenly Father owns everything puts us in the "Upper Income Bracket" of spiritual riches. Here are examples of our rich spiritual heritage:

~~~~~

...that he might make known the ***riches of his glory****...*
Romans 9:23

O the depth of the ***riches both of the wisdom and knowledge of God****! how unsearchable are his judgments, and his ways past finding out!*
Romans 11:33

...according to the ***riches of his grace****;*
Ephesians 1:7; 2:7

...that ye may know ...the ***riches of the glory of his inheritance in the saints,***
Ephesians 1:18; 3:16; Philippians 4:19; Colossians 1:27

But God, who is ***rich in mercy****...*
Ephesians 2:4

...preach ...the unsearchable ***riches of Christ****;*
Ephesians 3:8

~~~~~

There is no need for God's people to tuck their heads and feel inferior to any of the world's wealthy people. As the old song says,

"I know that I'm poor, but I've got a lot more than many rich folks that I know. I've got a home in the sky that money couldn't buy. I'm a Poor, Rich Man."[20]

Gem #161 June 9

Whatsoever thy ***hand findeth to do, do it with thy might;*** *for there is no work, nor device, nor knowledge, nor wisdom, in the grave, whither thou goest.*
Ecclesiastes 9:10

And ***whatsoever ye do, do it heartily, as to the Lord,*** *and not unto men; Knowing that of the Lord ye shall receive the reward of the inheritance: for ye serve the Lord Christ.*
Colossians 3:23-24

...and thy Father which ***seeth in secret*** *shall reward thee openly.*
Matthew 6:4, 6, 18

~~~~~

There are people who find great satisfaction in doing a job well, and they will even do more than is required because of their desire to serve. Then there are those who view serving as a dreaded duty and they get the job done, but not with enthusiasm or excellence. The Bible instructs us to do all things with excellence and without fanfare as though we are doing it unto the Lord instead of men. Sometimes it's hard to do things without receiving recognition for them, but Jesus promised He would openly reward our quiet, behind-the-scenes efforts when they are done unto Him.

Who can you find to quietly bless today?
Jesus is watching, and will come with rewards in His hand.

---

[20] Bud Chambers, born in Maud, OK in 1932, wrote over 3000 Gospel songs including "Poor Rich Man," "One More River," and "Born To Serve the Lord." He died in 2007 in Nashville, TN.
~~~~~

Gem #162 **June 10**

Moreover, brethren, I declare unto you the ***gospel*** *which I preached unto you, which also ye have received, and wherein ye stand;* ***By which also ye are saved,*** *if ye keep in memory what I preached unto you, unless ye have believed in vain. For I delivered unto you first of all that which I also received, how that* ***Christ died*** *for our sins according to the scriptures; And that* ***he was buried****, and that* ***he rose again*** *the third day according to the scriptures:*

1 Corinthians 16:1-4

In flaming fire taking vengeance on them that know not God, and that ***obey not the gospel*** *of our Lord Jesus Christ:*

2 Thessalonians 1:8

For ***I am not ashamed of the gospel of Christ****: for it is the power of God unto salvation to every one that believeth; to the Jew first, and also to the Greek.*

Romans 1:16

Whosoever therefore shall be ***ashamed of me*** *and of my words in this adulterous and sinful generation; of him also shall the Son of man be* ***ashamed****, when he cometh in the glory of his Father with the holy angels.*

Mark 8:38

~~~~~

Paul declared that **the Gospel which saves us consists of the Death, Burial and Resurrection of Jesus Christ,** and He pronounced a curse on anyone who obeyed any other gospel (Galatians 1:8-9). One day soon, God will take vengeance on those who do not obey the Gospel. So today, in agreement with the Apostle Paul, I unashamedly make the following declarations:

I am not ashamed to declare that I obeyed the Gospel of Jesus' Death when I *died* to my sinful nature and *repented* of all my sins. (Luke 13:3; Acts 2:38; Acts 17:30)
~~~~~

I am not ashamed to declare that I obeyed the Gospel of Jesus' Burial when I was *buried in the waters of baptism in the saving name of Jesus Christ* for the remission of my sins (John 3:5; Acts 2:38; Romans 6:4)

I am not ashamed to declare that I obeyed the Gospel of Jesus' Resurrection when I was filled with the Holy Ghost and spoke in other tongues as the Spirit spoke through me. (John 3:5; Acts 2:38; Romans 6:5)

The world is not ashamed to declare their evil, erroneous beliefs which only lead to death and eternal separation from God.

Let the Church unashamedly rise up and declare the Gospel of Christ, for there is power and salvation in the Gospel.

~~~~~

No Way We Are Not Ashamed[21]

We are the children of the King
We're not afraid to let our voices ring
Christ is our salvation; He's the light that shines
We are a chosen generation
Redeemed, sanctified, engrafted in the vine.

No way, we are not ashamed
Of the Gospel or His Name
Holy hands are lifted high
To the Name of Jesus Christ.

There's many voices in the wind
But only one that frees the soul from sin
Do you know Christ is still the answer
For the World today
There is no other Name so given
Unto a fallen man that he might be saved.

---

[21] Written and recorded by Carman Licciardello on his Mission 3:16 album in 1998.
~~~~~

Gem #163

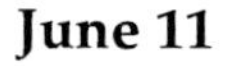

June 11

For our gospel came not unto you in word only, but also in power, and in the Holy Ghost, and in much assurance; as ye know what manner of men we were among you for your sake.
And ye became ***followers*** *of us, and of the Lord, having received the word in much affliction, with joy of the Holy Ghost.*
So that ye were ***ensamples*** *to all that believe in Macedonia and Achaia.*
1 Thessalonians 1:5-7

Let no man despise thy youth; but be thou an ***example of the believers****, in word, in conversation, in charity, in spirit, in faith, in purity.*
1 Timothy 4:12

Be ye ***followers*** *of* ***me****, even as I also am of Christ.*
1 Corinthians 1:11

Ye are our ***epistle*** *written in our hearts, known and read of all men:*
2 Corinthians 3:2

~~~~~

It is part of human nature to watch others and imitate what we see. Babies learn to talk by imitating the sounds they hear. They learn other skills by watching and imitating. The same principle is true in spiritual matters. We become a follower of Jesus by learning and obeying His Word and by following others who are examples of the principles outlined in God's Word. It is crucial that we follow those who are grounded in scripture and become examples of scriptural principles because some people will not pick up a Bible and read, but they will read our lives.

Who are you following?
What example are you showing to the world?
People are watching.
~~~~~

Gem #164 **June 12**

Open thou mine eyes, that I may behold ***wondrous*** *things out of thy law.*
Psalms 119:18

∼∼∼∼∼

It is enjoyable to watch little children experience something for the first time. Their eyes shine, and their faces are filled with wonder. They may clap their hands or jump up and down as they try to express their delight. The Psalmist tells us that wondrous things can be found in God's Law. Wondrous indicates something that excites wonder or amazement. When is the last time your eyes shone, or you excitedly clapped your hands over some amazing truth that you found in God's Word? If the Word doesn't fill you with wonder and amazement, it's time to ask God to open your eyes to the **wondrous** things that are found in His Law.

Gem #165 **June 13**

I love to tell the story Of unseen things above;
Of Jesus and His glory, Of Jesus and His love,
I love to tell the story, Because I know 'tis true,
It satisfies my longing, As nothing else can do.
(Chorus) I love to tell the story, T'will be my theme in glory
To tell the old, old story of Jesus and His love.[22]

∼∼∼∼∼

I love to talk about Jesus and His Word. I wonder who will need a word today from that old, old Story. I'm anticipating and eager to share.

---

[22] The well-loved hymn *I Love To Tell the Story* was written as a poem by Katherine Hankey (1834-1911), daughter of a wealthy English banker, during an illness she experienced at age 30. The words to the refrain and music to the song was written by William Fischer in 1869, but the song's fame was assured after its publication in 1875 in the influential *Gospel Hymns and Sacred Songs* hymnal by Phillip Bliss and Ira Sankey. (Information taken from "History of Hymns" by Dr. C. Michael Hawn, director of the sacred music program at Perkins School of Theology, Dallas, TX.)

Gem #166 **June 14**

Behold, ***all souls are mine****; as the soul of the father,*
so also the soul of the son is mine:
the soul that sinneth, it shall die.
Ezekiel 18:4

Now therefore, if ye will obey my voice indeed, and keep my covenant,
then ye shall be a peculiar treasure unto me above all people:
for ***all the earth is mine****:*
Exodus 19:5

For ***every beast of the forest is mine, and the cattle*** *upon a*
thousand hills. I know all the fowls of the mountains:
and the ***wild beasts of the field are mine****.*
If I were hungry, I would not tell thee:
for ***the world is mine****, and the fulness thereof.*
Psalms 50:10-12

~~~~~

God created the heavens, the earth, men and women and everything on the earth. As Creator, it all belongs to Him. However, He gave man dominion over all the earth and the animals (Genesis 1:28; Psalms 8:6). He does not force us to worship Him or support His Kingdom, but He does expect us to be good stewards over His possessions and give back a return on His investment. No doubt He is grieved over our selfish consumption of His bountiful blessings for our own desires and pleasure. A day of reckoning will come when the books will be opened, and we will be judged for the way we have lived our life and used the resources that He placed into our hands.

We had better give ourselves and our resources back to Him now so that we will hear Him say, "Well Done" when we stand before Him.
~~~~~

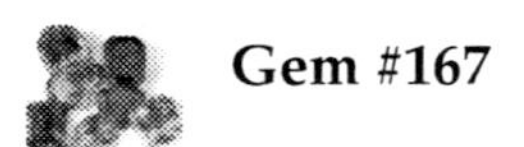

Gem #167 **June 15**

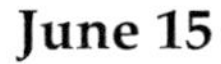

And [Job's] sons went and feasted in their houses, every one his day; and sent and called for their three sisters to eat and to drink with them. And it was so, when the days of their feasting were gone about, that Job sent and sanctified them, and rose up early in the morning, and offered burnt offerings according to the number of them all: for Job said, It may be that my sons have sinned, and cursed God in their hearts. Thus did Job continually.

Job 1:4-5

...he that begetteth a wise child shall have joy of him.

Proverbs 23:24

~~~~~

"**A good father** is one of the most unsung, unpraised, unnoticed, and yet one of the most valuable assets in our society."

Billy Graham

~~~~~

Although the third Sunday of June is set aside in America to honor the fathers in our families, today's culture puts very little value on traditional families that consist of a dad and mom and children. Single-parent homes have become the norm rather than the exception, and a large majority of these homes are parented by single mothers. These absent dads have left a gaping hole in the development of our nation's children.

Where are the praying dads who, like Job, would offer daily sacrifices for each one of his children just in case they might have sinned?

We desperately need fathers to take responsibility for the spiritual training of their families and not only pray for their wives and children, but also teach the children by example and instruction the power and value of prayer and living a Christian lifestyle.

Gem #168 **June 16**

Hear, ye children, the instruction of a ***father****,*
and attend to know understanding.
Proverbs 4:1

Children's children are the crown of old men;
and the glory of children are their ***fathers****.*
Proverbs 17:6

Remove not the ancient landmark, which thy ***fathers*** *have set.*
Proverbs 22:8

Hearken unto thy ***father*** *that begat thee,*
and despise not thy mother when she is old.
Proverbs 23:22

Honour thy ***father*** *and mother;*
which is the first commandment with promise;
Ephesians 6:2

~~~~~

In today's world of broken homes and severed relationships, the role of a ***father*** in the home is down-played. But the Bible teaches very strongly about the role that ***fathers*** play in leading the home, providing for the spiritual well-being as well as the physical needs of the wife and children, and loving the wife and children as God loved the Church. While the world would try to persuade us that homes without fathers or with two mothers are perfectly normal and acceptable, it is certainly not normal according to God's law. On the third Sunday of June, America celebrates Father's Day, and I want to pay tribute to all fathers everywhere who have cheerfully shouldered their God-given responsibilities for providing, nurturing, and training their children in the ways of God.

~~~~~

"One father is worth more than a hundred schoolmasters."
George Herbert

Gem #169 — June 17

The righteous shall ***flourish*** *like the palm tree: he shall grow like a cedar in Lebanon. Those that be planted in the house of the LORD shall* ***flourish*** *in the courts of our God. They shall still bring forth fruit in old age; they shall be* ***fat and flourishing****.*

Psalms 92:12-14

Blessed is the man that walketh not in the counsel of the ungodly, nor standeth in the way of sinners, nor sitteth in the seat of the scornful. But his delight is in the law of the LORD; and in his law doth he meditate day and night. And he shall be like a tree planted by the rivers of water, that ***bringeth forth his fruit in his season****; his leaf also shall not wither; and whatsoever he doeth shall prosper.*

Psalms 1:1-3

~~~~~

Our culture puts much emphasis on being fit; consequently people spend huge sums of money each year on gym memberships and the latest fad diet products. Although keeping ourselves fit and healthy is important for helping us to be able to perform God's purpose for our life, it is secondary to keeping our spirits healthy. The Psalmist pronounced a blessing on those who spend much time studying and meditating on the Word of God instead of spending time with ungodly people. Planting ourselves into a scripture-based church with a Holy Ghost-filled man of God is another ingredient which causes a person to flourish and be fruitful even into old age.

Is your spirit withered and dry?

Find a Church and a pastor, and commit to faithful attendance and support. Then commit to spending hours each day in study and meditation of God's Word. Your spiritual nature will then flourish and be productive in matters that have eternal value.
~~~~~

Gem #170 **June 18**

Therefore we ought to give the more earnest heed to the things which we have heard, lest at any time we should let them slip. For if the word spoken by angels was stedfast, and every transgression and disobedience received a just recompence of reward; How shall we escape, if we neglect so great salvation; which at the first began to be spoken by the Lord, and was confirmed unto us by them that heard him; God also bearing them witness, both with signs and wonders, and with divers miracles, and gifts of the Holy Ghost, according to his own will?

Hebrews 2:1-4

~~~~~

The greatest event in the history of humanity was the death of Jesus Christ to pay the penalty for our sins, and the next greatest event was the establishment of the Church on the Day of Pentecost for the purpose of empowering men and women to spread the good news of Jesus' payment for our sins. Since then, God has been pleased to confirm the preaching of the Gospel message of the death, burial and resurrection of Jesus with signs, wonders and miracles.

The book of Acts is rich with stories of lives which were changed after an encounter with the powerful message of redemption. Church history is also rich with stories of men and women whose lives were forever changed after they encountered and obeyed the Gospel. We should pay careful attention to our history and learn from the lessons of our past because God will reward obedience and transgressions with either life or death.

If we neglect to heed the teachings of our forefathers, they will slip from our grasp, and we will pay the penalty for our negligence.
~~~~~

Gem #171 **June 19**

Happy is the man that findeth wisdom,
and the man that getteth ***understanding.***
For the merchandise of it is better than the merchandise of silver,
and the gain thereof than fine gold. She is more precious than rubies:
and all the things thou canst desire are not to be compared unto her.
Length of days is in her right hand; and in her left hand riches and honour.
Her ways are ways of pleasantness, and all her paths are peace.
She is a tree of life to them that lay hold upon her:
and ***happy*** *is every one that retaineth her.*
Proverbs 3:13-18

Wisdom *is the principal thing; therefore get* ***wisdom****:*
and with all thy getting, get ***understanding****.*
Proverbs 4:7

If any of you lack ***wisdom****, let him ask of God, that giveth to all men liberally, and upbraideth not; and it shall be given him.*
James 1:5

~~~~~

We live in a pleasure-driven world. In the search for happiness, people will work two or three jobs to earn money to buy the latest technology gadget, appliance, tool, car, clothes, jewelry, toys, or you-name-it. Virtue and purity are wasted on unhealthy relationships in the search for love, acceptance and happiness. But true happiness does not consist of the "things" we acquire or the "relationships" we pursue. The Bible tells us to search for wisdom and acquire understanding. Possession of those virtues is more precious than jewels of silver, gold and rubies. The ways of wisdom are pleasant, peaceful, life-giving and honorable. Do you want to be happy? Then ask God for wisdom and understanding. He has a never-ending supply and is generous in passing it out to those who take the time to seek for it and apply it to their life. Only then will you find true happiness that will not be dependent on who you know or what you own.
~~~~~

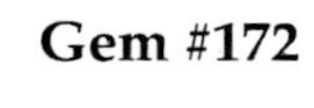

Gem #172 June 20

And [Moses] was there with the LORD forty days and forty nights...
And it came to pass, when Moses came down from mount Sinai...
that Moses wist not that the skin of his face shone
while he talked with him.
Exodus 34:28-29

Now when they saw the boldness of Peter and John, and perceived that
they were unlearned and ignorant men, they marvelled;
and they took knowledge of them, that they had been with Jesus.
Acts 4:13

And all that sat in the council, looking stedfastly on him,
saw [Stephen's] face as it had been the face of an angel.
Acts 6:15

~~~~~

What was one common denominator between Moses, Peter, John and Stephen? The time spent in the presence of God was manifested in their **faces**. In spite of persecution, imprisonment and even death, their **faces** reflected the beauty of the God they served. People took note that Moses had been with God, and in the New Testament, people noticed that the Christians had been with Jesus.

Americans spend billions of dollars each year on cosmetics in an attempt to enhance their appearance, but all that money could be saved if they would just spend time in the presence of the God who takes pleasure in His people and beautifies them with His salvation (Psalms 149:4).

What do people see in your face today?
~~~~~

Gem #173 **June 21**

Jesus answered and said unto her, Whosoever drinketh
of this water shall thirst again: But whosoever drinketh
of the water that I shall give him shall never thirst;
but the water that I shall give him shall be in him a
well of water springing up into everlasting life.
John 4:13-14

Therefore said the disciples one to another,
Hath any man brought him ought to eat?
Jesus saith unto them,
My meat is to do the will of him that sent me,
and to finish his work. Say not ye,
There are yet four months, and then cometh harvest?
behold, I say unto you, Lift up your eyes,
and look on the fields; for they are white already to harvest.
And he that reapeth receiveth wages, *and gathereth fruit*
unto life eternal: that both he that soweth
and he that reapeth may rejoice together.
John 4:33-36

~~~~~

In order to obtain food to satisfy our hunger, it is necessary to sow seed and harvest the food when it matures. Likewise, it is also necessary to obtain water to satisfy our thirst. Jesus said that we have been placed in the midst of a harvest field of souls. He has provided the meat of soul winning to satisfy our spiritual hunger and the living water of the Holy Ghost to satisfy our thirst. Wages are promised only to those who work in the harvest fields and labor to bring new souls into the Kingdom. Everyone has a part to play. If you expect to receive rewards in Heaven, then you must not consume all the rich blessings of the Lord on yourself, but get to work in the harvest field by sharing the water of life (the Holy Ghost) and the bread of life (God's Word) to a starving, dying world.
~~~~~

Gem #174 **June 22**

And there are also ***many other things which Jesus did,***
the which, if they should be written every one, I suppose that even the world itself could not contain the books that should be written. Amen.
John 21:25

...He that believeth on me, the works that I do shall he do also; and ***greater works*** *than these shall he do; because I go unto my Father.*
John 14:12

Ye are of God, little children, and have overcome them: because greater is he that is in you, than he that is in the world.
1 John 4:4

~~~~~

The Gospels give us a tiny glimpse into the ministry of Jesus in which miracles of healing, deliverance and provision occurred. People repented of their sins and lived different lives after encountering Jesus. John said that if everything Jesus did during His earthly life had been written, the world would not be able to contain all the books detailing His ministry. If that is true, the potential of the Church to do even greater works of healing, deliverance, provision, and conversion from sin is unlimited. God desires to work through His Church (Isaiah 43:13), but total surrender to Him is necessary.

How many lost people walk through your world each day? How many people are searching for relief from heavy burdens, healing from diseases, deliverance from addictions, or encouragement and answers to life's struggles?

The Church has the power and the answers to the world's needs. Let God flow through you today to perform ***greater works*** than those which Jesus did.
~~~~~

Gem #175 **June 23**

[Jesus] answered and said unto them, ***Give ye them to eat****...*
Mark 6:37

∼∼∼∼∼

Those of us who are church-goers hear the Word of God preached several times a week. If we are committed to daily Bible reading and study, then we are receiving additional spiritual nourishment. We attend camp meetings and conferences and other spiritually uplifting meetings and come away with enough spiritual food to feed a whole city, yet we often hoard these precious truths of God for ourselves. The world is perishing for lack of spiritual bread and water (the Word and the Holy Ghost). It is time to share our abundant spiritual nourishment with the world's hungry and thirsty and do our part to advance the Kingdom of God. Who can you share with today?

Gem #176 **June 24**

Thou art near, O Lord*; and all thy commandments are truth.*
Thy word is true from the beginning: and every one of
thy righteous judgments endureth for ever.
Psalms 119:151, 160

...he hath said, I will ***never leave*** *thee, nor* ***forsake*** *thee.*
Hebrews 13:5

∼∼∼∼∼

Many times I have heard the phrase, "Jesus is just as close as the mention of His name," but I have never heard anyone say, "Jesus is just as close as the mention of His Word." However, His Word contains everything we need for direction and answers. If you feel like He is far away, open up His Word and begin to read those amazing and wonderful words of Truth, and soon you will feel His presence, for He is just as close as the mention of His Word.

Gem #177 **June 25**

But his delight is in the law of the LORD;
and in his law doth he ***meditate*** *day and night.*
Psalms 1:2

My hands also will I lift up unto thy commandments, which I have loved;
and I will ***meditate*** *in thy statutes. O how love I thy law!*
it is my ***meditation*** *all the day.*
Psalms 119:48, 97

~~~~~

Because of the trouble on every hand, many people allow their thinking to be consumed with worry and fear, but the Bible tells us to **meditate** on God's Word at all times. The word "worry" is not even in the Bible, and the word "fret" only appears a handful of times, yet these words consume an inordinate amount of our thinking.

How about replacing worries over health with these words, *"I am the LORD that healeth thee"* (Exodus 15:26) and worries over finances with the words, *"My God shall supply all your need according to his riches in glory"* (Philippians 4:19). Find solace from fearful thoughts with the words, *"What time I am afraid, I will trust in thee"* (Psalms 56:3). When grief and weeping overwhelm you, remember these words, *"…weeping may endure for a night, but joy cometh in the morning"* (Psalms 30:5).

Search the scriptures for answers, and then ***meditate*** on those Truths. The Word will drive away all fears, worries, or frustrations.

What is consuming your thoughts?

Pick up God's Word and ***meditate*** on those life-giving truths.
~~~~~

Gem #178 **June 26**

Who gave himself for us, that he might redeem us from all iniquity, and purify unto himself a ***peculiar people****, zealous of good works.*
Titus 2:14

But ye are a chosen generation, a royal priesthood, an holy nation, a ***peculiar people****; that ye should shew forth the praises of him who hath called you out of darkness into his marvellous light;*
1 Peter 2:9

~~~~~

Peculiar means unusual, distinct from others, special, belonging exclusively to someone or something.

God's people have always had the distinction of being different from other people in the world. The Bible uses the term *"peculiar treasure"* and *"peculiar people"* on six occasions to define God's people.[23] In the Old Testament, there was never any question about who the Jews were. Their clothes were different; their diet was different; their crops in the fields were arranged differently than others; their homes had scriptures on the doors. They were distinctively separated in appearance and lifestyle from the nations around them. Likewise, the New Testament Church is also described as **peculiar**. If the Church dresses like the world, looks like the world, and lives like the world, then it has lost those **peculiar** characteristics of being distinct, special and belonging exclusively to God.

God is looking for those who are willing to be exclusively His in appearance, conversation and lifestyle.

Are you peculiar, or do you just fit in with everyone around you?

[23] Scriptures for additional study: Exodus 19:5; Deuteronomy 14:2; Deuteronomy 26:18; Psalms 135:4.
~~~~~

Gem #179 **June 27**

Be ye therefore followers of God, as dear children;
And walk in love, as Christ also hath loved us,
and hath given himself for us an offering and a sacrifice to God
for a sweetsmelling savour.
But fornication, and all uncleanness, or covetousness,
let it not be once named among you, as becometh saints;
Neither filthiness, nor foolish talking, nor jesting,
which are not convenient: but rather giving of thanks.
For this ye know, that no whoremonger, nor unclean person, nor covetous
man, who is an idolater, hath any inheritance in the kingdom of Christ
and of God. ***Let no man deceive you*** *with vain words:*
for because of these things cometh the wrath of God upon the
children of disobedience. Be not ye therefore partakers with them.
See then that ye ***walk circumspectly****, not as fools, but as wise,*
Redeeming the time, because the days are evil.
Wherefore be ye not unwise, but understanding
what the will of the Lord is.
Ephesians 5:1-7, 15-17

~~~~~

To be **circumspect** means to be discreet about private matters, prudent in providing for the future, to exercise good judgment in decision-making, and to be watchful, cautious, and on guard for things that would cause failure.

The entire fifth chapter of Ephesians gives a list of activities or attitudes to guard against in our Christian lifestyle. Paul stresses that if any of these characteristics are in our life, we will not inherit the Kingdom of God. Evil days are upon us, and traps are set daily for our destruction by the enemy of our souls.

It is imperative that we walk circumspectly and guard against any teaching that would cause us to drop our guard and allow the above-mentioned sins to prevent our inheriting of the rewards of the Kingdom.
~~~~~

Gem #180 **June 28**

I beseech you, brethren, (ye know the house of Stephanas, that it is the firstfruits of Achaia, and that they have ***addicted themselves to the ministry of the saints,)***
1 Corinthians 16:15

~~~~~

We usually think of addictions in relation to drugs, alcohol, smoking, pornography or some other vice. The dictionary says that someone who is addicted has devoted or given themselves psychologically or physically to something that is habit-forming. I have volunteered for over twelve years in our local county jail and have seen hundreds of women come through my Bible classes who had been arrested for drug use. Often their drug habits caused them to lose family, jobs, finances and homes. My aunt, a former high school counsellor for many years, has often told me that an addiction is a misplaced passion for something other than God. Paul tells us of a family in Achaia who had ***addicted themselves to the ministry of the saints.*** Many of us are so focused on our own little world that we have no time or desire to get involved in other people's needs and problems. What if we were to become less self-centered and more others-centered?

What would an addiction to the ministry of the saints look like in today's church? Would we spend time with an elderly person and listen to their stories? Would we volunteer to babysit some children at no charge, and give a frazzled mom an hour or two to grocery shop or just have some time to herself? Would we invite someone to our home for a home-cooked meal and some good, godly fellowship? How about sharing inspirational books that we have read to bless and inspire someone else? And most important of all, would a person ***addicted to ministry*** spend more time in prayer so that God could impress upon them what needs to be done?

Are you addicted to the ministry of the saints?
~~~~~

Gem #181 **June 29**

...let us ***put on the armour of light****. But* ***put ye on the Lord Jesus Christ****, and make not provision for the flesh...*
Romans 13:12, 14

Put on the whole armour of God*, that ye may be able to stand against the wiles of the devil.*
Ephesians 6:11

And that ye ***put on the new man,*** *which after God is created in righteousness and true holiness.*
Ephesians 4:24

And have ***put on the new man,*** *which is renewed in knowledge after the image of him that created him:* ***Put on*** *therefore, as the elect of God, holy and beloved, bowels of mercies, kindness, humbleness of mind, meekness, longsuffering; Forbearing one another, and forgiving one another, if any man have a quarrel against any: even as Christ forgave you, so also do ye. And above all these things* ***put on charity,*** *which is the bond of perfectness.*
Colossians 3:10, 12-14

~~~~~

Through the years, I've encountered people who think that once they have been converted, nothing more is required of them. However, that way of thinking is erroneous and very dangerous. A new convert has many things to learn in order to live a life that brings pleasure and honor to God. The Apostle Paul instructs the saints to **put on** some things to protect and identify themselves with their God. As soldiers, we ***put on armour*** to fight spiritual warfare. We also ***put on Jesus Christ*** which includes the virtues of mercy, kindness, humility, meekness, longsuffering, forbearance, forgiveness, and charity. There is no time to just sit down and wait for God to rapture us out of this life into His presence forever. Before we are qualified to inherit the next life, there are some things we must ***put on*** in order to accomplish the job we have been given.
~~~~~

 **Gem #182** 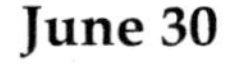 **June 30**

As he spake by the mouth of his ***holy prophets****, which have been since the world began:* ***That we should be saved from our enemies****, and from the hand of all that hate us;*

Luke 1:70-71

And he gave some, apostles; and some, ***prophets****; and some, evangelists; and some, pastors and teachers;* ***For the perfecting of the saints,*** *for the work of the ministry, for the edifying of the body of Christ: Till we all come in the unity of the faith, and of the knowledge of the Son of God, unto a perfect man, unto the measure of the stature of the fulness of Christ:*

Ephesians 4:11-13

~~~~~

Of the five senses of the body, eyesight is possibly the most important. The eyes see things that can protect and prevent danger from occurring in the body. Old Testament ***prophets*** were especially gifted with spiritual eyesight and insight into matters that the ordinary person would not perceive. The Bible contains numerous stories of ***prophets*** whose words raised the dead, performed many miracles, and brought victory in battles. Thousands of prophecies were recorded in the Bible. The ***prophets'*** calling also included the job of sounding the alarm when danger was near, and calling people to repentance when judgment was near. Often their warnings were ignored, and they even suffered persecution at the hands of the ones who rejected their warnings. Throughout its history, Israel could have avoided much heartache and judgment if they had obeyed the voices of their God-given ***prophets***. Likewise, God has placed ***prophets*** in the New Testament Church to perceive things that the ordinary person wouldn't see. Although their message may not be popular, God has given them to us for our protection. We are living in very dangerous times, and we would be wise to protect the ***prophets*** among us and heed their words, for they are sent to protect us.
~~~~~

Gem #183 **July 1**

Whether therefore ye eat, or drink, or whatsoever ye do,
do all to the glory of God.
1 Corinthians 10:31

What? know ye not that your body is the temple of the Holy Ghost which is in you, which ye have of God, and ye are not your own? For ye are bought with a price: therefore ***glorify God in your body, and in your spirit****, which are God's.*
1 Corinthians 6:19-20

That ye may with one mind and one mouth ***glorify God****, even the Father of our Lord Jesus Christ.*
Romans 15:6

~~~~~

While reading my Bible one morning, the phrase, ***"Do all to the glory of God"*** leaped out at me. My life should be lived in such a way that everything I do or say, and everywhere I go should bring glory to God.

That is a huge commitment!

Because my body is His Temple, every bite of food I put in my mouth should be something that will contribute to the nourishment and health of His Temple. Because my body is His physical representation to the world, my external appearance should reflect His glory to those who see me. Because my voice is His Word to the world, the words that I say should instruct, build up and restore hurting, broken, hopeless people. Because I am His visible representative in this world, the places I go should also testify to my commitment to a holy God.

Does your lifestyle glorify God?
~~~~~

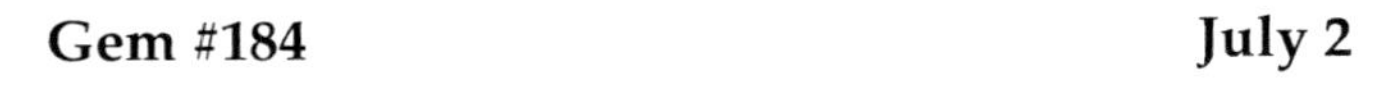

Gem #184 **July 2**

And when the day of Pentecost was fully come,
they were all with one accord in one place.
And they were ***all filled with the Holy Ghost,*** *and began to speak with other tongues, as the Spirit gave them utterance.*
Acts 2:1, 4

And they, continuing ***daily with*** *one* ***accord*** *in the temple,*
and breaking bread from house to house,
did eat their meat with gladness and ***singleness of heart,***
Acts 2:46

And when they had prayed, the place was shaken where they were assembled together; and they were ***all filled with the Holy Ghost,*** *and they spake the word of God with boldness. And the multitude of them that believed were of* ***one heart and one soul...***
Acts 4:31-32

...that ye stand fast in ***one spirit,*** *with* ***one mind striving together*** *for the faith of the gospel;*
Philippians 1:27

~~~~~

One Accord...One Heart...One Soul...Unity. The Early Church was a praying church. They were bold and powerful, and experienced outstanding miracles and explosive growth. What was one of the secrets to their power and explosive growth? It was Unity. They took very seriously Jesus' command to preach the Gospel to every creature, and everyone was focused on the same goal. Prayer meetings shook the buildings, and ***everyone*** in the place was filled with the Holy Ghost.

I wonder what the true Church could accomplish today if ***everyone*** set aside their personal agendas and worked ***together with one heart*** to spread the Gospel to the whole world.
~~~~~

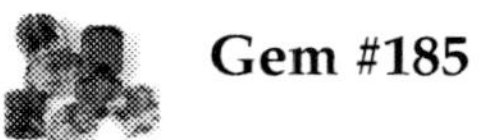

Gem #185 **July 3**

*Having **gifts** (faculties, talents, qualities) that differ according to the grace given us, let us **use them**: [He whose gift is] prophecy, [let him prophesy] according to the proportion of his faith; - [He whose gift is] practical service, let him give himself to serving; he who teaches, to his teaching; - He who exhorts (encourages), to his exhortation; he who contributes, let him do it in simplicity and liberality; he who gives aid and superintends, with zeal and singleness of mind; he who does acts of mercy, with genuine cheerfulness and joyful eagerness.*

Romans 12:6-8 (AMP)

*As each one has received a special **gift**, employ it in **serving one another** as good stewards of the manifold grace of God.*

1 Peter 4:10 (NASB)

~~~~~

The Bible likens the members of the Church to the various parts of the body. Every part of a body has a specific role to fulfill, and one body part cannot do another body part's job. Likewise, in the body of Christ, every member has been given gifts for the purpose of fulfilling God's ordained plan for that specific member. We are instructed to be good stewards of the gifts placed in our possession and use them to serve others. All gifts are of great importance and are vitally necessary for the smooth functioning of the body. Are you called to teach? Then study and share the information God gives you to the best of your ability. Are you gifted with compassion for the hurting and broken? Then use that gift to bring hope and healing to the members who cross your path in life. Are you called to lead? Then develop good people skills and become a leader that people are willing to follow.

What are your gifts?

Develop them and use them to the best of your ability to serve God and others.
~~~~~

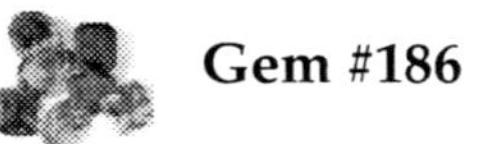

Gem #186 **July 4**

*Stand fast therefore in the **liberty** wherewith Christ hath made us **free**, and be not entangled again with the yoke of bondage.*
Galatians 5:1

~~~~~

On July 2, 1776, Congress voted to approve a complete separation from Great Britain. Two days afterwards – July 4th – the early draft of the Declaration of Independence was signed, albeit by only two individuals at that time: John Hancock, President of Congress, and Charles Thompson, Secretary of Congress. Four days later, on July 8, members of Congress took that document and read it aloud from the steps of Independence Hall, proclaiming it to the city of Philadelphia, after which the Liberty Bell was rung. The inscription around the top of that bell, Leviticus 25:10, was most appropriate for the occasion: *"Proclaim liberty throughout the land and to all the inhabitants thereof."*

What was the basis of American Independence? John Adams said, "The general principles on which the Fathers achieved independence were the general principles of Christianity."[24]

I am very thankful for my country and the men and women who have sacrificed greatly to give us the liberties and freedom we enjoy. But today I am even more grateful for the liberty and freedom that I have found in Jesus through the teaching and study of His Word, and I have no desire to ever become entangled again with the yoke of sin that I was born into.

It is my desire to share the message of truth and freedom with everyone who crosses my path in life for Jesus said,

"…the truth shall make you free" (John 8:32).

[24] "4th of July Article; David Barton; July 2006. wallbuilders.com.
~~~~~

 **Gem #187** **July 5**

Not slothful in business*; fervent in spirit; serving the Lord;*
Romans 12:11

Just balances, ***just weights****, a* ***just*** *ephah, and a* ***just*** *hin, shall ye have:*
I am the LORD *your God, which brought you out of the land of Egypt.*
Leviticus 19:36

He also that is ***slothful*** *in his work is brother to him that is a great waster.*
Proverbs 18:9

That ye be not ***slothful****, but followers of them who through*
faith and patience inherit the promises.
Hebrews 6:12

~~~~~

The Bible strongly condemns those who are lazy, refuse to work and are dishonest in business dealings with others. As Christians, it is not only important that we be well-versed in spiritual matters, but it is also imperative that we are exemplary in our financial and business dealings with others. As a self-employed business person for many years, I have dealt with plenty of people who have an entitlement mentality and think they should be given free or discounted services simply because they know me or go to church with me. Those with the entitlement mentality are the ones who take advantage of the ones providing the service and often neglect to pay their bill, or have to be reminded to pay.

In Ephesians 5, Paul lists many sins that should not be named among God's people. As children of light, we should be examples to unbelievers in our business affairs as much as in our spiritual affairs. That example includes living within our budget, paying our bills on time, giving our employer an honest day's labor for the wages we receive, and supporting the Church and those in need with the financial blessings we have been given.
~~~~~

Gem #188 **July 6**

*What time I am **afraid**, I will trust in thee.*
*In God have I put my trust: I will not be **afraid** what man can do unto me.*
Psalms 56:3, 11

*The LORD is my light and my salvation; whom shall I **fear**? the LORD is the strength of my life; of whom shall I be **afraid**?*
Psalms 27:1

And there shall be signs in the sun, and in the moon, and in the stars;
and upon the earth distress of nations, with perplexity;
*the sea and the waves roaring; **Men's hearts failing them for fear**,*
and for looking after those things which are coming on the earth:
for the powers of heaven shall be shaken.
And when these things begin to come to pass, then look up,
and lift up your heads; for your redemption draweth nigh.
Luke 21:25-26, 28

~~~~~

Every time I open up the news, there is renewed cause for alarm and fear. Fearful events are all around me. Stress! Job lay-offs! Broken Marriages! Murders! Child abuse! Crimes of every description! Natural disasters! Wars! Jesus said that the last days would be so perilous that men's hearts would literally fail because of fear. Heart attacks have become a leading cause of illness and death. God knew man's propensity to worry and fear, and He addressed fear hundreds of times in the Bible with words such as *"What time I am afraid, I will trust in thee."*

Although it seems like everything around me is shaking, I take consolation in the words of Jesus.

I will not be afraid!

I will look up, for my redemption is drawing nigh!
~~~~~

Gem #189 **July 7**

Mortify *therefore your members which are upon the earth; fornication, uncleanness, inordinate affection, evil concupiscence, and covetousness, which is idolatry: For which things' sake the wrath of God cometh on the children of disobedience: In the which ye also walked some time, when ye lived in them. But now ye also* ***put off*** *all these; anger, wrath, malice, blasphemy, filthy communication out of your mouth. Lie not one to another, seeing that ye have* ***put off*** *the old man with his deeds; And have* ***put on*** *the new man, which is* ***renewed*** *in knowledge after the image of him that created him:*

Colossians 3:5-10

That ye ***put off*** *concerning the former conversation the old man, which is corrupt according to the deceitful lusts; And be* ***renewed*** *in the spirit of your mind; And that ye* ***put on*** *the new man, which after God is created in righteousness and true holiness.*

Ephesians 4:22-24

~~~~~

The New Birth experience involves ***putting*** **on** Christ through the act of baptism in Jesus' name (Galatians 3:27) and being ***filled with*** Christ when we are filled with the Holy Ghost (John 14:17; Colossians 1:27). After experiencing the New Birth, Paul teaches that some characteristics of the old sinful life must be ***put off*** in order to develop into the Christian God desires for us to be. Because these characteristics are part of our sinful nature, we must daily make a conscious effort to remove them from our life and remove anything or anyone who would tempt us to put them back on. The tasks of ***removal and renewal*** are accomplished through daily habits of prayer, reading and study of the Word and submission to a pastor and other godly people.

Have you scheduled time today for removal and renewal?
~~~~~

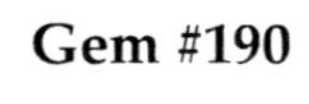

Gem #190 **July 8**

If ye then be risen with Christ, seek those things which are above, where Christ sitteth on the right hand of God. ***Set your affection on things above****, not on things on the earth. For ye are dead, and your life is hid with Christ in God.*

Colossians 3:1-3

Lay not up for yourselves treasures upon earth, where moth and rust doth corrupt, and where thieves break through and steal: But lay up for yourselves ***treasures in heaven****, where neither moth nor rust doth corrupt, and where thieves do not break through nor steal: For where your treasure is, there will your heart be also.*

Matthew 6:19-21

Blessed be the God and Father of our Lord Jesus Christ, which according to his abundant mercy hath begotten us again unto a lively hope by the resurrection of Jesus Christ from the dead, To an ***inheritance*** *incorruptible, and undefiled, and that fadeth not away,* ***reserved in heaven for you,***

1 Peter 1:3-4

~~~~~

"We may speak about a place where there are no tears, no death, no fear, no night; but those are just the benefits of Heaven. The beauty of Heaven is seeing God."

Max Lucado

~~~~~

As more and more of my friends and family leave earth to join the Heavenly hosts, my thoughts turn increasingly to the wonders that await me in my Heavenly home. My dreams and goals in this life are determined with Heaven in mind. One day soon, I hope to achieve that long-awaited dream. As much as I love my friends, family and my precious grandchildren, my affections are set on things above and on the treasures that await me in that land. I can hardly wait to see Jesus and the many family members and friends who have already completed their journey through this life.

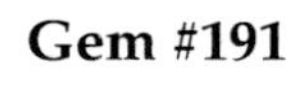 **Gem #191** **July 9**

Therefore also now, saith the LORD, turn ye even to me with all your heart, and with fasting, and ***with weeping, and with mourning****:*
And rend your heart, and not your garments, and turn unto the LORD your God: for he is gracious and merciful, slow to anger, and of great kindness, and repenteth him of the evil.

Joel 2:12-13

And Peter remembered the word of Jesus, which said unto him, Before the cock crow, thou shalt deny me thrice. And he went out, and ***wept*** *bitterly.*

Matthew 26:75

For ***Godly sorrow worketh repentance*** *to salvation...*

2 Corinthians 7:10

~~~~~

"Sorrow for sin is a perpetual rain, a sweet, soft shower, which to a truly saved man lasts all his life long...He is always sorrowful that he has sinned...He will never stop grieving until all sin has gone."

Charles Spurgeon

~~~~~

Although God is merciful and slow to anger, He cannot tolerate our sins against His righteousness. He requires repentance to put us in right standing with Him. It is not enough to just mouth the words, "I'm sorry." He is looking for those who will WEEP and mourn over their wrong-doing. After Peter's denial of Jesus, he wept bitter tears of remorse for his sin. His repentance brought him back into right-standing with God, and he became a very powerful preacher in the New Testament Church. It is godly sorrow that leads to repentance and salvation.

Do your sins against God produce the godly sorrow that results in tears of repentance?

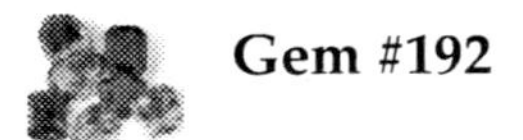

Gem #192 **July 10**

Thou therefore endure hardness, as a good soldier of Jesus Christ. No man that warreth entangleth himself with the affairs of this life; that he may please him who hath chosen him to be a soldier.
2 Timothy 2:3-4

This charge I commit unto thee, son Timothy, ...that thou by them mightest war a good warfare; Holding faith, and a good conscience; which some having put away concerning faith have made shipwreck:
1 Timothy 1:18-19

~~~~~

God has called His people to be soldiers in His army to fight against the evil perpetrated by Satan, the god of this world. Sometimes the battle gets fierce, and we need a break from the intensity of fighting. Our U.S. military understands the need to rotate its troops on the front line and give the weary fighters some time away for rest and relaxation. The same principle holds true in spiritual warfare. We can't fight all the time; we can't minister all the time. Weariness and frustration sometimes vents itself on those to whom we are ministering. To avoid accidentally wounding our own comrades in life's conflicts, there has to be times when we step away from the fight, and step away from the incessant demands of the crowd to regroup. Your time of regrouping might be spent engaging in a hobby or traveling; perhaps you just turn off the phone and the email and spend time with your grandchildren. Time spent in relaxation and renewal is not wasted time. Even Jesus periodically took time away from ministry to regroup and renew (Matthew 14:13-23).

Are you weary, frustrated, or discouraged? It's time to step off the front lines and schedule some R & R.
~~~~~

 **Gem #193** **July 11**

So thou, O son of man, I have set thee a ***watchman*** *unto the house of Israel; therefore thou shalt hear the word at my mouth, and* ***warn them*** *from me.*

Ezekiel 33:7

And I will give you ***pastors*** *according to mine heart, which shall* ***feed you*** *with knowledge and understanding.*

Jeremiah 3:15

And he gave some, apostles; and some, prophets; and some, evangelists; and some, ***pastors*** *and teachers;* ***For the perfecting of the saints****, for the work of the ministry, for the edifying of the body of Christ:*

Ephesians 4:11-12

~~~~~

"As a pastor, I have a deep desire to lead people to God and encourage people to pray, read the Bible, and carry their faith into every part of their lives."

Adam Hamilton

~~~~~

Long before the invention of electronic security alarm systems, cities employed **watchmen** to guard the citizens and warn them about any approaching danger. Old Testament prophets were also called **watchmen** because it was their responsibility to watch and warn God's people about anything that would jeopardize their spiritual well-being. Jeremiah and Paul called these **watchmen, pastors,** whose job it was to feed the people with knowledge and understanding and equip them for the work of the ministry. God has gifted **pastors** with special insight into matters that the average person in the Church doesn't see. They **watch** for our souls and will give an account before God for each person they pastor. It is our responsibility to pray for our pastors (2 Thessalonians 3:1) and obey them (Hebrews 13:17).

Do you have the security of a watchman/pastor in your life?

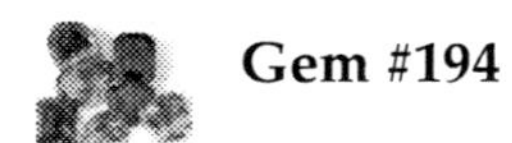

Gem #194 **July 12**

It is of the LORD's ***mercies*** *that we are not consumed,*
because his compassions fail not. They are new every morning:
great is thy faithfulness*. The LORD is my portion, saith my soul;*
therefore will I hope in him. The LORD is good unto them that wait for him,
to the soul that seeketh him. It is good that a man should both hope
and quietly wait for the salvation of the LORD.
Lamentations 3:22-26

I will sing of the ***mercies*** *of the LORD for ever:*
with my mouth will I make known thy ***faithfulness*** *to all generations.*
Psalms 89:1

Like as a father pitieth his children, so the LORD pitieth them that fear him.
For he knoweth our frame; he remembereth that we are dust.
Psalms 103:13-14

~~~~~

One morning shortly after my husband died, I woke up feeling like a failure and very useless. Of course, the longer I thought on these kinds of thoughts, the worse I felt. Finally, the Lord got my attention and impressed me to pick up my Bible and read the page where my bookmark was. I knew my bookmark was in the book of Lamentations, and I wondered what in the world the Lord would want to say to me from that sad book. As I read through chapter three, the words from verses 22-26 jumped out at me. Because the Lord is the Creator of us all and He makes the rules, He could consume every one of us the moment we do something wrong. But His compassion for our human weakness is unfailing. If I will just repent every time I transgress His laws, He will wipe my slate clean, and I can begin every day with a fresh, clean slate.

As I start this new day, my slate is clean and my hope is in God. Great is His faithfulness!
~~~~~

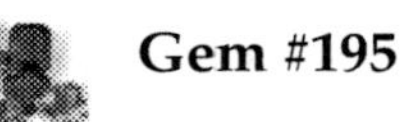

Gem #195 **July 13**

And I will fasten him as a ***nail in a sure place****; and he shall be for a glorious throne to his father's house. And they shall* ***hang upon him*** *all the glory of his father's house, the offspring and the issue, all vessels of small quantity, from the vessels of cups, even to all the vessels of flagons. In that day, saith the LORD of hosts, shall the* ***nail that is fastened in the sure place*** *be removed, and be cut down, and fall; and the burden that was upon it shall be cut off: for the LORD hath spoken it.*

Isaiah 22:23-25

~~~~~

Many years ago I heard a sermon on this passage of scripture. The minister said we were all nails fastened into some kind of foundation. If we are driven into wood, our nail can support much weight, but if we are driven into something flimsy like sheetrock, then heavy things will rip our nail out of its foundation. Isaiah prophesied that Hilkiah would be a nail that was fastened in a sure place, and the spiritual heritage of David and succeeding generations would hang on his nail.

You can drive your nail into Prayer, Bible Study and the things of God, or you can drive it into the world's lures of prestige, prosperity and thrill-seeking. Your children and others whom you influence are hanging on your nail and will follow your example. If your foundation is sure, those hanging on your nail are secure, but if you get ripped out of your foundation, everyone hanging on your nail will fall with you.

How will you influence those on your nail?

Is your nail fastened in a sure place?
~~~~~

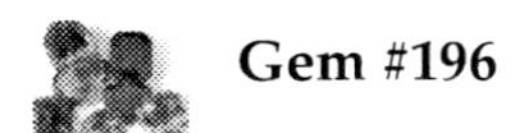

Gem #196

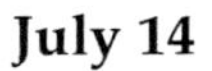

July 14

Togetherness is defined as being in a condition of contact, unity, compactness or coherence. The Bible uses the term **together** over 460 times. God did not intend for life to be lived in isolation. There is power in numbers. More hands get the job done quicker. More missions contributions send more missionaries to more countries. God has one Church with many members who work **together** to accomplish His purpose of preaching the Gospel to every creature. Here are just a few of the tasks that the Church is called to accomplish **together**.

1. The Early Church was **together** and had all things in common (Acts 2:44).
2. The Early Church assembled **together** for prayer (Acts 3:1; 4:31; 12:12)
3. The Holy Ghost in the individual members has quickened and raised them up to sit **together** in heavenly places in Christ Jesus (Ephesians 2:5-6).
4. The members are knit **together** in love (Colossians 2:2, 19).
5. The members are tempered **together** into one body (1 Corinthians 12:21-22, 24).
6. The members are built and framed **together** into a holy temple and habitation for God's Spirit (Ephesians 2:21-22)
7. The members labor **together** to build the Kingdom (1 Corinthians 3:9)
8. The members strive **together** for the faith of the Gospel (Philippians 1:27)
9. At the rapture, the members will be caught up **together** to live forever with God (1 Thessalonians 4:17; 5:10).

Are you trying to live your faith alone? If so, you are prey to every wolf and deceptive spirit whose purpose is to destroy you. Find a body of true believers and work **together** with them to build God's Kingdom on earth.

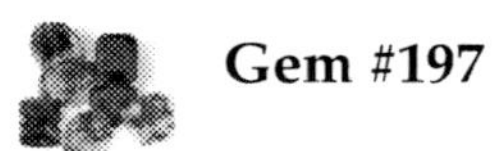

Gem #197 **July 15**

And [Elijah] said, I have been very jealous for the LORD *God of hosts: because the children of Israel have forsaken thy covenant, thrown down thine altars, and slain thy prophets with the sword; and I, even* ***I only, am left****; and they seek my life, to take it away. And the* LORD *said unto him, Go, …anoint Hazael to be king over Syria: And Jehu the son of Nimshi shalt thou anoint to be king over Israel: and Elisha …shalt thou anoint to be prophet in thy room. Yet I have left me seven thousand in Israel, all the knees which have not bowed unto Baal, and every mouth which hath not kissed him. So he departed thence, and found Elisha the son of Shaphat, who was plowing …and Elijah passed by him, and cast his mantle upon him. …Then [Elisha] arose, and went after Elijah, and ministered unto him.*

1 Kings 19:14-16, 18-19, 21

~~~~~

Ministering to hard-headed people can be physically and mentally exhausting and sometimes, life-threatening as well. Elijah's contest against the false prophets of Baal had successfully demonstrated the power of Jehovah God over the false god, Baal. This victory over evil should have put Elijah on an emotional high, yet when wicked Jezebel heard that her false prophets had been slain, she vowed to kill Elijah. Terrified, Elijah ran for his life. When he finally stopped running and encountered God, he lamented that he was the **only one** left who was standing for what was right, although in the previous chapter, Obadiah, servant of Ahab, had reminded Elijah that he feared God and had hidden 100 prophets from wicked Jezebel (1 Kings 18:3-4, 12-13). The Lord also told Elijah there were 7,000 people in Israel who had not bowed to Baal. Situations are seldom as dreadful as we think in our moments of exhaustion and fear. God gave Elijah several assignments to complete, one of which was to find Elisha and invest time in training him to be Elijah's successor. *"Elijah moments"* are common to us all, but God has a solution to help us get through those temporary times.

1) Get some rest (1 Kings 19:5).
~~~~~

2) Eat some nourishing food (1 Kings 19:6-8).
3) Talk to God (1 Kings 19:9-18).
4) Take the focus off of yourself and invest in others (1 Kings 19:19-21).

Are you experiencing an ***"Elijah moment"***? Try applying God's ***"Elijah moment"*** solution.

Gem #198 **July 16**

And Joses, who by the apostles was surnamed ***Barnabas,***
(which is, being interpreted, ***The son of consolation,****) a Levite,*
and of the country of Cyprus, Having land, sold it,
and brought the money, and laid it at the apostles' feet.
Acts 4:36-37

~~~~~

Barnabas' name meant "The Son of Consolation" or "**One who encourages**." Are you known for being an encourager to others? Sometimes just a simple word of encouragement or a kind act goes a long way in restoring hope to someone who is facing tough times. Look around and find someone to encourage today.

~~~~~

"**Encouragement** is a necessary fuel for the Christian race. Without encouragement, as a runner without water, no one could endure the often grueling stretch for long. As we make our journey, we learn that encouragement is a two-way street. We give encouragement to others and so receive it ourselves from other believers and even from God Himself. A little encouragement goes a long way in strengthening the weary and motivating those whose faith is languishing. We often find that the spiritual encouragement we receive from the prayers of those around us rejuvenates us for the second mile. In some cases, that is another twelve years in prison for our faith. In other cases, it is merely the ability to endure another day." ~ **Extreme Devotion, Voice of the Martyrs**

Gem #199 **July 17**

*And it came to pass in those days, that he went out into a mountain to pray, and continued **all night in prayer** to God.*
Luke 6:12

*...The **effectual fervent prayer** of a righteous man availeth much.*
James 5:16

"You can do more than pray after you have prayed,
but you cannot do more than pray until you have prayed."
John Bunyan

"In fact, I have so much [work] to do that I shall have to spend the first three hours in prayer."
Martin Luther

"Why is there so little anxiety to get time to pray? Why is there so little forethought in the laying out of time and employments, so as to secure a large portion of each day for prayer? Why is there so much speaking, yet so little prayer? Why is there so much running to and fro, yet so little prayer? Why so much bustle and business, yet so little prayer? Why so many meetings with our fellow men, yet so few meetings with God? Why so little being alone, so little thirsting of the soul for the calm, sweet hours of unbroken solitude, when God and His child hold fellowship together, as if they could never part? It is this want that not only injures our own growth in grace, but makes us such unprofitable servants of Christ."
William Reid

~~~~~

I am convicted this morning as I read these scriptures and quotes about Jesus and other mighty men whose prayers shook the kingdom of darkness and forever changed the face of history.

Lord, help me to become mighty in prayer!
~~~~~

Gem #200 **July 18**

Thou wilt keep him in perfect ***peace****, whose mind is stayed on thee: because he trusteth in thee. Trust ye in the LORD for ever: for in the LORD JEHOVAH is everlasting strength:*

Isaiah 26:3-4

Peace *I leave with you, my* ***peace*** *I give unto you: not as the world giveth, give I unto you. Let not your heart be troubled, neither let it be afraid.*

John 14:27

Now the God of hope fill you with all joy and ***peace*** *in believing, that ye may abound in hope, through the power of the Holy Ghost.*

Romans 15:13

~~~~~

In a world of ever-increasing wars and violence, the cries for **peace** become more and more urgent. Peace treaties between warring nations are made and broken. Fear abounds. Who will be the next victim of a rapist, a child molester, a gunman or a drunk driver?

In a world filled with hatred and violence, God knew that humanity would need reassurance, so the subject of peace is addressed over 400 times in the Bible. I am calmed by the reassuring words of Isaiah and Jesus which say that if I can look beyond the chaos and confusion of this world into the face of the One who loves me most, my fears will be changed to **peace**. Not the peace treaties the world invents, but the **peace** of God that is born of trust and produces strength to fight every fear.

Are you troubled and afraid? Get your mind on Jesus and put your trust in Him…

"And the ***peace of God****, which passeth all understanding, shall keep your hearts and minds through Christ Jesus."*

Philippians 4:7
~~~~~

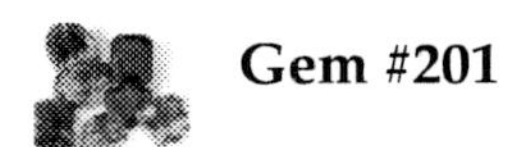

Gem #201 **July 19**

Come unto me, all ye that labour and are heavy laden,
and I will give you ***rest****. Take my yoke upon you, and learn of me;*
for I am meek and lowly in heart: and ye shall find ***rest*** *unto your souls.*
For my yoke is easy, and my burden is light.
Matthew 11:28-30

For with stammering lips and another tongue will he speak to this people.
To whom he said, This is the ***rest*** *wherewith ye may cause the weary to*
rest*; and this is the refreshing: yet they would not hear.*
Isaiah 28:11-12

It is vain for you to rise up early, to sit up late, to eat the
bread of sorrows: for so he giveth his beloved ***sleep****.*
Psalms 127:2

~~~~~

Most of us live life in the fast lane and become victims of perpetual weariness in mind and body. There are dangers of living in a constant state of weariness. We may be too busy to eat and receive the nourishment our body needs, so we become a target for illness. Too many tasks steal our sleep and deprive the body of the rest it needs to heal and restore. Weariness can produce frustration and cause us to complain and say hurtful things to others. Our judgment becomes clouded, and we make unwise decisions. Even doing good works can produce weariness (Galatians 6:9).

What is the solution? Jesus has ordained that we eat properly and get adequate sleep to nourish and restore our physical bodies, and He has given His Holy Spirit to dwell inside us to refresh our spiritual nature.

Are you weary in mind and body? Get some food and sleep and spend some time with Jesus through prayer and study of His Word. Then your body and your spirit will be revived.
~~~~~

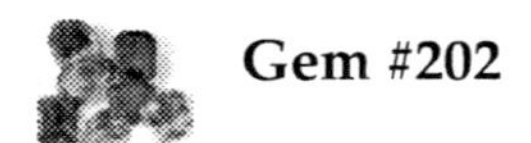 **Gem #202** **July 20**

Finally, brethren, whatsoever things are true, whatsoever things are honest, whatsoever things are just, whatsoever things are pure, whatsoever things are lovely, whatsoever things are of good report; if there be any virtue, and if there be any praise,
think on these things.
Philippians 4:8

*In the multitude of **my thoughts** within me thy comforts delight my soul.*
Psalms 94:19

*The **thoughts** of the righteous are right:*
but the counsels of the wicked are deceit.
Proverbs 12:5

*Commit thy works unto the LORD, and thy **thoughts** shall be established.*
Proverbs 16:3

*The **thoughts** of the diligent tend only to plenteousness;*
but of every one that is hasty only to want.
Proverbs 21:5

*For as he **thinketh** in his heart, so is he:…*
Proverbs 23:7

~~~~~

THOUGHTS! Those mental reflections can fill us with joy, excitement or anticipation, or they can fill us with dread, discouragement or frustration. Solomon taught that our ***thoughts*** reveal what we are on the inside, and Paul gave us a list of guidelines to use as a measuring stick to determine if our ***thoughts*** are appropriate. Anything that doesn't represent truth, honesty, justice, purity, loveliness, goodness, virtue or praise must be banished!!

What kind of ***thoughts*** will you entertain today?
~~~~~

Gem #203 **July 21**

And all the angels stood round about the throne,
and about the elders and the four beasts,
and fell before the throne on their faces, and ***worshipped God,***
Revelation 7:11

And I saw another angel fly in the midst of heaven, having the everlasting gospel to preach unto them that dwell on the earth, and to every nation, and kindred, and tongue, and people, Saying with a loud voice, Fear God, and give glory to him; for the hour of his judgment is come:
and ***worship him that made heaven, and earth,***
and the sea, and the fountains of waters.
Revelation 14:6-7

And the four and twenty elders and the four beasts fell down and ***worshipped God*** *that sat on the throne, saying, Amen; Alleluia.*
Revelation 19:4

~~~~~

As I read my devotional reading today from the seventh chapter of Revelation, my thoughts turned to some old songs about Heaven that remind me that *"This World Is Not My Home, I'm just a-passin' through"* and *"When We All Get To Heaven, What a day of rejoicing that will be." "Soon and Very Soon" "I'll Fly Away"* to a place where *"No Tears In Heaven Will Be Known." "What a Day That Will Be When My Jesus I Shall See." "O Happy Day!" "I'm Longing For Home, for the sun's going down. I long to go where, sweet rest can be found. I'm just about through with this old house of clay. I'm leaving this world for Glory someday."*

Are you longing for Heaven today?

"It Won't Be Long, then we'll be leaving here. It won't be long, We'll be going home."
~~~~~

Gem #204 **July 22**

She stretcheth out her hand to the poor;
yea, she reacheth forth her hands to the needy.
Proverbs 31:20

*...**Do good, and lend**, hoping for nothing again;*
*and your reward shall be great... **Give**, and it shall be given unto you;*
good measure, pressed down, and shaken together, and running over,
shall men give into your bosom. For with the same measure
that ye mete withal it shall be measured to you again.
Luke 6:35, 38

~~~~~

During my morning devotion, I sat down at the piano and opened up the hymn book to a song titled, ***"Make Me A Blessing."*** Here are the words.

1. Out in the highways and byways of life,
Many are weary and sad;
Carry the sunshine where darkness is rife,
Making the sorrowing glad.

Cho. Make me a blessing, Make me a blessing
Out of my life may Jesus shine;
Make me a blessing, O Savior, I pray,
Make me a blessing to someone today.[25]

~~~~~

As I sang and prayed my way through the words of that song, I was reminded of Jesus' words that it is ***more blessed to give than to receive.*** We are so prone to ask for blessings for ourselves that we sometimes forget that God blesses those who bless others.

Today, instead of asking God to bless you, ask instead for Him to make you a blessing to someone else.

---

[25] Lyrics by Ira B. Wilson and music by George S. Schuler. 1924.

Gem #205 **July 23**

Blessed be the Lord, who daily loadeth us with ***benefits****,*
even the God of our salvation. Selah. He that is our God is the
God of salvation; and unto GOD the Lord belong the issues from death.
Psalms 68:19-20

Bless the LORD, O my soul, and forget not all his ***benefits****:*
Who forgiveth all thine iniquities; who healeth all thy diseases;
Who redeemeth thy life from destruction; who crowneth thee with
lovingkindness and tender mercies; Who satisfieth thy mouth
with good things; so that thy youth is renewed like the eagle's.
Psalms 103:2-5

~~~~~

Often, before we engage in a job or activity, we ask the question, "How will this ***benefit*** me?" or "What ***benefits*** does this job have to offer in addition to salary?" It seems we are always looking for opportunities to invest our time and energy into that will provide a good return on our investment. God offers the best ***benefit*** plan ever invented, and these ***benefits*** are in effect every day.

How about these ***benefits***? Salvation from death; Forgiveness for all sins; Healing for all diseases; Redemption from eternal punishment; Continual rewards of lovingkindness and tender mercies; satisfaction with good things and daily renewal.

How do you obtain these ***benefits***? The price is total surrender of your will to His.

Are you ready to invest your life into this plan? Its ***benefits*** provide eternal returns.
~~~~~

 **Gem #206** 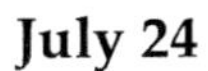 **July 24**

Wherefore remember, that ye being in time past ***Gentiles*** *in the flesh, who are called Uncircumcision by that which is called the Circumcision in the flesh made by hands; That at that time ye were without Christ, being* ***aliens*** *from the commonwealth of Israel, and* ***strangers*** *from the covenants of promise, having no hope, and without God in the world: But now in Christ Jesus ye who sometimes were far off are made nigh by the blood of Christ.*

Ephesians 2:11-13

\~~~~~

If I, as a Gentile, had been born before Calvary, I would have had no hope of establishing a relationship with my Creator. But Jesus came into the world for the express purpose of reaching out to all the aliens and strangers who were without God and without hope. Through His blood that was shed at Calvary, I now have a personal relationship with God, and I possess the hope of spending eternity with Him after this life. I'm thankful today for Calvary and the blood of Jesus.

Gem #207 **July 25**

For as many of you as have been ***baptized into Christ have put on Christ.***

Galatians 3:27

To whom God would make known what is the riches of the glory of this mystery among the Gentiles; which is ***Christ in you, the hope of glory:***

Colossians 1:27

\~~~~~

When we are baptized in Jesus' name, we have put on Christ just as we put on our clothes. We are surrounded with Him. But when we are filled with the Holy Ghost, we become filled with Christ so that He is in us and on us; totally immersed in Christ, our hope of glory.

"Water Baptism put you into Christ.
Spirit Baptism puts Christ into you." ~ **Doug Pierce**

 **Gem #208** **July 26**

Let your light so shine before men, that they may ***see your good works, and glorify your Father*** *which is in heaven.*
Matthew 5:16

Having your conversation honest among the Gentiles: that, whereas they speak against you as evildoers, they may ***by your good works,*** *which they shall behold,* ***glorify God*** *in the day of visitation.*
1 Peter 2:12

Looking for that blessed hope, and the glorious appearing of the great God and our Saviour Jesus Christ;
Who gave himself for us, that he might redeem us from all iniquity, and purify unto himself a peculiar people, ***zealous of good works.***
Titus 2:13-14

~~~~~

Little children often need some kind of incentive to promote good behavior. It might be something as simple as giving them money, a special treat or some special privilege. Some children simply love the attention they receive from doing something good, so that is enough motivation.

Now what about us who are adults? What is our motivation for doing good works? Do we enjoy hearing people praise us for the good things we do? Do we do good, expecting some type of payment for our works?

Jesus and Peter very specifically said that our good works should represent God and cause others to glorify the God we serve.

Do people see God in your good works and give glory to Him instead of you?
~~~~~

 **Gem #209** **July 27**

Behold, ***I come quickly****: hold that fast which thou hast,*
that no man take thy crown.
Revelation 3:11

Behold, ***I come quickly****: blessed is he that keepeth the sayings*
of the prophecy of this book. And, behold, ***I come quickly****; and*
my reward is with me, to give every man according as his work shall be.
He which testifieth these things saith, Surely ***I come quickly****. Amen.*
Even so, come, Lord Jesus.
Revelation 22:7, 12, 20[26]

~~~~~

During Jesus' earthly ministry, He spoke often of His death, resurrection and ascension back into Heaven. He promised to return to His followers in the form of the Holy Ghost so they would be empowered to carry on the work He had started. He also taught them to watch for His soon physical return, at which time He would come with rewards in His hand for those who had worked and faithfully followed His teachings.

Because it has been about two thousand years since Jesus instructed His followers to watch for His soon coming, many have lost hope in the promise of His coming and are living their lives according to their own desires. However, Peter prophesied of these times in 2 Peter 3 and reminded us that God keeps His promises and will return soon to reward those who are working and watching. What may seem like a long time according to man's calculations is simply a short time according to God's calculations. According to His time-clock, it has only been about two days since He went away. (A thousand years is as one day – 2 Peter 3:9.) Don't become weary in watching, for He will return soon. Are you ready?

---

[26] Related scriptures on the subject: Matthew 24:36-44; 25:1-13; Mark 13:33-37; Luke 21:28-36; Revelation 3:3; 16:5.
~~~~~

Gem #210 **July 28**

And it came to pass after these things, that God did tempt Abraham, and said unto him, ***Abraham****: and he said, Behold,* ***Here I am.***
Genesis 22:1

And God spake unto Israel in the visions of the night, and said, ***Jacob, Jacob****. And he said,* ***Here am I.***
Genesis 46:2

And when the LORD saw that he turned aside to see, God called unto him out of the midst of the bush, and said, ***Moses, Moses****. And he said,* ***Here am I.***
Exodus 3:4

*Also [****Isaiah****] heard the voice of the Lord, saying, Whom shall I send, and who will go for us? Then said I,* ***Here am I;*** *send me.*
Isaiah 6:8

And there was a certain disciple at Damascus, named Ananias; and to him said the Lord in a vision, ***Ananias****. And he said, Behold,* ***I am here, Lord.***
Acts 9:10

~~~~~

Jesus told His disciples that the world was a harvest field for preaching the Gospel, and He was looking for laborers to work in His field (Matthew 9:37-38; Luke 10:2; John 4:35-38). The Bible is full of stories of men and women who were called of God to lead, to preach, or to perform a special task. Many heard His voice and answered the call, but there were also many more who chose their own will over God's. God is still looking for those whose heart is perfect toward Him (2 Chronicles 16:9) so He can use them to bring in the harvest.

He is calling today. Are you listening and available?
~~~~~

Gem #211 **July 29**

But if ye have bitter envying and strife in your hearts, glory not, and lie not against the truth. This wisdom descendeth not from above, but is earthly, sensual, devilish. For where envying and strife is, there is ***confusion*** *and every evil work.*
But the wisdom that is from above is first pure, then peaceable, gentle, and easy to be intreated, full of mercy and good fruits, without partiality, and without hypocrisy. And the fruit of righteousness is sown in peace of them that make peace.

James 3:14-18

For God is not the author of ***confusion****, but of peace, as in all churches of the saints. Let all things be done decently and in order.*

1 Corinthians 14:33, 40

~~~~~

Confusion is defined as a state of bewilderment, perplexity, chaos, embarrassment, or inability to distinguish between right and wrong.

James taught how to distinguish between devilish wisdom and the wisdom that comes from God. Devilish wisdom springs from a root of bitter envying and strife which produces confusion and evil works, whereas the wisdom that comes from God produces purity, peacefulness, gentleness, mercy, good fruits, impartiality, and virtuous character. Paul taught that God was the author of peace and put His stamp of approval on decency and order.

So if you find yourself in a state of confusion, check your heart and determine the root cause of the matter, for God is not the author of confusion.

My prayer today comes from the psalmist:

In thee, O LORD, do I put my trust: let me never be put to ***confusion****.*

Psalms 71:1
~~~~~

Gem #212 **July 30**

... [Jesus said,] I am come that they might have ***life****,*
and that they might have it more ***abundantly****.*
John 10:10

Knowing this, that our ***old man is crucified*** *with him, that the body of sin might be destroyed, that henceforth we should not serve sin. For he that is dead is freed from sin.*
Romans 6:6-7

I am ***crucified with Christ****: nevertheless I live; yet not I, but Christ liveth in me: and the life which I now live in the flesh I live by the faith of the Son of God, who loved me, and gave himself for me.*
Galatians 2:20

And they that are Christ's have ***crucified the flesh*** *with the affections and lusts.*
Galatians 5:24

~~~~~

We often hear these catchy phrases indicating how we should live life, i.e., *"Live it up," "Eat, drink and be merry,"* or *"Enjoy life to the fullest."* Jesus did say that He came to give us abundant life, but His and Paul's instructions for living an abundant life were not in agreement with today's definition of abundant living. The world says to try it, touch it, taste it, or experience it. Seek pleasure, seek thrills, seek wealth, or seek happiness. But God's way to abundance requires death to self, death to the flesh, and death to sin. Although many times material blessings do come our way, God didn't promise that our rewards would be earned in this life. He said for us to lay up treasures in Heaven rather than on earth.

Are you willing to die to self so that Christ may live and shine through you? The choice is yours.
~~~~~

Gem #213 **July 31**

And the angel of the Lord spake unto Philip, saying, Arise, and go toward the south unto the way that goeth down from Jerusalem unto Gaza, which is desert. And he arose and went: and, behold, a man of Ethiopia, an eunuch of great authority under Candace queen of the Ethiopians, who had the charge of all her treasure, and had come to Jerusalem for to worship, Was returning, and sitting in his chariot read Esaias the prophet. Then the Spirit said unto Philip, Go near, and join thyself to this chariot. And Philip ran thither to him, and heard him read the prophet Esaias, and said, ***understandest thou what thou readest?*** *And he said, How can I, except some man should guide me? And he desired Philip that he would come up and sit with him.*

Acts 8:26-31

But sanctify the Lord God in your hearts: and ***be ready always to give an answer to every man*** *that asketh you a reason of the hope that is in you with meekness and fear:*

1 Peter 3:15

~~~~~

The Bible is a spiritual book and can only be accurately understood by those who are filled with the Spirit and spend time studying, researching, praying and committing the Word to memory (Psalms 119:111; Corinthians 2:12-14). When we were born into the Kingdom of God, it was not God's intent that we spend the rest of our days being fed the things of God by others. It is our responsibility to grow up and commit ourselves to studying and learning everything we can learn about the Word and the lifestyle of a Christian so we can accurately explain it to others. There are millions of people in the world who, like the Ethiopian eunuch, read the Bible and cannot understand what it means. It is up to the Holy Ghost-filled believers to enlighten them. The Ethiopian eunuchs in your world are awaiting your answers to their questions. Are you willing to make room in your schedule to spend hours learning the Word so you will *"be ready always to give an answer to every man that asketh"*?
~~~~~

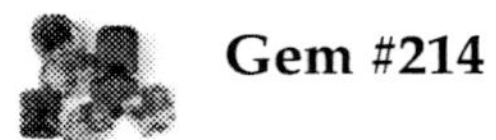

Gem #214 **August 1**

Then they that feared the LORD spake often one to another: and the LORD hearkened, and heard it, and a book of remembrance was written before him for them that feared the LORD, and that thought upon his name. And they shall be mine, saith the LORD of hosts, in that day when I make up my jewels; and I will spare them, as a man spareth his own son that serveth him. Then shall ye return, and discern between the righteous and the wicked, between him that serveth God and him that serveth him not.

Malachi 3:16-18

~~~~~

There are those who call themselves Christians, yet they rarely talk about the things of God. When you are around them, you hear about their problems, current sports or movie heroes, politics, their vacations, their job, their favorite restaurants, their favorite places to shop or other miscellaneous topics that are unrelated to God and His Word.

The prophet Malachi said that God was listening to the conversations of His people, and He had a book in which was written the names of all those who talked often to one another about Him, and whose thoughts were on His name. Everyone whose name is written in that book is a special jewel belonging to God and will be spared from the wrath that God will pour out on the inhabitants of the earth when He returns to set up His Millennial Kingdom.

Does your daily conversation include comments about God and His goodness to you and your family? God is listening and writing.
~~~~~

Gem #215 **August 2**

That Christ may dwell in your hearts by faith; that ye, being ***rooted and grounded in love,*** *May be able to comprehend with all saints what is the breadth, and length, and depth, and height; And to know the* ***love*** *of Christ, which passeth knowledge, that ye might be filled with all the fulness of God.*
Ephesians 3:17-19

A new commandment I give unto you, That ye ***love*** *one another; as I have* ***loved*** *you, that ye also* ***love one another****. By this shall all men know that ye are my disciples, if ye have* ***love one to another****.*
John 13:34-35

Seeing ye have purified your souls in obeying the truth through the Spirit unto unfeigned ***love*** *of the brethren, see that ye* ***love one another*** *with a pure heart fervently:*
1 Peter 1:22[27]

~~~~~

Rooted and Grounded in Love! Our ability to comprehend the infinite mysteries of God is limited to the depth of the roots of love in our life.

Little love = little understanding. Great love = great understanding. The words love and charity appear over 460 times in the Bible, so this subject is apparently a key component of our spiritual growth and lifestyle.

Are you hungry to know the deep things of God?

Nurture the roots of love, and your understanding will soar, for love is the foundation of understanding!

---

[27] Additional scriptures on this subject: John 15:12, 17; Romans 12:10; 13:8; Galatians 5:13; Ephesians 4:2; 1 Thessalonians 3:12; 4:9; Hebrews 10:24; 1 Peter 3:8; 1 John 3:11, 23; 4:7, 11-12; 2 John 1:5
~~~~~

Gem #216 **August 3**

And this is the ***promise*** *that he hath* ***promised*** *us, even* ***eternal life****.*
1 John 2:25

My sheep hear my voice, and I know them, and they follow me:
And ***I give unto them eternal life****; and they shall never perish,*
neither shall any man pluck them out of my hand.
John 10:27-28

For the wages of sin is death; but the ***gift of God is eternal life***
through Jesus Christ our Lord.
Romans 6:23

In hope of ***eternal life, which God****, that cannot lie,*
promised *before the world began;*
Titus 1:2

And for this cause he is the mediator of the new testament,
that by means of death, for the redemption of the transgressions
that were under the first testament, they which are called
might receive the ***promise of eternal inheritance****.*
Hebrews 9:15

~~~~~

Human life is precious because it is so temporary. James compared life to a vapor which appears for a brief time and then vanishes away (James 4:14). Because life is so short, it is imperative that we live it in accordance with the teachings of the Bible so that when it is over, we will inherit the promise of eternal life. I have staked my whole existence on the promises given in the Bible by a God who cannot lie.

One day soon, life on this earth as we know it will be over, and if we have obeyed God's commandments, we will live again in His presence forever. Oh Happy Day!
~~~~~

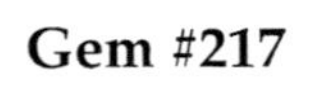 **Gem #217** **August 4**

All scripture is given by inspiration of God*, and is profitable for doctrine, for reproof, for correction, for instruction in righteousness: That the man of God may be perfect, thoroughly furnished unto all good works.*
2 Timothy 3:16-17

Knowing this first, that no prophecy of the scripture is of any private interpretation. For the prophecy came not in old time by the will of man: but ***holy men of God spake as they were moved by the Holy Ghost****.*
2 Peter 1:20-21

Search the scriptures*; for in them ye think ye have eternal life: and they are they which testify of me.*
John 5:39

~~~~~

First of all, we must remember that all scripture was written by holy men of God who were inspired by the Holy Ghost. Those words of life are not subject to personal interpretation. God gives understanding to those who are full of the Spirit (1 Corinthians 2:9-14) and those who commit time to search out the treasures contained in the scriptures. It is within those pages that we learn the doctrinal tenets that save us. Those pages also reprove us when we do wrong and teach us how to correct the wrongs we do. And finally, they teach us how to become righteous in order to inherit eternal life. Everything in that Book is given for the purpose of maturing us and equipping us to do the work of God.

Do you want to mature in your walk with God? The road to maturity is found in studying and applying the teachings of that Holy Book (2 Timothy 2:15).
~~~~~

Gem #218 **August 5**

The eternal God is thy refuge, and underneath are the ***everlasting arms****:*
and he shall thrust out the enemy from before thee;
and shall say, Destroy them.

Deuteronomy 32:27

~~~~~

This verse provided the inspiration for the composition of the well-known hymn ***"Leaning On The Everlasting Arms"*** by A. J. Showalter and Elisha Hoffman. While writing notes to two of his friends who had suffered recent bereavements, author and businessman, Mr. Showalter included Deuteronomy 32:27 in his remarks of comfort. After finishing his letters, the thought occurred to him that this verse would provide a fine theme for a hymn. Suddenly inspired, he proceeded to write down the words to the chorus. He then consulted his friend, Rev. Elisha Hoffman, a pastor and composer of more than 2,000 gospel songs, and asked him to write some verses to go with his chorus. The completed hymn was published in 1887 in the *Glad Evangel for Revival, Camp and Evangelistic meetings Hymnal.*[28]

~~~~~

What a fellowship, what a joy divine,
Leaning on the everlasting arms.
What a blessedness, what a peace is mine.
Leaning on the everlasting arms.
Leaning, leaning, safe and secure from all alarms.
Leaning, leaning, leaning on the everlasting arms.

~~~~~

It is reassuring to remember that in times of sickness, grief, or trouble, we can find refuge in God's everlasting arms.

---

[28] Kenneth W. Osbeck, *Amazing Grace: 366 Inspiring Hymn Stories for Daily Devotions* (Grand Rapids, MI: Kregel Publications, 1990) 87.
~~~~~

 **Gem #219** 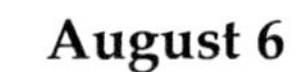 **August 6**

Every day *will I bless thee; and I will praise thy name for ever and ever.*
Psalms 145:2

And my tongue shall speak of thy righteousness and of thy praise
all the day long.
Psalms 35:28

In God we boast ***all the day long****, and praise thy name for ever. Selah.*
Psalms 44:8

Let my mouth be filled with thy praise and with thy honour ***all the day.***
Psalms 71:8

While I live *will I praise the LORD: I will sing praises unto my God*
while I have any being.
Psalms 146:2

~~~~~

We are busy people and live by strict schedules. We wear watches on our arms and have clocks on our walls, in our cars and on our phones to remind us of the time so we can allocate selected amounts of time for each of the day's appointments and tasks. Yet the most important priority of every day is to bless and praise the Lord. That does not mean just a hurried "Thank you Jesus, for this day" when I open my eyes in the morning and before I close them at night. The Psalmist said he would not only praise the Lord *every day*, but he would also praise the Lord *all the day long for as long as he lived.*

Praise to our God *every day, throughout the day* is the standard that has been set for living a victorious, overcoming life.

Have you scheduled ***"praise breaks"*** throughout your day?
~~~~~

Gem #220 **August 7**

Bear ye one another's burdens*, and so fulfil the law of Christ.*
Galatians 6:2

We then that are strong ought to ***bear the infirmities of the weak****,*
and not to please ourselves.
Romans 15:1

~~~~~

We are soldiers fighting for God's cause, and every day, soldiers get wounded in the fight. Often their wounds are not fatal, but they are unable to remove themselves from the battle to a place of safety so their wounds can receive attention, and they can recover. When we are in the heat of the battle, it is easy to neglect the needs of our fallen comrades due to our instinct to save our own lives. However, God has called us to bear one another's burdens rather than doing what pleases ourselves. Many around us are wounded and hurting; they are crying for someone to pick them up and bring them to a place of safety so they can recover and fight again.

Will you ignore the cries of wounded soldiers around you, or will you risk your life to save someone else? We are our brother's keeper.

Gem #221 **August 8**

And when the day of Pentecost was fully come, they were all with one accord in one place. And suddenly there came a sound from heaven as of a rushing mighty wind, and it filled all the house where they were sitting.
And there appeared unto them cloven tongues like as of fire,
and it sat upon each of them.
And they were all ***filled with the Holy Ghost,***
and began to ***speak with other tongues,***
as the Spirit gave them utterance.
Acts 2:1-4
~~~~~

While Peter yet spake these words, the Holy Ghost fell on all them which heard the word. And they of the circumcision which believed were astonished...because that on the Gentiles also was poured out the ***gift of the Holy Ghost****.*
For they heard them ***speak with tongues and magnify God.***
Acts 10:44-46

...while Apollos was at Corinth, Paul ...came to Ephesus: and finding certain disciples, He said unto them, Have ye received the Holy Ghost since ye believed? And they said unto him, We have not so much as heard whether there be any Holy Ghost.
And when Paul had laid his hands upon them, the ***Holy Ghost*** *came on them; and they* ***spake with tongues****, and prophesied.*
Acts 19:1-2, 6

~~~~~

On August 8, 1965, I knelt at an altar at Apostolic Temple in Houston, Texas and was filled with the Holy Ghost and spoke in tongues for the very first time. Such intense feelings of joy overwhelmed me that night. I felt so clean and new. That experience has been renewed hundreds of times over the years as I have continued the practice of speaking in tongues in my personal prayer life. I'm thankful today that as a little 9 year old girl, I received the Holy Ghost exactly as they did in the book of Acts. Believing in Jesus alone is not enough. Jesus said that all believers should receive the Holy Ghost (John 7:38-39). The Holy Ghost gives power to witness (Acts 1:8), leads us into all Truth (John 16:13), puts us in the family of God (Romans 8:9), and will change us to immortality at the coming of Jesus (Romans 8:11). Today I ask the same question that the Apostle Paul asked the group of believers in Acts 19.

"Have you received the Holy Ghost since you believed?"
~~~~~

Gem #222 **August 9**

And ***these words****, which I command thee this day,*
shall be in thine heart: *And thou shalt* ***teach them diligently***
unto thy children*, and shalt talk of them when thou sittest in thine house,*
and when thou walkest by the way, and when thou liest down,
and when thou risest up.
And when thy son asketh thee in time to come, saying,
What mean the testimonies, and the statutes, and the judgments,
which the LORD our God hath commanded you?
Then thou shalt say unto thy son…
And the LORD commanded us to do all these statutes, to fear the LORD our God, for our good always, that he might preserve us alive, as it is at this day. And it shall be our righteousness, if we observe to do all these commandments before the LORD our God, as he hath commanded us.
Deuteronomy 6:6-7, 20-21, 24-25

~~~~~

God's words must be so engrained in our heart that we can answer our children's "Why do we do this?" or "Why don't we do that?" questions with scriptural answers. Too often parents don't know the Word themselves, so they give lame answers such as, "This is what our pastor teaches," or "Our church disapproves of that," or "This was the way my parents raised me."

The Word has answers, and it is imperative that parents know what they believe and are able to explain it to their children. Moses said that God's laws were given for our good, for our preservation and for our righteousness.

Can you explain to your children and others who have questions why you believe what you believe? If not, it's time to spend time in prayer and serious study. Those who look to us for information deserve answers.
~~~~~

Gem #223

August 10

I have declared ***my ways****, and thou heardest me: teach me thy statutes.*
I thought on ***my ways****, and turned my feet unto thy testimonies.*
I have kept thy precepts and thy testimonies:
for ***all my ways*** *are before thee.*
Psalms 119:26, 59, 168

Thou compassest my path and my lying down,
and art acquainted with ***all my ways****.*
Psalms 139:3

I said, I will take heed to ***my ways****, that I sin not with my tongue:*
I will keep my mouth with a bridle, while the wicked is before me.
Psalms 39:1

~~~~~

Habits are those routine ways of life that are performed almost automatically. Things like brushing our teeth before bed, combing our hair when we awake, saying please and thank you, putting on seatbelts before driving, looking both ways before crossing a street and numerous other practices are just normal ways of daily life.

Although most of our habits are automatic and public, sometimes we have secret habits that we take great care to conceal from other eyes. Yet, even though we may conceal some of our ways from others, the Bible says that God knows all our ways. Nothing is hidden from Him.

It is time for me to take inventory of our daily habits.

Do *all my ways* please God? He is watching and keeping records.
~~~~~

 **Gem #224**  **August 11**

Marvel not at this: for the hour is coming, in the which all that are in the graves shall hear his voice, And shall come forth; ***they that have done good, unto the resurrection of life; and they that have done evil, unto the resurrection of damnation.***
John 5:28-29

And I saw the dead, small and great, stand before God;
and the books were opened: and another book was opened,
which is the book of life: and ***the dead were judged out of those things which were written in the books****, according to their works.*
And ***whosoever was not found written in the book of life***
was cast into the lake of fire.
Revelation 20:12, 15

~~~~~

Repetition. We learn by doing things over and over until they become habits. We also learn by hearing and seeing things over and over until we understand and obey the message. The Bible has two very important teachings that are repeated over and over throughout the Old and New Testaments. The teaching of Heaven promises eternal life to those who love God and obey His commandments during their earthly life. The fearful teaching of Hell promises eternal separation from God in the lake of fire to those who do not love God and disobey His teachings. Although these teachings are repeated hundreds of times in the Bible, the vast majority of people choose to disregard the teaching of Hell and live according to their own will, wrongly believing that a God of love would not condemn a person to an eternity in Hell. Make no mistake. The God of love and mercy will change into a God of vengeance and judgment for those who have ignored His laws.

We must learn what the Bible says and obey it fully to escape the coming wrath of God.
~~~~~

Gem #225 **August 12**

Thy word is a lamp unto my feet, and a ***light*** *unto my path. The entrance of thy words giveth* ***light****; it giveth understanding unto the simple.*

Psalms 119:105, 130

The people that walked in darkness have seen a great light: they that dwell ***in*** *the land of the shadow of death, upon them hath the* ***light*** *shined.*

Isaiah 9:2

Then spake Jesus again unto them, saying, I am the ***light*** *of the world: he that followeth me shall not walk in darkness, but shall have the* ***light*** *of life.*

John 8:12

Ye are the ***light*** *of the world. A city that is set on an hill cannot be hid. Let your* ***light*** *so shine before men, that they may see your good works, and glorify your Father which is in heaven.*

Matthew 5:14, 16

For ye were sometimes darkness, but now are ye light in the Lord: walk as children of ***light****:*

Ephesians 5:8

~~~~~

The Bible teaches that God is ***light***, and His Word is ***light***. We are instructed to be ***lights*** in our world. The only way our dark sinful nature can be transformed into ***light*** is for us to develop a relationship with God and His Word. The more time we spend in God's presence and in the study of His Word, the more darkness is pushed out of our lives, and the brighter our ***light*** shines before the world. The world gets darker everyday, and the people who walk in darkness are desperately searching for ***light***.

Does your relationship with God and knowledge of His Word shine brightly to those who cross paths with you?
~~~~~

Gem #226 **August 13**

The L*ORD shall* ***preserve thee*** *from all evil: he shall* ***preserve*** *thy soul.*
The L*ORD shall* ***preserve*** *thy going out and thy coming in*
from this time forth, and even for evermore.
Psalms 121:7-8

~~~~~

In 2004, I spent seven weeks in Bolivia, South America with missionary friends Rev. Darrell Collins and his wife Cindy. I attended the dedication of a church built in memory of my deceased husband and taught several lessons at the Bible school in Cochabamba. I also traveled to several cities with the Collins and attended leadership training sessions taught by Rev. Collins. One day, a flat tire on the vehicle forced us to pull off the road. I snapped a picture of the exploded tire and left the camera dangling by its strap on my right arm while I watched Rev. Collins change the tire. Suddenly, a Bolivian ran up to me and grabbed my camera, broke the strap off my arm, quickly jumped on a waiting motorcycle, and sped off. I was stunned!

Later that evening, I opened my Bible to Psalms 121 and verse 5 just jumped out at me.

"The L*ORD is thy keeper: the* L*ORD is thy shade upon thy* ***right*** *hand."*

My camera had been dangling from my ***right*** arm. Although I had lost my camera and many irreplaceable pictures that were on the card inside, my life had been preserved. The camera was replaced by my travel insurance when I returned home, but my life would have been irreplaceable. I wonder how many times God permits a small loss in our life in order to prevent the greater loss of our life.

My confidence is in God's promise to preserve me from all evil.
~~~~~

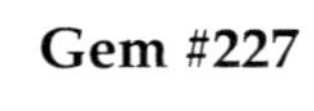

Gem #227 **August 14**

Ask, and it shall be given you; seek, and ye shall find; knock, and it shall be opened unto you: For ***every one that asketh receiveth****; and he that seeketh findeth; and to him that knocketh it shall be opened.*

Matthew 7:7-8; Luke 11:9-10

And ***whatsoever ye shall ask*** *in my name, that will I do, that the Father may be glorified in the Son. If ye shall a****sk any thing in my name,*** *I will do it.*

John 14:13-14

~~~~~

On many occasions in the Gospels, Jesus told His followers that they could ask anything in prayer in His name, and they would receive whatever they asked. That's a pretty huge promise. Yet many times we are frustrated in prayer because we ask things of God over and over, and do not receive what we ask from Him. Why? After searching the scriptures, I found five reasons why we may not receive what we ask from God.

1) **Unbelief** blocks God's hand from giving us the petitions we desire of Him. (Matthew 21:22; Mark 9:23; 11:24) Faith pleases God and is a prerequisite for receiving anything from Him (Hebrews 11:6; Matthew 21:21; Mark 11:23)

2) Prayers that are **not in accordance with God's will** are not answered as we wish (1 John 5:14-15). Jesus taught us by example to pray, "Not my will, but thine be done" (Matthew 26:39, 42; Luke 22:42).

3) **Disobedience** to God's laws prohibits Him from granting our requests (John 15:7-10).

4) **We do not ask** (James 4:2). We get caught up in trying to do everything ourselves, and we simply do not ask until we have exhausted all our own resources.
~~~~~

5) **Prayers asked with a wrong motive** will not be answered as we desire (James 4:3). Or when we do ask, we think only of what will benefit our self instead of what will bring honor and glory to God.

Do you want to see more answers to your prayers? Then make sure that they are in alignment with God's Word, and He will take great delight in granting your petitions.

Gem #228 **August 15**

Ye are our epistle written in our hearts, known and read of all men: Who also hath made us able ministers of the new testament; not of the letter, but of the spirit: for the letter killeth, but the spirit giveth life.
2 Corinthians 3:2, 6

~~~~~

Some people will never pick up a Bible and read it for themselves. God has ordained for His people to be epistles or letters written to the world.

Do you know and obey His Word well enough that your life reflects God's values and principles to those who are watching you?

Are you able to minister His teachings to others?

You may be the only Bible some people in your sphere of influence will ever read.

Learn it. Live it. People are reading you.
~~~~~

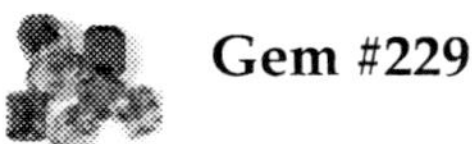

Gem #229 **August 16**

That he might sanctify and ***cleanse it with the washing of water by the word,*** *That he might present it to himself a glorious church…*
Ephesians 5:25-27

Wherewithal shall a young man ***cleanse*** *his way?*
by taking heed thereto ***according to thy word.***
Psalms 119:9

[Jesus said,] Now ye are ***clean through the word*** *which*
I have spoken unto you.
John 15:3

~~~~~

The world in which we live is a sinful, dirty environment, and it is impossible to live our lives without some of its filth attaching itself to us. We are exposed to ungodly talk in the work place, immodesty in store displays in the shopping malls, and temptations to sin from the billboards on the highways. Many other examples could be given of the sinfulness around us that grieves our spirit and causes us to feel unclean. Thankfully, the Bible remedy for washing away all these evil influences is to spend more time in the Word.

Has the world's influence left you feeling dirty? Pick up the Bible and read, and let its pure, holy Words wash that filthiness right off of you.

~~~~~

"How can a young person in this decadent society hope to lead a pure life? How can one avoid wandering from the Truth? By mastering God's Word. By allowing it to control his or her life. The way to master the Word is to memorize it. Then when the spiritual battles come, the Sword of the Spirit can be wielded at a moment's notice, without fumbling for words!"
Don Wyrtzen[29]

---

[29] Don Wyrtzen, *A Musician Looks at the Psalms* (Grand Rapids, MI: Daybreak Books, 1988) 311.

Gem #230 **August 17**

The scripture for today in my daily devotional book came from Psalms 27:4. The words ***"one thing"*** jumped out at me and out of curiosity, I decided to research other places in which that phrase occurred. I discovered that phrase encompasses a wide spectrum of subjects relating to God and His promises as well as setting priorities and acquiring spiritual virtues in our lives. Here are the results of my search.

~~~~~

God Keeps Every Promise – *"...know in all your hearts and in all your souls, that not* ***one thing*** *hath failed of all the good things which the LORD your God spake concerning you; all are come to pass..."* ~ **Joshua 23:14**

Priority of Worship – *"****One thing*** *have I desired of the LORD, that will I seek after; that I may dwell in the house of the LORD all the days of my life, to behold the beauty of the LORD, and to enquire in his temple."* ~ **Psalms 27:4**

Death of Physical Body – *"For that which befalleth the sons of men befalleth beasts; even one thing befalleth them: as the one dieth, so dieth the other; yea, they have all one breath; so that a man hath no preeminence above a beast... All go unto* ***one place****; all are of the dust, and all turn to dust again."* ~ **Ecclesiastes 3:19-20**

Priority of Jesus First – *"Then Jesus beholding him loved him, and said unto him,* ***one thing*** *thou lackest: go thy way, sell whatsoever thou hast, and give to the poor, and thou shalt have treasure in heaven: and come, take up the cross, and follow me."* ~ **Mark 10:21; Luke 18:22**

Priority of Learning Before Serving – *"But* ***one thing*** *is needful: and Mary hath chosen that good part, which shall not be taken away from her."* ~ **Luke 10:42**

Unshakeable Faith – *"He answered and said, ...****One thing*** *I know, that, whereas I was blind, now I see."* ~ **John 9:25**
~~~~~

Determination - *"...this **one thing** I do, forgetting those things which are behind, and reaching forth unto those things which are before, I press toward the mark for the prize of the high calling of God in Christ Jesus."* ~ **Philippians 3:13-14**

God's Timing vs. Man's Timing - *"But, beloved, be not ignorant of this **one thing**, that one day is with the Lord as a thousand years, and a thousand years as one day."* ~ **2 Peter 3:8**

Gem #231 **August 18**

And whatsoever ye do in word or deed, **do all in the name of the Lord Jesus**, giving thanks to God and the Father by him.
Colossians 3:17

~~~~~

In 2013, I attended a General Conference of the United Pentecostal Church International in St. Louis. The theme of the week was ***"In The Name."*** Every song and sermon followed the theme of the name of Jesus. Amazing things happened that week. There is power, salvation, healing and miracles, authority, deliverance, revelation, and eternal life in that name. Demons and civil authorities fear the power of that name, and untold multitudes have suffered persecution for that name.

I am thankful I know His name is Jesus. Since I was baptized in Jesus' name and filled with the Holy Ghost[30] according to Bible teachings, I possess all the power and authority of that name.

---

[30] Matt. 10:22; 24:9; Mk. 13:13; Lk. 21:17; Acts 3:1-6; 4:5-12, 30; 5:40; 16:16-18; 19:13-17; John 20:31. For additional scriptural support of these comments, see April 11 and August 8.
~~~~~

 **Gem #232** **August 19**

The ***Lord is my rock,*** *and* ***my fortress,*** *and* ***my deliverer;***
my God, my strength, *in whom I will trust;* ***my buckler,***
and ***the horn of my salvation,*** *and* ***my high tower.***
Psalms 18:2

~~~~~

We often use various terms to describe what God means to us. Writers of the Bible used a variety of subjects to testify of God's operation in their lives. Moses, Isaiah and the Psalmist testified that God was their strength, their song, and their salvation (Exodus 15:2; Psalms 118:14; Isaiah 12:2). Jeremiah said God was his strength, his fortress, his refuge, and his portion (Jeremiah 16:19; Lamentations 3:24). The Apostle Paul said God was his helper (Hebrews 13:6). Other descriptions of God that were recorded in the Psalms include my shepherd (Psalms 23:1), my light (Psalms 27:1), my shield (Psa. 28:7) and my defence (Psalms 94:22).

We used to sing a little chorus when I growing up that said,

He is my Everything. He is my All.
He is my Everything, both great and small.
He gave His life for me, made Everything new.
He is my Everything. Friend, how about you?

What adjectives can you use to describe what God means to you today?

Just fill in the blanks. God is everything you can describe and so much more.
~~~~~

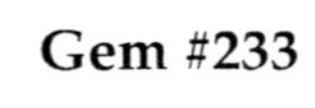

Gem #233 August 20

Give*, and it shall be given unto you; good measure, pressed down, and shaken together, and running over, shall men give into your bosom. For with the same measure that ye mete withal it shall bemeasured to you again.*

Luke 6:38

But this I say, He which soweth sparingly shall reap also sparingly; and he which soweth bountifully shall reap also bountifully. Every man according as he purposeth in his heart, so let him ***give****; not grudgingly, or of necessity: for* ***God loveth a cheerful giver****.*

2 Corinthians 9:6-7

~~~~~

We often think of Luke 6:38 in terms of giving money to receive more money in return. Although that principle is true, the law of giving and receiving involves so much more than just the giving of money. When Jesus spoke those words, He was not talking about money at all. He was teaching about giving love to our enemies, doing good to those who hate us, giving of our possessions to those who ask for them, giving forgiveness to those who wrong us and extending mercy to those who don't deserve it.

The rewards of giving are tied to the laws of sowing and reaping. Paul said if you sow sparingly, you will reap sparingly; but if you sow bountifully, you will reap bountifully. If you give love, you receive love. If you give forgiveness, you receive forgiveness. If you sow good deeds, you reap good deeds.

God is searching for cheerful, bountiful givers so He can give back to them good measure, pressed down, shaken together and running over.
~~~~~

Gem #234 **August 21**

*So that a man shall say, Verily there is a **reward for the righteous**: verily he is a God that judgeth in the earth.*
Psalms 58:11

*The wicked worketh a deceitful work: but to him that soweth righteousness shall be a sure **reward**.*
Proverbs 11:18

*Whoso despiseth the word shall be destroyed: but he that feareth the commandment shall be **rewarded**.*
Proverbs 13:13

*For the Son of man shall come in the glory of his Father with his angels; and then he shall **reward** every man according to his works.*
Matthew 16:27

*And, behold, I come quickly; and my **reward** is with me, to give every man according as his work shall be.*
Revelation 22:12

~~~~~

Sometimes it seems like the unrighteous are the most prosperous and get all the breaks in life while the righteous lack the finer things of life. That has been a fact of life ever since sin entered the world. The Psalmist said his foot almost slipped when he looked around and saw the prosperity of the wicked (Psalms 73). Jesus warned that His people would experience tribulation and would be hated for His name's sake (Matthew 10:22; John 16:33). Fortunately, our sojourn on this earth is simply a preparation ground for the next life. The Bible assures us over and over again that there will be ***rewards*** for the righteous. You may be poverty-stricken in this life, but God is keeping very good records, and when He returns for His Church, every person will receive ***rewards*** for their obedience to God's commandments and for the good works they have done in this life.
~~~~~

Gem #235

August 22

*Study to shew thyself approved unto God, a workman that needeth not to be ashamed, rightly dividing the **word of truth**.*
2 Timothy 2:15

*And many **false prophets** shall rise, and shall deceive many. For there shall arise **false Christs**, and **false prophets**, and shall shew great signs and wonders; insomuch that, if it were possible, they shall deceive the very elect.*
Matthew 24:11, 24

*Beloved, believe not every spirit, but try the spirits whether they are of God: because many **false prophets** are gone out into the world.*
1 John 4:1

~~~~~

I recently had a conversation with a person who had spent years studying various world religions and philosophies so he could know what they believed and converse with them on their level. As I listened to him talk, his thought processes were far removed from the truths contained in the Bible. I was challenged to prove that the Bible is Truth. No scripture I quoted could satisfy the question to prove that the Bible is true. I have heard that bank tellers do not waste their time studying counterfeit money to prove what is genuine. They become so familiar with the real thing that they are instantly able to recognize a counterfeit. In the same manner, I refuse to open my spirit up to the deceptions taught in Eastern religions, cults and worldly philosophies. I believe that the Bible is Truth, and the more I study it and absorb its teachings into my spirit, the more qualified I will be to recognize deceptive teachings. Deception abounds in today's Christian churches, and Jesus and other Bible writers warned us about false prophets and false teachings. Studying the deceptive teachings is NOT the answer to recognizing them. Studying the Words of Truth found in the Bible will equip you to recognize and reject anything that disagrees with that book.
~~~~~

Gem #236 **August 23**

Give ear, O my people, to my law:
***incline your ears** to the words of my mouth.*
Psalms 78:1

***Incline your ear,** and come unto me: hear, and your soul shall live;*
and I will make an everlasting covenant with you,
even the sure mercies of David.
Isaiah 55:3

∼∼∼∼∼

The phrase "***incline your ear***" is not one we hear used in modern-day conversations, but in times past, it was an idiom which meant to listen willingly or favorably. When God asks us to ***incline our ears*** to something He has to say, we should pay attention, for He has some nuggets of truth to share with us.

Do you desire the riches of the Kingdom? Then ***incline your ear*** to the Words in the Holy Bible, and you will experience the greatest adventures of your life.

Gem #237 **August 24**

*...by love **serve** one another. For all the law is fulfilled in one word,*
even in this; Thou shalt love thy neighbour as thyself.
Galatians 5:13-14

∼∼∼∼∼

The gifts and talents God has given me are not for my own personal benefit alone. He expects me to use them to bless and minister to others. We do not well when we isolate ourselves from the needs and hurts of others.

Lord, use me to bless the needy and hurting who pass through my world.

Gem #238 **August 25**

Be kindly affectioned one to another with brotherly love;
in honour ***preferring one another;***
Romans 12:10

I charge thee before God, and the Lord Jesus Christ, and the elect angels, that thou observe these things without ***preferring one before another,*** *doing nothing by partiality.*
1 Timothy 5:21

~~~~~

At first glance, these two scriptures might seem to contradict one another. Paul told the Romans to honor and prefer one another, yet he told Timothy not to prefer one before another. How do we reconcile Paul's teaching in these two scriptures? A closer look at the phrase "doing nothing by partiality" in 1 Timothy 5:21 gives the key to understanding Paul's teaching to Timothy. In short, we should not show partiality in choosing who to love, who to show kindness to, or who to honor. God's way is to promote and prefer others above ourselves. James said it this way.

"My brethren, have not the faith of our Lord Jesus Christ, the Lord of glory, with respect of persons. For if there come unto your assembly a man with a gold ring, in goodly apparel, and there come in also a poor man in vile raiment; And ye have respect to him that weareth the gay clothing, and say unto him, Sit thou here in a good place; and say to the poor, Stand thou there, or sit here under my footstool: Are ye not then partial in yourselves, and are become judges of evil thoughts? If ye fulfil the royal law according to the scripture, Thou shalt love thy neighbour as thyself, ye do well: But if ye have respect to persons, ye commit sin, and are convinced of the law as transgressors."
James 2:1-4, 8-9

How about finding someone who often gets overlooked when honors are passed out and show them special treatment today?
~~~~~

Gem #239 **August 26**

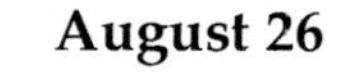

And when Joseph's brethren saw that their father was dead, they said, Joseph will peradventure hate us, and will certainly requite us all the evil which we did unto him. And they sent a messenger unto Joseph, saying, Thy father did command before he died, saying, So shall ye say unto Joseph, Forgive, I pray thee now, the trespass of thy brethren, and their sin; for they did unto thee evil: and now, we pray thee, forgive the trespass of the servants of the God of thy father. And Joseph wept when they spake unto him. And his brethren also went and fell down before his face; and they said, Behold, we be thy servants. And Joseph said unto them, Fear not: for am I in the place of God? But as for you, ye thought evil against me; but God meant it unto good, to bring to pass, as it is this day, to save much people alive.

Genesis 50:15-20

And we know that all things work together for good to them that love God, to them who are the called according to his purpose.

Romans 8:28

~~~~~

The story is told of a missionary[31] who, afflicted with multiple sclerosis, found it impossible to drive to her speaking engagements while she was home on furlough. Her dad, an unbeliever, offered to drive for her. After sitting in services several times a week, he was convicted and gave his heart to God. Our way of thinking would be to ask God to heal the missionary so she could be more mobile and effective in her work. We probably would have asked God to give Joseph's brothers a loving attitude toward their baby brother rather than to sell him into slavery. But God looks beyond our personal comfort or pleasure to the bigger need of salvation for everyone. How can your pain, betrayal, and disappointments in life be used for God's glory and another's salvation? Keep your spirit pure and your attitude right, and God will receive glory, and others will benefit from your disappointments in life.

---

[31] Robert Morgan, *All To Jesus* (Nashville, TN: B & H Publishing Group, 2008) 145.
~~~~~

Gem #240 **August 27**

*That he may **incline our hearts** unto him, to walk in all his ways, and to keep his commandments, and his statutes, and his judgments…*
1 Kings 8:58

***Incline my heart** unto thy testimonies, and not to covetousness. I have **inclined mine heart** to perform thy statutes always…*
Psalms 119:36, 112

~ ~ ~ ~ ~

When faced with making certain choices, we say we are ***inclined*** to do one thing or another. Many voices in our lives attempt to influence our choices and preferences by promising enticing rewards if we choose that path. God's Word has outlined a plan for living, and He calls us to ***incline our hearts*** toward Him and His ways. He has promised exciting rewards for those who prefer and obey His plan. While His way may not produce the immediate rewards promised by the alluring worldly voices, the eternal rewards He offers have no comparison to anything the world has to offer. Will you ***incline your heart*** toward the temporary enticements of the worldly voices, or toward God and His eternal rewards?

Gem #241 **August 28**

*And he spake a parable unto them to this end, that men ought **always to pray**, and not to faint;*
Luke 18:1

~ ~ ~ ~ ~

"**Prayer**, more than any other single activity, is what places us in the flow of the Spirit. When we pray, hearts get convicted, sin gets confessed, believers get united, intentions get encouraged, people receive guidance, the Church is strengthened, stubbornness gets melted, wills get surrendered, evil gets defeated, grace gets released, illness gets healed, sorrows are comforted, faith is born, hope is grown, and love triumphs." ~ **John Ortberg**

Gem #242 **August 29**

***Remember**, O LORD, thy tender mercies and thy lovingkindnesses;*
for they have been ever of old.
***Remember** not the sins of my youth,*
nor my transgressions: according to thy mercy
***remember** thou me for thy goodness' sake, O LORD.*
Psalms 25:6-7

*He hath not dealt with us after our sins; nor rewarded us according to our iniquities. For as the heaven is high above the earth, so great is his mercy toward them that fear him. As far as the east is from the west, so far hath he removed our transgressions from us. Like as a father pitieth his children, so the LORD pitieth them that fear him. For he knoweth our frame; he **remembereth** that we are dust.*
Psalms 103:10-14

~~~~~

Memory is a very powerful force, and in times of conflict and disappointments in life, it is encouraging to ***remember*** God's provision and deliverance in our past. However, during those times of extreme pressure, stress, financial losses or grief, I find dozens of examples in the Bible where people cried out to God and asked Him to ***remember*** them in their hard trials.

Sometimes we may feel like we are fighting our battles alone, and God has forgotten our address, but we must not allow those feelings of doubt to overcome us, for the Bible also gives us numerous reminders that God ***remembers*** us, and His mercies and provision for His people are unending.

Are you in a tough spot in your life right now?

It is perfectly Biblical to cry out to God and say, "Remember me," and it is also perfectly Biblical for God to respond back and say, "Yes, I remember you, and I will see you through this difficult time."
~~~~~

Gem #243

August 30

The law of the LORD is perfect, converting the soul: the testimony of the LORD is sure, making wise the simple. The statutes of the LORD are right, rejoicing the heart: the commandment of the LORD is pure, enlightening the eyes. The fear of the LORD is clean, enduring for ever: the judgments of the LORD are true and righteous altogether. More to be desired are they than gold, yea, than much fine gold: sweeter also than honey and the honeycomb. Moreover by them is thy servant warned: and in keeping of them there is great reward.

Psalms 19:7-11

~~~~~

The purpose of God's Word can be summed up in these five verses. Conversion. Acquisition of Wisdom. Cause for Rejoicing. Enlightenment. Endurance. Truth. Values. Tasty. Warnings. Rewards.

We spend a lifetime searching for meaning and fulfillment through education, careers, relationships, or acquisition of material goods; yet without immersion in the laws of God, all these other things come up short of satisfying the God-designed hunger in our hearts. His Word is more important than gold and sweeter than any dessert we can consume, and the rewards for living by its teachings have eternal value.

Are you searching for something to satisfy, but cannot quite put your finger on what you want? I suspect the missing ingredient is the Word of God.

Read it, study it, live it, talk it, share it. It is the Word of Life.
~~~~~

 **Gem #244** **August 31**

I'll Take Jesus First Of All

1. Houses and land I may not own Many riches be unknown
A little person in this world I may be.
I can't keep up with the styles, But I know I'm God's own child
I'll take Jesus first, and that's enough for me.
Cho. I'll take Jesus first of all, He will answer me when I call
For I know I have a soul He set free.
I am God's own child by birth,
That's the highest honor on this earth.
I'll take Jesus first and that's enough for me.
2. Some may live on wealth and pride, But I'm poor and satisfied.
Great Jehovah owns this world, don't you see?
Underneath His sheltering wings, I'm as happy as a king.
I'll take Jesus first, and that's enough for me.
3. I can remember the time and the place
When I sought my Savior's face.
Then I found Him at an altar on my knees.
There He caught my falling soul, It's just better felt than told
I'll take Jesus first, and that's enough for me.

~~~~~

Recently while going through my Mother's old songbook of songs she used to sing, I found this song. Many memories flooded my mind of the teachings of my parents during my years at home. Putting Jesus first was a core teaching in our family, i.e. reading our Bible every day, memorizing scriptures regularly, praying every day, attending Church every time something was scheduled. Jesus said in Matthew 6:31-33 that we should not worry about what to eat, what to wear, etc, but to seek first His kingdom, and everything else would fall into place.

Today is my mother, Gloria's birthday, and I honor her and my dad, Hubert for their life-time of faithful commitment to their God.
~~~~~

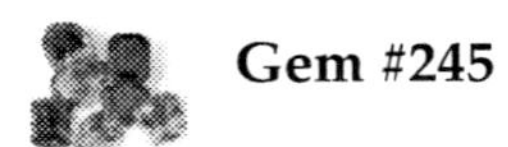 **Gem #245** **September 1**

And David was greatly distressed; for the people spake of stoning him
because the soul of all the people was grieved,
every man for his sons and for his daughters:
but ***David encouraged himself*** *in the LORD his God.*
1 Samuel 30:6

The LORD is my strength and my shield; my heart trusted in him,
and ***I am helped****: therefore my heart greatly rejoiceth;*
and with my song will I praise him.
Psalms 28:7

~~~~~

The Bible teaches us to:

- Bless others (1 Peter 3:9)
- Comfort them (Isaiah 40:1; 2 Corinthians 2:7; 1 Thessalonians 5:14)
- Bear their burdens (Galatians 6:2)
- Edify them and build them up (Romans 14:19; Ephesians 4:29; 1 Thessalonians 5:11).

But there are times in our life when we get down, and no one is available to help us back up. David found himself in such a dilemma when the Amalekites had raided Ziklag and taken It is in times like these that we must use our own resources to ***encourage ourselves*** in the Lord. It may be as simple as singing a song or reading some encouraging verses in the Bible. Maybe you can open a journal of recorded victories or answered prayers and read what God has done in the past. It is important that you have some means of ***encouragement*** in your arsenal of weapons so that you can fight back when the enemy brings you down and no one is there to help you back up.
~~~~~

Gem #246 **September 2**

But Jesus beheld them, and said unto them,
With men this is impossible;
but ***with God all things are possible.***
Matthew 19:26

And ***God is able*** *to make all grace abound toward you;*
that ye, always having all sufficiency in all things,
may abound to every good work:
2 Corinthians 9:8

Now unto him that is able *to do exceeding abundantly above all that we ask or think, according to the power that worketh in us,*
Ephesians 3:20

~~~~~

The Bible teaches us in the Old and New Testaments that *God* ***is able*** to do anything that is needed, ***for anyone*** who needs it, ***any time*** it is needed. His abilities are not the issue, for they are unlimited. Our doubt is the issue, for doubt limits His ability to supply the need. What else does the Bible say about God's abilities?

...***able*** to deliver us from the burning fiery furnace...***able*** to make him stand...***able*** even to subdue all things unto himself...***able*** to keep that which I have committed unto Him...***able*** to succour them that are tempted...***able*** to save him from death...***able*** to save them to the uttermost...***able*** to raise him up...***able*** to save and to destroy...***able*** to keep you from falling.[32]

So cast away your doubts and bring Him your needs. ***He is able and willing.***

Just ask and believe.

---

[32] Daniel 3:17; Romans 14:4; Philippians 3:21; 2 Timothy 1:12; Hebrews 2:18; 5:7; 7:25; 11:19; James 4:12; Jude 1:24
~~~~~

Gem #247 **September 3**

The LORD is my shepherd; I shall not want. He maketh me to lie down in green pastures: he leadeth me beside the still waters. He restoreth my soul: he leadeth me in the paths of righteousness for his name's sake. Yea, though I walk through the valley of the shadow of death, I will fear no evil: for thou art with me; thy rod and thy staff they comfort me. Thou preparest a table before me in the presence of mine enemies: thou anointest my head with oil; my cup runneth over. Surely goodness and mercy shall follow me all the days of my life: and I will dwell in the house of the LORD for ever.

Psalms 23:1-6

~~~~~

Psalms 23 has always been one of my favorite chapters in the Bible. My Aunt Rachel helped me to memorize it when I was 5. Through the years, I have learned to pray its promises for myself and others.

I take comfort in the fact that because the Lord is my Shepherd, my needs are met, and He provides nourishment and quiet times for reflection. When I'm at my wit's end, He provides restoration for my frustrations and leads me in righteous paths. When life-threatening crises occur in my life, He calms my fears and reminds me of His nearness. He disciplines me when I step off the path of righteousness. When I'm surrounded with evil, He prepares good things for me and pours the Holy Ghost anointing over my head in such abundance that it flows out of me to touch and break the yokes of others who are bound. I am protected by His goodness and mercy all my life, and I love living in the household of God's family.

I am thankful today for my Heavenly Shepherd. My life with Him is full and complete.
~~~~~

Gem #248 **September 4**

Wherefore lay apart all filthiness and superfluity of naughtiness,
and receive with meekness the engrafted ***word,***
which is able to save your souls.
James 1:21

And that from a child thou hast known the ***holy scriptures, which are able to make thee wise unto salvation*** *through faith which is in Christ Jesus. All scripture is given by inspiration of God, and is profitable for doctrine, for reproof, for correction, for instruction in righteousness: That the man of God may be perfect, thoroughly furnished unto all good works.*
2 Timothy 3:15-17

~~~~~

"This precious Word of God has made clear many a perplexity, has illumined many a dark road, has cheered many a lonesome way, has soothed many a deep sorrow, has guided and upheld many a faltering step, and has crowned with victory many a feat of arms in the great battle with Satan, the world, and sin."
Octavious Winslow

~~~~~

The Holy Scriptures are an extension of our Holy God, and they are able to give us the wisdom we need to be saved. That wisdom can only come through diligent study and obedience to the teachings we learn through our studies. Every word in that book is profitable to equip us to do the work we have been called to do.

So love it, study it, and obey it, and those lifestyle changes will save you and reward you with eternal life.

Gem #249 **September 5**

The righteous shall ***be glad in the Lord****, and shall trust in him; and all the upright in heart shall glory.*
Psalms 64:10

Although the fig tree shall not blossom, neither shall fruit be in the vines; the labour of the olive shall fail, and the fields shall yield no meat; the flock shall be cut off from the fold, and there shall be no herd in the stalls: Yet ***I will rejoice in the Lord****, I will joy in the God of my salvation. The* LORD *God is my strength, and he will make my feet like hinds' feet, and he will make me to walk upon mine high places…*
Habakkuk 3:17-19

~~~~~

Life has a way of throwing discouraging circumstances at us which could bring us down if we would let them, but the prophet Habakkuk told us that when the crops failed and famine afflicted the land, he would rejoice in the Lord. When he lost his flocks, he promised to rejoice in the Lord because it is God who strengthened him to walk through the tough places in life and come through them with a spring in his steps and a praise on his lips.

The Psalmist said that when the enemy's tongue is like a sword to accuse the righteous, and he lays traps to destroy them (Psalms 64:3-5), the righteous person trusts in the Lord and maintains a spirit of gladness.

Are people gossiping about you? Are you worried about the escalating cost of groceries, utilities, gasoline and other necessities of life?

Just cast all those cares on Jesus, and rejoice in the Lord. He will put a spring in your step and lift you up into His high places of strength and encouragement.
~~~~~

Gem #250 **September 6**

And the L*ORD God took the man, and put him into the garden of Eden to dress it and to keep it. And the* L*ORD God commanded the man, saying, Of every tree of the garden thou mayest freely eat: But of the tree of the knowledge of good and evil,* ***thou shalt not eat of it****: for in the day that thou eatest thereof thou shalt surely die.*
Genesis 2:15-17

Ye shall walk after the L*ORD your God, and fear him, and keep his commandments, and* ***obey*** *his voice, and ye shall serve him, and cleave unto him.*
Deuteronomy 13:4

And Samuel said, Hath the L*ORD as great delight in burnt offerings and sacrifices, as in* ***obeying the voice of the*** **L*ORD****? Behold,* ***to obey is better than sacrifice****, and to hearken than the fat of rams. For rebellion is as the sin of witchcraft, and stubbornness is as iniquity and idolatry…*
1 Samuel 15:22-23

Keep ***my commandments****, and live; and* ***my*** *law as the apple of thine eye.*
Proverbs 7:2

If ye love me, keep my commandments.
John 14:15

~~~~~

"The first doctrine of the Bible is not faith; it's not hope; it's not love; it's not grace. It's **obedience**."
Ken Raggio

~~~~~

The thread of obedience is woven into the fabric of Bible teachings from the very beginning of time. Disobedience robbed Adam and Eve of their Garden paradise, and disobedience in sacrificial offerings brought their son, Cain into disfavor with God. Moses' single act of disobedience in striking the rock instead of speaking to it prevented him from entering the Promised Land. Achan disobeyed Joshua's order to give all the spoils of Jericho to the Lord by keeping several things for himself, and he lost his life. Saul's disobedience in battle prevented his descendants from inheriting the royal throne of Israel. Uzzah disobeyed the law that forbade him from touching the Ark of the Covenant, and he was killed.

God is serious about His laws, and He expects them to be obeyed. If we expect to reap the rewards of the righteous, then we musy study the Bible and heed its teachings. Only then can we expect to be rewarded for the things we have done in this earthly life.

Gem #251 **September 7**

And he said unto them, How is it that ye sought me?
wist ye not that I must be about my ***Father's business****?*
Luke 2:49

"One reason we are so harried and hurried is that we make yesterday and tomorrow our business, when all that legitimately concerns us is today. If we really have too much to do, there are some items on the agenda which God did not put there. Let us submit the list to Him and ask Him to indicate which items we must delete. There is always time to do the will of God. If we are too busy to do that, we are too busy."
Elisabeth Elliot

~~~~~

Lord, help me to submit my daily list to You and quit trying to do things You did not mean for me to do. There are only so many hours in my day. Help me to do the things that You have ordained specifically for me to do and say no to the rest. In Jesus' name.
~~~~~

Gem #252 **September 8**

Then Peter began to say unto him, Lo, we have ***left all****, and have followed thee. And Jesus answered and said, Verily I say unto you, There is no man that hath left house, or brethren, or sisters, or father, or mother, or wife, or children, or lands, for my sake, and the gospel's, But he shall receive an hundredfold now in this time, houses, and brethren, and sisters, and mothers, and children, and lands, with persecutions; and in the world to come eternal life.*

Mark 10:28-30

And after these things he went forth, and saw a publican, named Levi, sitting at the receipt of custom: and he said unto him, Follow me. And he ***left all****, rose up, and followed him.*

Luke 5:27-28

~~~~~

While reading stories today about the missionaries David Livingstone and Alexander Mackay, who left everything behind to share the Gospel with the people of Africa and Uganda, I was convicted about my comfortable lifestyle surrounded by my children and grandchildren. Although God doesn't call every Christian to leave home to evangelize foreign countries or even distant cities in our own country, He does require all of us to spread the Gospel to everyone who hasn't heard or obeyed it. Am I willing to *leave* my comfortable bed in the middle of the night to intercede in prayer for the lost? Am I willing to *leave* my carefully constructed daily schedule to go out of my way to spend time with the homeless, inmates in jail, children without fathers, the elderly in nursing homes, or shut-ins who can't attend church? It's so easy to get caught up in making a living and living life that we forget that everything in this life is simply a preparation time for the next life.

Lord, help me today to be willing to *leave all* to accomplish the task of spreading the Gospel and obtaining the hundredfold reward and eternal life that has been promised to those who have made that kind of commitment.
~~~~~

Gem #253 **September 9**

Now when he had left speaking, he said unto Simon, Launch out into the deep, and let down your nets for a draught. And Simon answering said unto him, Master, we have toiled all the night, and have taken nothing: nevertheless at thy word I will let down the net. And when they had this done, they inclosed a great multitude of fishes: and their net brake.

Luke 5:4-6

*And let us not be weary in well doing: for in due season **we shall reap**, if we faint not.*

Galatians 6:9

*They that sow in tears shall **reap in joy**.*

Psalms 125:5

~~~~~

Jesus commanded us to go out into the world and preach the Gospel to every creature. Sometimes it seems that our labors do not produce any results, but God's Word promises a harvest if we will not lose hope.

In reading several missionary stories today, I learned that William Carey labored seven years in India before baptizing his first convert. The first American missionary, Adoniram Judson, worked seven years in Burma before seeing his first convert. Robert Morrison labored seven years in China before getting his first convert. Missionaries Henry Nott and his wife labored twenty-two years in Tahiti before baptizing their first convert.[33]

So are you frustrated with the seemingly slow return on your investments of time, prayer, study, witnessing and labor for souls?

Keep letting down your nets, for God sees your labor of love for the lost, and in due season, **you will reap** if you don't faint.

---

[33] Robert Morgan, All To Jesus (B&H Publishing Group, Nashville, TN; 2012) Day 157.
~~~~~

Gem #254 **September 10**

School shootings, wars, destructive tornadoes, kidnappings, murders, terrorist bombings, plane crashes, poverty, starvation, cancer, heart attacks, strokes, disease-resistant germs, lay-offs, bankruptcies, escalating prices. The list could go on and on. How do we avoid anxiety and depression when we are bombarded with such devastating news stories every day?

The wise King Solomon gives us a solution for avoiding despair in the face of bad news.

A ***merry*** *heart maketh a cheerful countenance: but by sorrow of the heart the spirit is broken. All the days of the afflicted are evil: but he that is of a* ***merry*** *heart hath a continual feast.*
Proverbs 15:13, 15

A ***merry*** *heart doeth good like a medicine: but a broken spirit drieth the bones.*
Proverbs 17:22

So how can we be merry in the midst of problems? Again, the Bible has solutions.

Thou wilt shew me the path of life: in ***thy presence*** *is fulness of joy; at* ***thy*** *right hand there are pleasures for evermore.*
Psalms 16:11

For you have made him most blessed forever; You have made him ***exceedingly glad with Your presence****.*
Psalms 21:6

Prayer! That powerful tool that we have been given is often used as a last resort, but spending time in His presence brings renewal, pleasure, gladness, and fullness of joy.

The Bible gives us another solution to ward off the heaviness brought on by life's stresses.

*I **rejoice at thy word**, as one that findeth great spoil.*
Psalms 119:162

*Thy **words** were found, and I did eat them; and **thy word** was*
*unto me the **joy** and **rejoicing of mine heart**:*
for I am called by thy name, O LORD God of hosts.
Jeremiah 15:16

God's Word is packed with words of life that, when read and obeyed, will dispel gloom and dispense hope and gladness.

Another important solution to the problem of downcast spirits is mentioned dozens of times in Scripture.

*Serve the LORD with **gladness**: come before **his presence** with **singing**.*
Psalms 100:2

Is any among you afflicted? let him pray.
*Is any **merry**? let him **sing** psalms.*
James 5:13

Sing! Make music! Paul and Silas were beaten and thrown into jail for preaching and working a miracle in a young girl's life, yet in the midst of pain and imprisonment, they sang praises to God, and God responded to their praise by sending an earthquake that loosed their bonds and resulted in the conversion of the jailer and his family. Music rewires our brain, and the right kind of music has the ability to lift us out of the depths of despair and bring gladness back into our spirit. So are you downhearted due to the pressures of life? Pick up your Bible and read; spend time in God's presence through prayer; and sing songs of praise to God. Before you know it, those feelings of gloom and doom will be banished!

Gem #255 **September 11**

[3] I will call upon the LORD, who is worthy to be praised: so shall I be saved from mine enemies. [4] The sorrows of death compassed me, and the floods of ungodly men made me afraid. [5] The sorrows of hell compassed me about: the snares of death prevented me. [6] In my distress I called upon the LORD, and cried unto my God: he heard my voice out of his temple, and my cry came before him, even into his ears. [13] The LORD also thundered in the heavens, and the Highest gave his voice; hail stones and coals of fire. [14] Yea, he sent out his arrows, and scattered them; and he shot out lightnings, and discomfited them. [17] He delivered me from my strong enemy, and from them which hated me: for they were too strong for me. [19] He brought me forth also into a large place; he delivered me, because he delighted in me. [20] The LORD rewarded me according to my righteousness; according to the cleanness of my hands hath he recompensed me. [29] For by thee I have run through a troop; and by my God have I leaped over a wall. [35] Thou hast also given me the shield of thy salvation: and thy right hand hath holden me up, and thy gentleness hath made me great. [36] Thou hast enlarged my steps under me, that my feet did not slip. [37] I have pursued mine enemies, and overtaken them: neither did I turn again till they were consumed. [38] I have wounded them that they were not able to rise: they are fallen ***under my feet.*** *[39] For thou hast girded me with strength unto the battle: thou hast subdued* ***under me*** *those that rose up against me. [40] Thou hast also given me the necks of mine enemies; that I might destroy them that hate me. [41] They cried, but there was none to save them: even unto the LORD, but he answered them not. [42] Then did I beat them small as the dust before the wind: I did cast them out as the dirt in the streets. [46] The LORD liveth; and blessed be my rock; and let the God of my salvation be exalted. [47] It is God that avengeth me, and subdueth the people* ***under me.*** *[48] He delivereth me from mine enemies: yea, thou liftest me up above those that rise up against me: thou hast delivered me from the violent man. [49] Therefore will I give thanks unto thee, O LORD, among the heathen, and sing praises unto thy name.*

Psalms 18

(selected verses)

~~~~~
~~~~~

September 11, 2001. That day is forever etched into the memory of most Americans. On that day, my friend Donna and I had driven to the home of another friend, Treasa, to teach her a Bible study. We were visiting for a few minutes before starting our lesson when I received a phone call from my son telling me that a plane had just crashed into one of the twin towers in New York City. While we were talking, he told me that another plane had crashed into the second tower. We then turned on the news and watched reruns of the two plane crashes in addition to receiving more disturbing reports of the crash into the Pentagon in Washington, D.C. and the crash of the plane in Pennsylvania. Our Bible study session turned into an intercessory prayer meeting for our nation. Since that day, our nation has been involved in a war against terrorists who blatantly disregard human life and conspire to destroy anyone who dares to disagree with their evil philosophies.

Since the fall of Satan and his rebellious angels, there has been war between God and Satan, and specifically, since the fall of Adam and Eve to Satan's temptation, Satan has had billions of human vehicles through whom he has attempted to work and blatantly express his vendetta against God. As people of God, we must recognize that the war against Satan's evil devices will not end until Jesus Christ returns and permanently casts him into the lake of fire. Until that time, we must be alert to Satan's devices and fight the good fight of faith. God is our defender, and gives us the assurance that our enemies are simply defeated foes ***under our feet***. Psalms 18 is one of my favorite chapters to pray for myself or someone else who is involved in the heat of a spiritual battle.

Do you sometimes feel overwhelmed at the increasing intensity of the war against "spiritual terrorists"? In those times, you must call on the Lord and pray the promises of His Word. Then you will recognize that Satan and all his minions are nothing more than defeated foes ***under your feet***.

Gem #256 **September 12**

That Christ may dwell in your hearts by faith;
that ye, being rooted and grounded in love, May be able to comprehend
with all saints what is the breadth, and length, and depth, and height;
And to know the love of Christ, which passeth knowledge,
that ye might ***be filled with all the fullness of God.***
Ephesians 3:17-19

And even as they did not like to retain God in their knowledge,
God gave them over to a reprobate mind, to do those things which are not
convenient; ***Being filled with*** *all unrighteousness, fornication,*
wickedness, covetousness, maliciousness; full of envy, murder, debate,
deceit, malignity; whisperers, Backbiters, haters of God, despiteful, proud,
boasters, inventors of evil things, disobedient to parents,
Without understanding, covenantbreakers, without natural affection,
implacable, unmerciful: Who knowing the judgment of God,
that they which commit such things are worthy of death,
not only do the same, but have pleasure in them that do them.
Romans 1:28-32

~~~~~

The Bible speaks frequently about the kinds of things that fill us. We can spend our days filling ourselves with unrighteousness and other evil attributes as listed in Romans 1. The end of that journey is death and eternal separation from God. No other person receives blessing or benefit from a life lived in that way. On the other hand, we can allow God to fill us with His Holy Spirit and spend our days studying His ways and allowing Him to fill us with His love, wisdom, joy, knowledge, fruits of righteousness and all the fullness of God. A life lived in this way will bless others, leave a legacy for succeeding generations, and reap the greatest benefit of eternal life with God after this earthly life is completed.

What is filling your life? Your eternal destiny and the destinies of those you influence are at stake.
~~~~~

Gem #257 **September 13**

Fret not *thyself because of evildoers, neither be thou envious against the workers of iniquity.* [2] *For they shall soon be cut down like the grass, and wither as the green herb.* [7] *Rest in the LORD, and* ***wait*** *patiently for him:* ***fret not*** *thyself because of him who prospereth in his way, because of the man who bringeth wicked devices to pass.* [9] *For evildoers shall be cut off: but those that* ***wait*** *upon the LORD, they shall inherit the earth.* [10] *For yet a little while, and the wicked shall not be: yea, thou shalt diligently consider his place, and it shall not be.* [11] *But the meek shall inherit the earth; and shall delight themselves in the abundance of peace.* [22] *For such as be blessed of him shall inherit the earth; and they that be cursed of him shall be cut off.* [29] *The righteous shall inherit the land, and dwell therein for ever.* [34] ***Wait*** *on the LORD, and keep his way, and he shall exalt thee to inherit the land: when the wicked are cut off, thou shalt see it.*

Psalms 37:1-2, 9-11, 22, 29, 34

~~~~~

The Apostle Paul warned the Church to beware of evil men, for in the last days, they would become worse and worse, deceiving not only themselves, but also others in the process (2 Timothy 3:13). Because of the abundance of evil around us, it would be easy to fret and give in to fear. But God's Word assures us that evildoers and workers of iniquity will be cut off. The key word for the Church is ***wait.***

In God's timing, all evildoers will be punished, and in the Millennial Kingdom, the meek, the righteous, and those who have lived according to God's way will be exalted to inherit the land.

Do you feel insignificant among the rich, elite, and famous people of the world? Just wait. In time, God will exalt His people and appoint them as rulers over the world.
~~~~~

Gem #258 **September 14**

Know ye that the LORD *he is God: it is* ***he that hath made us****,*
and not we ourselves; we are his people, and the sheep of his pasture.
Psalms 100:3

For ye are ***bought with a price****: therefore glorify God in your body,*
and in your spirit, which are God's.
1 Corinthians 6:20

But ye are a ***chosen*** *generation, a royal priesthood, an* ***holy*** *nation…*
1 Peter 2:9

But now being made free from sin, and become ***servants to God****,*
ye have your fruit unto holiness, and the end everlasting life.
Romans 6:22

I will extol thee, ***my God, O king****;*
and I will bless thy name for ever and ever.
Psalms 145:1

~~~~~

The world teaches us to be self-sufficient, develop self-esteem, and become independent, living life according to our own desires and pleasures. However, these teachings are foreign and contradictoryto the teachings of the Bible. Through study of that Holy Book, I learn that God is my Father, for He created me. When Satan stole God's creation from Him through the sin of Adam and Eve, God bought them back to Himself through His death on the cross. He established the Church and chose obedient people to represent Him and His teachings on earth. Therefore, I belong to God, 1) as His creation, 2) as His purchase, and 3) as His conquest because I have voluntarily surrendered my life to be a servant to my heavenly King and am willing to do His bidding, not mine, for as long as He lets me live on this earth. Are you trying to do your own thing in this earthly life? Give it up and surrender to your owner, the Lord Jesus Christ and receive the ultimate prize of eternal life with Him.
~~~~~

Gem #259 **September 15**

Let no ***corrupt communication*** *proceed out of your mouth,*
but that which is good to the use of edifying,
that it may minister grace unto the hearers.
And grieve not the holy Spirit of God,
whereby ye are sealed unto the day of redemption.
Let all bitterness, and wrath, and anger, and ***clamour****, and* ***evil speaking****,*
be put away from you, with all malice:
And be ye kind one to another, tenderhearted, forgiving one another,
even as God for Christ's sake hath forgiven you.
Ephesians 4:29-32

Set a watch, O LORD, before my mouth*; keep the door of my lips.*
Incline not my heart to any evil thing, to practise wicked works
with men that work iniquity: and let me not eat of their dainties.
Psalms 141:3-4

Death and life are in the power of the ***tongue****:*
and they that love it shall eat the fruit thereof.
Proverbs 18:21

The subject of the spoken word is addressed hundreds of times in the Bible because the words that come out of our mouth have tremendous power to influence those who hear us speak. Words can give life and build up, or they can tear down and destroy. Paul taught the church to guard the communication that proceeded from their mouths and make sure that they were not dishonest, lacking in integrity or evil. He also addressed clamor, which is a vehement expression of dissatisfaction. The Psalmist prayed for God to set a watch before his mouth so that he was not influenced to speak like the wicked people around him. Before you speak today, ***Think!!*** Will these words edify, benefit, uplift, or minister grace to those who hear you?

The power to harm or heal is in your tongue. God is listening!

Gem #260 **September 16**

*He hath shewed his people the **power** of his works... The works of his hands are verity [Truth] and judgment; all his commandments are sure. They stand fast for ever and ever, and are done in truth and uprightness.*

Psalms 111:6-8

~~~~~

Between September 9, 2013 and September 16, 2013, Boulder, Colorado and surrounding mountain communities received over 17 inches of rain in what newscasters reported as a 1,000-year rain and a 100-year flood. Because I had graduated from High School in Boulder, Colorado, I was especially interested in every news article I could find about the flooding in the area. I spent hours reading news and looking at pictures and videos of the terrible damages resulting from the flooding in Boulder. While reading numerous accounts of people's harrowing escapes from rising floodwaters and mudslides, the recurring theme of people putting themselves in danger to help others in danger provided a reassuring note among the agonizing accounts of devastation and loss. When all the damages were assessed, 4 lives had been lost, 345 homes were destroyed, 557 were damaged, 1,102 people were evacuated by air and 707 by road. About 150 miles of roads were damaged with an estimated cost of $150 million to replace them.[34]

When I read the above verse about the ***power*** of God's works, I remembered the images I had seen of the rushing flood waters taking everything in their path. God's works are ***powerful,*** and they show humanity not only His Truth, but also His Judgment. I do not ever want to forget that God is the Supreme Ruler over all the earth, and I am responsible to live every day by every Word He has spoken.

---

[34] *Eight Day, 1,000-year Rain, 100-year Flood: The story of Boulder County's Flood of 2013.* Extensive article detailing day-by-day occurrences during this disastrous storm. http://www.dailycamera.com/news/boulder-flood/ci_24148258/boulder-county-colorado-flood-2013-survival-100-rain-100-year-flood.
~~~~~

Gem #261 **September 17**

Their ***idols*** *are silver and gold, the work of men's hands.*
They have mouths, but they speak not: eyes have they, but they see not:
They have ears, but they hear not: noses have they, but they smell not:
They have hands, but they handle not: feet have they, but they walk not:
neither speak they through their throat. ***They that make them***
are like unto them; *so is every one that trusteth in them.*
Psalms 115:4-8

Thou shalt have ***no other gods*** *before me. Thou shalt not make unto thee*
any graven image, or any likeness of any thing that is in heaven above,
or that is in the earth beneath, or that is in the water under the earth.
Thou shalt not bow down thyself to them, nor serve them:
for I the LORD thy God am a jealous God…
Exodus 20:3-5

I am the LORD: that is my name: and ***my glory will I not give***
to another, *neither my praise* **to** *graven images.*
Isaiah 42:8

~~~~~

Idolatry: excessive or blind adoration, reverence or devotion to a person or thing. God's hatred for idol worship is a prevailing theme throughout the Bible. As Creator, He desires and deserves all the worship and praises of His created beings. The modern-day emphasis on "self" with its teachings on self-esteem, self-development, self-care, self-discipline, self-improvement, etc., has transferred our focus from glorifying God to glorifying man. When we idolize our self, we lose any opportunity for influencing others to worship God, for the Psalmist says that those who make lifeless idols become lifeless just like the idol they created. We may think we are doing Kingdom work by promoting positive thinking and self-improvement teachings, but that kind of teaching is lifeless and leads to glorification of self rather than God. It is time to return to the basics of worshipping God only and letting His life-giving Word transform us into the people we are supposed to be.
~~~~~

Gem #262 **September 18**

For there shall arise false Christs, and false prophets, and shall shew great signs and wonders; insomuch that, if it were possible, they shall ***deceive the very elect****.*

Matthew 24:24

Let us hold fast the profession of our faith without wavering; (for he is faithful that promised;) And let us consider one another to provoke unto love and to good works:

Not forsaking the assembling of ourselves together,

as the manner of some is; but exhorting one another: and so much the more, as ye see the day approaching.

Hebrews 10:23-25

~~~~~

Jesus warned of false Christs and false prophets who would arise, and through great signs and wonders would deceive many. He also warned against following after signs and wonders rather than the teachings of His Word (Mark 8:12). We are living in a day of great deception. Men and women in pulpits have created false doctrines through twisting the scriptures, and because their followers do not know the Word, they blindly follow these false teachers. We had better know the Word and attach ourselves to a Church that preaches the whole Word. Furthermore, the writer of Hebrews makes us responsible to provoke each other to do the right thing. It's not enough that I save only myself, but I must also reach for others who are being led astray and see that they are restored and walking in Truth. Evil days are here, and there is protection in God's Word, God's people, God's Spirit, and God's ministers. Being Holy Ghost filled alone is not enough to save us. We must also be connected to the Word, the Church and a Pastor. God put these safeguards in place for our protection and our salvation.

~~~~~

"If the whole church goes off into deception, that will in no way excuse us for not following Christ."

Leonard Ravenhill

Gem #263 **September 19**

*My tears have been my meat day and night, while they continually say unto me, Where is thy God? When I remember these things, **I pour out my soul** in me…*
Psalms 42:3-4

*Trust in him at all times; ye people, **pour out your heart** before him: God is a refuge for us. Selah.*
Psalms 62:8

***I poured out my complaint** before him; I shewed before him my trouble.*
Psalms 142:2

*LORD, in trouble have they visited thee, they **poured out a prayer** when thy chastening was upon them.*
Isaiah 26:16

*Arise, cry out in the night: in the beginning of the watches **pour out thine heart** like water before the face of the LORD: lift up thy hands toward him for the life of thy young children…*
Lamentations 2:19

~~~~~

Our modern lifestyle measures success in terms of performance or acquisition of degrees, honors or possessions. In order to meet the level of expectations, we often work long hours and neglect prayer and private devotions; time for family is minimized; and time for rest and relaxation is given low priority. As the pressures to perform and meet deadlines increase, our ***cup*** of frustration becomes a ***bucket*** of stress, anxiety, anger, or even depression, and when the bucket gets full and overflows, woe be unto the person who becomes the recipient of that avalanche of problems. It is in these overwhelming times that the Bible instructs us to ***pour out our hearts in prayer*** to God, for He alone has answers for our situation and refreshment for our spirit.
~~~~~

Are you in one of those pressure-cooker moments of life? Instead of pouring out your frustration on your husband, wife, children, friends, or some unsuspecting victim, run boldly to the throne of grace, for it is there that you will find grace to help in your time of need (Hebrews 4:16).

Gem #264 **September 20**

*For **God so loved the world, that he gave his only begotten Son**, that whosoever believeth in him should not perish, but have everlasting life.*

John 3:16

*Hereby perceive we the love of **God,** because he **laid down his life** for us: and we ought to lay down our lives for the brethren.*

1 John 3:16

*And without controversy great is the mystery of godliness: **God was manifest in the flesh**, justified in the Spirit, seen of angels, preached unto the Gentiles, believed on in the world, received up into glory.*

1 Timothy 3:16

~~~~~

There is no controversy between John 3:16 and 1 John 3:16 because John had already stated in John 1:1 that the Word was God, and in the 14th verse of chapter 1, he stated that God became flesh and lived among men so they could behold His glory. He further stated in John 14:9 that those who saw Jesus were actually seeing the Father. Paul made it very clear in his letter to Timothy that ***it was God who came in flesh,*** was believed on by those who heard Him, and ascended back into Heaven after His resurrection from the dead. God did not send a separate person to die for our sins. He loved us so much that He, the eternal, invisible Spirit took on flesh and blood, and ***laid down His life*** for our sins.
~~~~~

Gem #265 **September 21**

Now thanks be unto God, which always causeth us to triumph in Christ, and maketh manifest the ***savour*** *of his knowledge by us in every place. For we are unto God a sweet* ***savour*** *of Christ, in them that are saved, and in them that perish: To the one we are the* ***savour*** *of death unto death; and to the other the* ***savour*** *of life unto life. And who is sufficient for these things? For we are not as many, which corrupt the word of God: but as of sincerity, but as of God, in the sight of God speak we in Christ.*

2 Corinthians 2:14-17

~~~~~

The sense of smell allows us to identify spicy or sweet flavors in food or to distinguish when a food is spoiled. The smell of freshly mowed grass is a fragrant scent of summertime. The sense of smell can also protect and save lives in the case of identifying smoke when a building is on fire.

The Bible tells us that God's people are the ***sweet savour*** *of Christ* to the world. God is actually revealed to unbelievers through our victorious Christian lifestyle. Our steadfast faith in God and triumph over every hard trial that we experience is the savour or magnet that draws hungry souls to salvation and a Christian lifestyle. On the other hand, a little corrupting or changing of the Word here and there will present an appealing savour to some who are looking for an easier way into the Kingdom, but that savour which is so pleasant to the flesh will result in death and eternal separation from God.

What kind of ***savour*** are you presenting to the world? Does your Christian witness bring life or death to others? Eternal destinies are at stake.
~~~~~

Gem #266 **September 22**

Thou shalt have no other gods before me. Thou shalt not make unto thee any graven image… Thou shalt not take the name of the Lord thy God in vain… Remember the sabbath day, to keep it holy. Honour thy father and thy mother… Thou shalt not kill. Thou shalt not commit adultery. Thou shalt not steal. Thou shalt not bear false witness against thy neighbour. Thou shalt not covet…

Exodus 20:3-4, 7-8, 12-17

~~~~~

For several thousand years, the Ten Commandments have formed the basis for human governments and human relationships between God and others. Here in the United States, they have been etched in stone and placed in parks and inside government buildings. They have been written on plaques and have been hung on walls in homes, churches and places of business. I daresay that no other teachings have shaped and influenced both ancient and modern civilizations as much as the Ten Commandments. However, our increasingly lawless and godless society has begun to feel threatened by those rules, and many have raised their voices in protest, demanding that these reminders of God's laws be removed from public view. I am reminded of the Old Testament King Jehoiakim, who thought he could destroy the Word of God by cutting up the pages with his penknife and throwing them into the fire (Jeremiah 36:20-24). Jeremiah simply wrote them again and added additional words of punishment against the king for his wicked deeds.

Evil men in our day may try their hardest to remove all traces of Godly influence from our government, our laws, our schools, and even our churches, but God's Word is true and will never be destroyed by those who refuse to obey it. So even though it looks like evil is prevailing over righteousness, don't be dismayed. In the end, God's Word will triumph, and everyone who has obeyed it will be rewarded.
~~~~~

Gem #267 **September 23**

And to you who are troubled rest with us, when the Lord Jesus shall be revealed from heaven with his mighty angels, In flaming fire taking vengeance on them that know not God, and that obey not the gospel of our Lord Jesus Christ: Who shall be punished with everlasting destruction from the presence of the Lord, and from the glory of his power; When he shall come to be glorified in his saints, and to be admired in all them that believe (because our testimony among you was believed) in that day.

2 Thessalonians 1:7-10

~~~~~

Moses was the first one to teach about the fires of Hell in Deuteronomy 32. After that, the subject is mentioned numerous times in the Bible. Modern-day Christianity doesn't like to hear teaching about Hell being the destination for all who refuse to obey the Gospel, so many of the modern English translations of the Bible have totally removed the word Hell from their pages. Even the New King James Version has replaced the word Hell with the words Hades or Sheol which changes the severity of Hell from everlasting punishment and separation from God into simply a place of the dead.

Make no mistake! Even though it may not be popular or politically correct to tell people they are going to Hell if they do not obey the Gospel and live according to Biblical teachings, the fact remains that it is a strong Bible teaching, and one day soon, Jesus will return to take vengeance on all who do not know Him and have not obeyed the Gospel. I do not want to be on the vengeance side of God in that day.

Have you obeyed the Gospel as taught in John 3:5, Acts 2:38, and 1 Corinthians 15:1-4? It is your escape route from the eternal torments of Hell.
~~~~~

Gem #268 **September 24**

And Jesus …said unto them, Every kingdom …and every … house ***divided*** *against itself shall not stand:*
Matthew 12:25

Now I beseech you, brethren, mark them which cause ***divisions*** *and offences contrary to the doctrine which ye have learned; and avoid them.*
Romans 16:17

For ye are yet carnal: for whereas there is among you envying, and strife, and ***divisions****, are ye not carnal, and walk as men?*
1 Corinthians 3:3

Now I beseech you, brethren, by the name of our Lord Jesus Christ, that ye all speak the same thing, and that there be no ***divisions*** *among you…*
1 Corinthians 1:10

~~~~~

"United We Stand, Divided We Fall." This popular phrase based on Jesus' teaching in Matthew 12 has reverberated through history as a reminder that unity brings strength and victory, whereas division weakens and destroys. In Patrick Henry's final public address two months before he died, he stated, "United we stand, divided we fall. Let us not split into factions which must destroy that union upon which our existence hangs." The Apostle Paul wove the thread of Jesus' teaching into his epistles to the Romans and Corinthians on several occasions. He accused the Corinthians of being carnal because of the factions that were causing strife and division in the Church. He begged them to speak the same thing and be unified in mind and judgment. Today's Christian Church is being attacked on every side and tempted to remove ancient landmarks of doctrine which have made it invincible through the years. Its only hope of survival in the perilous last days of this age is for its members to take a strong stand for Truth and unite together against every force that comes against it, for "United We Stand, Divided We Fall."
~~~~~

Gem #269 **September 25**

And the whole multitude sought to ***touch*** *him:*
for there went virtue out of him, and healed them all.
Luke 6:19

...they shall ***lay hands*** *on the sick, and they shall recover.*
Mark 16:18

Is any sick among you? let him call for the elders of the church; and let them pray over him, ***anointing him with oil in the name of the Lord:*** *And the prayer of faith shall save the sick, and the Lord shall raise him up; and if he have committed sins, they shall be forgiven him.*
James 5:14-15

~~~~~

Of the five senses of the body, the sense of ***touch*** is the most powerful in communicating and even transferring faith, hope, comfort, or encouragement. In times of grief, a touch on the arm or a hug can bring comfort. Touching fans the flames of romance between a man and woman. When a child hurts himself, a kiss and a hug help to make it all better.

In the Bible, there are dozens of illustrations of the power of ***touch*** to heal the sick. Although the spoken word is powerful, Jesus taught us to lay hands on the sick for their recovery. James furthered that teaching by instructing the elders to anoint with oil in the name of Jesus when praying for the sick, for virtue and faith are transferred when the person is touched.

Do you need healing today? Let your prayers reach out and touch Jesus, or call for faith-filled men or women of God to lay hands on you and pray for your healing in Jesus' name.
~~~~~

Gem #270 **September 26**

And the LORD *turned the captivity of Job, when he prayed for his friends: also the* LORD *gave Job twice as much as he had before.*

Job 42:10

Ye have heard that it hath been said, Thou shalt love thy neighbour, and hate thine enemy. But I say unto you, Love your enemies, bless them that curse you, do good to them that hate you, and pray for them which despitefully use you, and persecute you; That ye may be the children of your Father which is in heaven: for he maketh his sun to rise on the evil and on the good, and sendeth rain on the just and on the unjust.

Matthew 5:43-45

~~~~~

Job was a wealthy man who was known all over the east, not only for his wealth, but also for his generosity in helping others who were in need (Job 29). Yet when hard times came to him, and he lost his wealth and his children, several of his "friends" came to interrogate him in order to extract a confession of wrongdoing from him for all the misfortunes that had come upon him. After twelve chapters of their accusations and scathing remarks, God finally came to Job's rescue and demanded that the "friends" offer a sacrifice to God and have Job pray for God to accept them. God turned Job's captivity ***after*** he prayed for his friends.

Jesus taught a similar lesson when He instructed us to love our enemies, bless those who curse us, do good to those who hate us, and most importantly, pray for our persecutors.

Have you experienced reverses in life due to accusations and lies told against you by someone you trusted? It just might be that God is waiting for you to pray for your tormentors ***before*** He sends relief to your situation.
~~~~~

Gem #271 **September 27**

Great peace have they which ***love thy law****:*
and ***nothing shall offend them****.*
Psalms 119:165

And I will delight myself in thy commandments, which I have loved. My hands also will I lift up unto thy commandments, which I have loved; and I will meditate in thy statutes.
Psalms 119:47-48

O how ***love I thy law****! it is my meditation all the day.*
Psalms 119:97

Therefore I ***love thy commandments*** *above gold;*
yea, above fine gold.
Psalms 119:127

Thy ***word*** *is very pure: therefore thy servant* ***loveth it.***
Psalms 119:140

Jesus pronounced judgment on those who offended others (Matthew 18:6; Mark 9:42; Luke 17:2), and Paul also taught us not to do anything to offend or cause someone to stumble in their walk with God (Romans 14:13, 21; 1 Corinthians 8:9, 13). However, the Psalmist expressed his love For God's law eleven times in Psalms 119 and in verse 165, he said that **nothing could offend those who love God's law**. Many people walk around with chips on their shoulders and blame others when they fall away from God. Could it be that if more people would develop a love affair with God's Word, there would be a whole lot less stumbling, offenses, and backsliding?

Protect yourself today from offense
by falling in love with God's Word.

Gem #272 **September 28**

In those days there was no king ***in*** *Israel,*
but every man did that which was ***right in his own eyes.***
Judges 17:6

Where no counsel is, the people fall:
but ***in the multitude of counsellors there is safety.***
Proverbs 11:14

The way of a fool is ***right in his own eyes****:*
but he that hearkeneth unto counsel is wise.
Proverbs 12:15

All the ways of a man are ***clean in his own eyes****;*
but the Lord weigheth the spirits. There is a way that seemeth right unto a man, but the end thereof are the ways of death.
Proverbs 16:2, 25

Every way of a man is ***right in his own eyes****:*
but the Lord pondereth the hearts.
Proverbs 21:2

~~~~~

Some of the most bizarre stories in the Bible are recorded in the book of Judges during the period of time when Israel had sporadic judges instead of consistent Godly leadership. In the absence of judges, everyone did whatever was right in their own eyes. The wise King Solomon taught in several of the Proverbs that it was dangerous to rely on our own instincts to determine what was right and wrong. Everyone needs accountability in their lives to weigh out what should and should not be done. Our basic accountability guidelines are found in the Bible. Ignorance of its teachings will get us in big trouble with God and man. Another safeguard in our life is the five-fold ministry of the Church (Ephesians 4:11-13) which is given to train and equip the Church members for service. And finally, when we submit our plans and desires to Godly elders,
~~~~~

spouses, or friends (Ephesians 5:21; Titus 2), we can avoid making unwise choices in our life. Do not go through life being a "lone ranger." Establish consistent prayer and Bible study habits; then submit yourself to the direction of a Godly pastor and other Godly leaders for *"in the multitude of counsellors there is safety."*

Gem #273 **September 29**

Lead me *in thy truth, and* ***teach me:*** *for thou art the God of my salvation; on thee do I wait all the day.*
Psalms 25:5

Teach me *to do thy will; for thou art my God: thy spirit is good;* ***lead me*** *into the land of uprightness.*
Psalms 143:10

And [Jesus] saith unto them, Follow me, and I will make you ***fishers of men****.*
Matthew 4:19

~~~~~

"It is the good property of all Christ's faithful servants
to come when they are called,
and to follow their Master wherever He leads them."
Matthew Henry

~~~~~

Just when I think I have everything all planned out, my whole world caves in around me. In those times, I must surrender my ideas and say, *"nevertheless, not my will, but thine be done."* (Luke 22:42)

His Way, not mine.

Lead me Lord, and teach me how to be a more effective fisher of men.

Gem #274 **September 30**

Remember the former things of old: for I am God, and there is none else...
Declaring the end from the beginning*, and from ancient times the things that are not yet done, saying, My counsel shall stand, and I will do all my pleasure:*
Isaiah 46:9-10

[4] And there went out a champion out of the camp of the Philistines, named Goliath, of Gath, whose height was six cubits and a span. [10] And the Philistine said, I defy the armies of Israel this day; give me a man, that we may fight together. [11] When Saul and all Israel heard those words of the Philistine, they were dismayed, and greatly afraid. [16] And the Philistine drew near morning and evening, and presented himself forty days. [32] And David said to Saul, Let no man's heart fail because of him; thy servant will go and fight with this Philistine. [34] And David said unto Saul, Thy servant kept his father's sheep, and there came a lion, and a bear, and took a lamb out of the flock: [36] Thy servant slew both the lion and the bear: and this uncircumcised Philistine shall be as one of them, seeing he hath defied the armies of the living God. [50] So David prevailed over the Philistine with a sling and with a stone, and smote the Philistine, and slew him...
1 Samuel 17:4, 10-11, 16, 32, 34, 36, 50

~~~~~

God was not caught off guard during the 40 days that Goliath challenged Israel to produce a man to fight with him. Many years before that famous battle, God had prepared a young shepherd boy to bring victory to the nation. While Goliath was educating himself in the ways of warfare to fight the Philistines' enemies, young David was educating himself in the ways of worship and praise to his God along with honing his skills in slingshot skills to protect his flock. When the time was right, David, with confidence in his God and his sling, slew the giant and brought glory to the God of Israel. What battle are you facing? Does it seem like no answers are in sight? Just remember, the God who knows the end from the beginning, has already foreseen this challenge and has prepared an answer that will bring victory to you and glory to Him.
~~~~~

Gem #275 **October 1**

Why art thou cast down, O my soul? and why art thou disquieted within me? hope thou in God: for I shall yet ***praise*** *him, who is the health of my countenance, and my God.*
Psalms 42:11

Heal me, O LORD, and I shall be healed; save me, and I shall be saved: for thou art my ***praise****.*
Jeremiah 17:14

~~~~~

Two months after my husband died, I was sitting in a Sunday service in Raleigh, North Carolina with my son when I heard the song *"Praise His Name"* for the first time. When I heard the lines, "You can praise the hurt away if you'll just praise His name," I thought, "What does that girl know about praising hurt away? She's young and hasn't experienced tremendous hurt like I've just experienced." I rejected the song, but on October 26, 2001, I awoke with such severe pain in my body that I began crying and told the Lord I could not stand the pain any longer. I had experienced much pain in my hands and arms after the death of my husband nine months earlier, and often the pain would wake me during the night. Through my tears I remembered the song, *"Praise His Name"* by Jeff & Sheri Easter, which I had rejected months before, and I felt the Lord speak to my spirit, asking me to prove the truth of His Word by praising the hurt away. I got up and opened my computer Bible program and began researching what the Bible has to say about praise (248 times in 216 verses). Several hours later, after reading and praying these verses to God, I admitted the truth of those lines in the song. Praise really does take the hurt away. God did a miraculous work in my body, and I have been able to sleep without pain since that day.

What hurtful situations are you facing today? Get out your Bible and start quoting praise scriptures, and I promise you, God will respond to your need through your praise.
~~~~~

Gem #276 **October 2**

Labour not to be rich*: cease from thine own wisdom.*
Proverbs 23:4

And having food and raiment ***let us be therewith content.***
But they that will be rich fall into temptation and a snare,
and into many foolish and hurtful lusts,
which drown men in destruction and perdition.
For the love of money is the root of all evil:
which while some coveted after, they have erred from the faith,
and pierced themselves through with many sorrows.
But thou, O man of God, ***flee these things****;*
and follow after righteousness, godliness, faith, love, patience, meekness.
1 Timothy 6:8-11

~~~~~

Today's culture puts strong emphasis on the privileges of wealth and encourages everyone to work hard, save more, and acquire more in order to attain the elite status of the wealthy. That mindset has even crept into the Church, and more and more preachers are preaching "prosperity gospels" to build their churches and line their pocketbooks with the contributions of their members.

While the Bible contains hundreds of scriptures that discuss money, I cannot find anywhere that teaches me to "sow" money into the Kingdom so I can "reap" more money for myself. Contentment with a simple lifestyle is sadly lacking in modern-day churches. The early Church model was to live simply and share excess resources with missionaries and others who were in need.

It is time to get back to the early Church pattern and find contentment in simplicity; then build the Kingdom with our excess.
~~~~~

Gem #277 October 3

...the LORD said unto me, Gather me the people together, and I will make them hear my words, that they may learn to fear me all the days that they shall live upon the earth, and that they may ***teach their children.***

Deuteronomy 4:10

And these words, which I command thee this day, shall be in thine heart: And thou shalt ***teach*** *them diligently* ***unto thy children****,*
and shalt talk of them when thou sittest in thine house, and when thou walkest by the way, and when thou liest down, and when thou risest up.
And thou shalt bind them for a sign upon thine hand,
and they shall be as frontlets between thine eyes.
And thou shalt write them upon the posts of thy house, and on thy gates.

Deuteronomy 6:6-9

Therefore shall ye lay up these my words in your heart and in your soul, and bind them for a sign upon your hand, that they may be as frontlets between your eyes. And ye shall ***teach them your children****, speaking of them when thou sittest in thine house, and when thou walkest by the way, when thou liest down, and when thou risest up. And thou shalt write them upon the door posts of thine house, and upon thy gates.*

Deuteronomy 11:18-20

And he said unto them, Set your hearts unto all the words which I testify among you this day, which ye shall ***command your children*** *to observe to do, all the words of this law.*

Deuteronomy 32:46

~~~~~

During Moses' final words with the children of Israel, he stressed on four occasions that they were to teach and command their children to obey the laws of God in order to receive God's blessings on their lives. We live in a society that puts a high premium on education. We will work long hours and even take on extra jobs to ensure that we have the required funds to educate our children for their future careers. Moses instructed the parents to first of all, put
~~~~~

the laws of God in their own hearts. Then they were to teach them to their children every day, throughout the day. They were even to post signs and pictures in their homes to remind the children of the ways of God.

What kind of pictures hang on the walls of your home? What kind of games do you play with them? What kinds of topics do you discuss with them? We started teaching our children to memorize scriptures as soon as they learned to talk, and we played hours and hours of Bible Trivia during our Friday night family game nights. Now I make up scripture songs to sing with my grandchildren to encourage memorization of scriptures. I wonder how much more powerful the Church would be if we spent as much time educating our children about the laws and ways of God as we do about the information that is so valued by the world. Although it's important to teach our children to read and write and communicate effectively, we should not neglect their spiritual education, for that education will benefit them for eternity, whereas secular education will benefit them only during their temporary time here on earth.

Gem #278 **October 4**

And that from a child thou hast known the holy scriptures, which are able to make thee wise unto salvation through faith which is in Christ Jesus.
2 Timothy 3:15

~~~~~

My whole life of 50+ years has been spent in memorizing and learning the Word, seeking God and His will for my life. This Christian lifestyle is all I've ever known. I have staked my whole existence on the belief that the Bible is true and that obedience to its teachings will reap eternal rewards in the life beyond this one. By the world's standards, I've missed out on many thrilling things life has to offer, but I don't regret separating myself from those things and focusing on the eternal prize. As an old song once said…

"It's a good life living for the Lord."
~~~~~

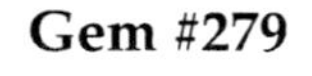

Gem #279 **October 5**

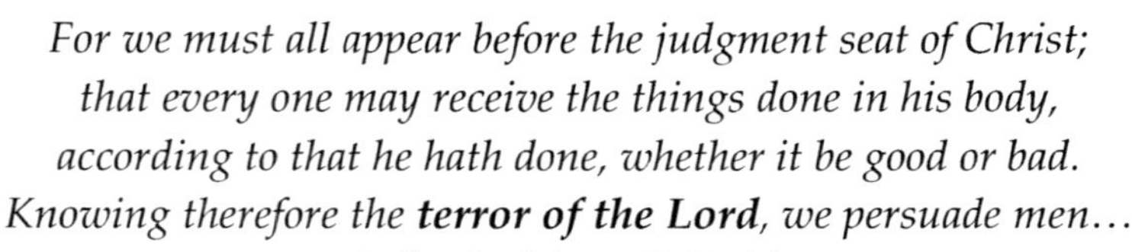

For we must all appear before the judgment seat of Christ;
that every one may receive the things done in his body,
according to that he hath done, whether it be good or bad.
Knowing therefore the ***terror of the Lord****, we persuade men…*
2 Corinthians 5:10-11

And I saw a great white throne, and him that sat on it, from whose face the earth and the heaven fled away; and there was found no place for them. And I saw the dead, small and great, stand before God; and the books were opened: and another book was opened, which is the book of life: and the dead were judged out of those things which were written in the books, according to their works. And whosoever was not found written in the book of life was cast into the ***lake of fire****.*
Revelation 20:11-12, 15

~~~~~

As a young girl, I remember many sermons about the fires of Hell and the torment and eternal separation from God that would be experienced in that place. The word pictures of those flames were so vivid that people would run to the altar and repent for fear of dying and going to that awful place. Now, as a much older woman, I find it rare to hear a sermon about the terror or wrath of God that would send disobedient sinners to the hot, flaming fires of Hell. We have become so inundated with the false teachings of God's unconditional love that the Biblical teaching of a God of wrath, terror and judgment against sinners has become lost in the shuffle.

Have we succumbed to the current apathy toward the teaching of Hell? Are we really convinced that sinners will be sentenced to that awful place on Judgment Day? If we really believe that real people will go to a real Hell, then we need to rediscover the Biblical sense of urgency to persuade men and women to obey the Gospel[35] to avoid going to that awful place.

[35] John 3:3-8; Acts 2:37-39; 1 Corinthians 15:1-4
~~~~~

Gem #280 **October 6**

*The Lord is not slack concerning his promise, as some men count slackness; but is longsuffering to us-ward, **not willing that any should perish,** but that all should come to repentance.*

2 Peter 3:9

And I saw heaven opened, and behold a white horse; and he that sat upon him was called Faithful and True, and in righteousness he doth judge and make war. His eyes were as a flame of fire, and on his head were many crowns; and he had a name written, that no man knew, but he himself. And he was clothed with a vesture dipped in blood: and his name is called The Word of God. And the armies which were in heaven followed him upon white horses, clothed in fine linen, white and clean. And out of his mouth goeth a sharp sword, that with it he should smite the nations: and he shall rule them with a rod of iron: and he treadeth the winepress of the fierceness and wrath of Almighty God. And he hath on his vesture and on his thigh a name written, KING OF KINGS, AND LORD OF LORDS.

Revelation 19:11-16

~~~~~

Two prevailing themes of the Bible are those of God's ***mercy*** and God's ***wrath***. We tend to hear many more sermons about the mercy and longsuffering of God than we do about His judgment and wrath, but in actuality, the Bible contains more scriptural warnings about God's judgment and wrath on those who disobey His laws than it does the more comforting scriptures detailing His mercy and longsuffering. While it is true that our God is v-e-r-y longsuffering toward our propensity to be headstrong and do things our way, the fact remains that in the end, He will have His way. We had better make sure that we know the rules that are outlined in the rule book, the Holy Bible, and live our lives according to those rules because the God of mercy and long-suffering will one day show Himself to be the God of judgment and wrath.

I don't want to be on the wrong side of God in that day.
~~~~~

Gem #281

October 7

That the ***trial of your faith****, being much more precious than of gold that perisheth, though it be tried with fire, might be found unto praise and honour and glory at the appearing of Jesus Christ:*

1 Peter 1:7

Beloved, think it not strange concerning the ***fiery trial*** *which is to try you, as though some strange thing happened unto you: But rejoice, inasmuch as ye are partakers of Christ's sufferings; that, when his glory shall be revealed, ye may be glad also with exceeding joy.*

1 Peter 4:12-13

My brethren, count it all joy when ye fall into divers temptations; Knowing this, that the trying of your faith worketh patience. Blessed is the man that endureth temptation: for ***when he is tried****, he shall receive the crown of life, which the Lord hath promised to them that love him.*

James 1:2-3, 12

~~~~~

Test time! When I was in school, those words often produced feelings of anxiety. Was I ready? Would all my note-taking and study prepare me for it? Would I make a good grade? God also gives us information through pastors, teachers, Bible study, and personal experiences. Then He periodically gives us a test to determine our progress. Although these times of trial and testing are not always pleasant, we do have the assurance that they are more precious to our growth process than any amount of gold or material possessions we can acquire. Peter tells us that the proper response to our fiery trials is rejoicing, and James assures us that our hard trials will ultimately result in being blessed with a crown of life from the Lord.

Are you experiencing a fiery trial right now? Don't let it get you down. Instead, rejoice because your successful passing of those tests will earn you a crown of life, and you will spend eternity in the presence of your Lord.
~~~~~

Gem #282 **October 8**

*Praise ye the LORD. Blessed is the man that feareth the LORD, that **delighteth** greatly in his commandments.*
Psalms 112:1

[14] *I have **rejoiced** in the way of thy testimonies, as much as in all riches.*
[16] *I will **delight** myself in thy statutes: I will not forget thy word.*
[24] *Thy testimonies also are my **delight** and my counselors.*
[35] *Make me to go in the path of thy commandments; for therein do I **delight**.*
[47] *And I will **delight** myself in thy commandments, which I have loved.*
[77] *Let thy tender mercies come unto me, that I may live: for thy law is my **delight**.*
[162] *I **rejoice** at thy word, as one that findeth great spoil.*
[174] *I have longed for thy salvation, O LORD; and thy law is my **delight**.*
Psalms 119:14, 16, 24, 35, 47, 77, 162, 174

~~~~~

Oh the richness of God's living Word! I have read it from beginning to end dozens of times throughout my life and have memorized hundreds of verses, yet those living words never fail to speak life, hope and encouragement to me when I need it. I cannot tell you how many times while reading my Bible, certain words seem to stand out, and I gain a new understanding on a familiar passage of scripture. No matter how many times I read it, those words are fresh and new every day. I can truly say with the Psalmist that the words contained in the pages of the Holy Bible are my delight. I treasure that book more than any other possession I own.

Do you find delight in the teachings of God's Word?
~~~~~

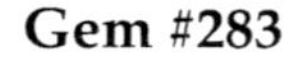 **Gem #283** **October 9**

*The **angel** of the LORD encampeth round about them that fear him, and delivereth them.*

Psalms 34:7

*For he shall give his **angel**s charge over thee, to keep thee in all thy ways.*

Psalms 91:11

But to which of the angels said he at any time, Sit on my right hand, until I make thine enemies thy footstool? Are they not all ministering spirits, sent forth to minister for them who shall be heirs of salvation?

Hebrews 1:13-14

*And I beheld, and I heard the voice of many **angel**s round about the throne and the beasts and the elders: and the number of them was ten thousand times ten thousand, and thousands of thousands;*

Revelation 5:11

~~~~~

Stories of angelic visitations abound in both the Old and New Testaments. They not only worship God, but they also are sent forth as ministering spirits to minister to those who shall be heirs of salvation: God's family of born-again believers. While we do not know the exact number of angels who are available to do the Lord's bidding, Jesus said in Matthew 26:53 that He could have called more than twelve legions of angels to deliver Him from the cross if He had chosen to do so. (A legion ranges from 3,000 – 6,000, so 36,000 – 72,000 angels were available to deliver Him.) But the number is not the important point. The greater message is that God's army of angelic hosts is more than adequate to defend all of His children from the unrelenting attacks of the devil and his angels.

Are you feeling the heat of enemy attacks against you? Just call on the Lord, and He will send however many angels are necessary to put the enemy on the run.
~~~~~

Gem #284 **October 10**

So we, numerous as we are, are one body in Christ (the Messiah) and individually we are parts one of another [mutually dependent on one another]. Having gifts (faculties, talents, qualities) that differ according to the grace given us, let us use them: [He whose gift is] prophecy, [let him prophesy] according to the proportion of his faith; [He whose gift is] practical service, let him give himself to serving; he who teaches, to his teaching; He who exhorts (encourages), to his exhortation; he who contributes, let him do it in simplicity and liberality; he who gives aid and superintends, with zeal and singleness of mind; he who does acts of mercy, with genuine cheerfulness and joyful eagerness.

Romans 12:5-8 (AMP)

~~~~~

In several places of the New Testament, the Church of God is likened to a body with each member performing different functions. When we are born, God places certain gifts in our life so that we can fulfill our divine purpose in life. Consider these functions of the gifts:

The **Teachers** are the **mind** of the body and are gifted at researching and acquiring information to share with the body.

The **Prophets** are the **eyes** of the body and are gifted with perception beyond what others see. Their responsibility is to watch for things that would harm the body and protect them.

The **Exhorters** are the **mouth** of the body and are gifted encouragers and public speakers.

The **Superintendents** are the **shoulders** of the body, shouldering the responsibility of administrative tasks. They are skilled in identifying the gifts of others and delegating tasks according to everyone's area of expertise.
~~~~~

The **Merciful** people are the **heart** of the body and are gifted with compassion for members who are hurting or in need. Once a need is identified, they are quick to step in and do what is necessary to alleviate the hurt. They are especially gifted in intercessory prayer.

The **Contributors** are the **arms** of the body who specialize in giving generously of time, resources and energy with no strings attached. Often, they are especially blessed financially because they give generously to the financial needs of the body without storing up wealth for themselves.

The **Practical Servers** are the **hands** of the body, and they are especially gifted in working with their hands. They are not leaders, but they are loyal followers who know how to get things done quickly and efficiently.

Often we get placed in areas of involvement that are in conflict with our gifting, and we dread doing the jobs we have been assigned. What are your areas of giftedness? If you will learn what God has gifted you to do and work in your proper place in the body, then the body will function like a well-oiled machine to expand the Kingdom of God on earth.

Gem #285 **October 11**

This is the day which the Lord hath made; we will rejoice and be glad in it.
Psalms 118:24

~~~~~

God has given you a brand new day to worship Him and advance His Kingdom. 1,440 minutes are allotted to you today.

How will you spend them? Choose carefully, for once the minutes are spent, they cannot be recalled and spent again.
~~~~~

Gem #286 **October 12**

I am crucified with Christ: nevertheless I live; yet not I,
but Christ liveth in me: and the life which I now live in the flesh
I live by the faith of the Son of God, who loved me, and gave himself for me.
Galatians 2:20

If ye then be risen with Christ, seek those things which are above,
where Christ sitteth on the right hand of God.
Set your affection on things above, not on things on the earth.
For ye are dead, and your life is hid with Christ in God.
Colossians 3:1-3

~~~~~

IF – This tiny two-letter conjunction lays down conditions for something to happen. It appears 1,595 times in the King James Version of the Bible. Often we use the term "If only" to express regret over bad decisions or missed opportunities. In these two scripture passages, Paul is asking us to search our hearts and evaluate our purpose in being a Christian.

Have we really crucified our sinful nature? Have we really died to our former sinful lifestyle? Have we really risen from the dead and become a new creature in Christ?

IF the answer to those three questions is yes, then our affections should be on Heavenly matters rather than worldly matters. Instead of asking, How much *stuff* can I accumulate here?, we should ask, How can I influence others to become dead to sin and alive in Christ?

IF I really am crucified and risen in Christ, then I should seek for eternal things that will remain with me in the life to come.

Where are your affections today?
~~~~~

Gem #287 **October 13**

Trust in him at all times; ye people, pour out your heart before him:
God is a ***refuge*** *for us. Selah.*
Psalms 62:8

I will say of the LORD, He is my ***refuge*** *and my fortress:*
my God; in him will I trust.
Psalms 91:2

In the fear of the LORD is strong confidence: and his children
shall have a place of ***refuge****.*
Proverbs 14:26

~~~~~

In our culture that stresses self-reliance and independence, it's easy to put our trust in bank accounts, doctors, attorneys, college degrees, jobs, or friends, but at some point, all of these crutches will fail us. The only sure refuge in times of trouble or need is God. If we will run to Him first, He will console us in our troubles and provide for all our losses.

~~~~~

"Where does your security lie? Is God your refuge, your hiding place, your stronghold, your shepherd, your counselor, your friend, your redeemer, your saviour, your guide? If He is, you don't need to search any further for security."
Elisabeth Elliot

"The all-victorious Christ is like a great rock in a weary land, to whose shelter we may flee in every time of sorrow or trial, finding quiet **refuge** and peace in him."
J. R. Miller

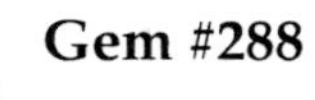 **Gem #288** **October 14**

But ye shall receive power, after that the Holy Ghost is come upon you: and ye shall be witnesses *unto me both in Jerusalem, and in all Judaea, and in Samaria, and unto the uttermost part of the earth.*

Acts 1:8

And when the day of Pentecost was fully come, they were all with one accord in one place. And suddenly there came a sound from heaven as of a rushing mighty wind, and it filled all the house where they were sitting. And there appeared unto them cloven tongues like as of fire, and it sat upon each of them. And they were ***all filled with the Holy Ghost, and began to speak with other tongues,*** *as the Spirit gave them utterance.*

Acts 2:1-4

And when Paul had laid his hands upon them, the ***Holy Ghost came on them; and they spake with tongues****, and prophesied.*

Acts 19:6

Now the God of hope fill you with all joy and peace in believing, that ye may abound in hope, through the ***power of the Holy Ghost****.*

Romans 15:13

~~~~~

Holy Ghost Power! It all started on the Day of Pentecost some two thousand years ago. After being filled with the power of the Holy Ghost, fearful disciples were turned into fearless, bold, flaming ambassadors of the Gospel! Jealous religious leaders tried to silence them with imprisonment, beatings and threats, but they ignored the pain and humiliation and boldly continued their witness to the whole world. Then evil emissaries of Satan tried to stamp out the Christians by torturing and killing them, but nothing could stop the spread of the Gospel.

Have you experienced the power of the Holy Ghost? If not, God is waiting to fill you in the same way that the disciples and other believers received it in the book of Acts. Just ask!
~~~~~

Gem #289  **October 15**

*Art not thou our God, who didst drive out the inhabitants of this land…, and gavest it to the seed of **Abraham thy friend** for ever?*
2 Chronicles 20:7

*But thou, Israel, art my servant,…the seed of **Abraham my friend**.*
Isaiah 41:8

*And the scripture was fulfilled which saith, **Abraham** believed God… and he **was called the friend of God**.*
James 2:23

*For I know **[Abraham], that he will command his children and his household after him,** and they shall keep the way of the LORD, to do justice and judgment; that the LORD may bring upon Abraham that which he hath spoken of him.*
Genesis 18:19

~~~~~

On three different occasions, the Bible calls Abraham a friend of God. What special characteristic gave him such favored status with God? James gives us a clue with his statement that Abraham believed God. Absolute faith in the words of God even when circumstances made it seem impossible for God's words to be fulfilled. Moses also gave us a clue in Genesis 18:19. Not only did Abraham believe the words of God, but he also taught them to his children and his household so that everyone associated with him would keep the ways of the Lord.

Friendship with God comes with conditions attached. Jesus told His disciples that they could be His friends and learn His secrets "IF ye do **whatsoever** I command you" (John 15:14-15). Do you want to be one of God's favorites and learn the secrets that are reserved only for His friends? Then pick up His Word and learn His ways, His commandments, and His laws. Believe them and obey them. Then and only then, will He be willing to call you His friend.
~~~~~

Gem #290 **October 16**

Now then we are ***ambassadors for Christ****, as though God did beseech you by us: we pray you in Christ's stead, be ye reconciled to God.*
2 Corinthians 5:20

And [pray] for me, that utterance may be given unto me, that I may open my mouth boldly, to make known the mystery of the gospel,
For which I am an ***ambassador in bonds****:*
that therein I may speak boldly, as I ought to speak.
Ephesians 6:19-20

And whatsoever ye do in word or deed, ***do all in the name of the Lord Jesus,*** *giving thanks to God and the Father by him.*
And ***whatsoever ye do, do it heartily****, as to the Lord, and not unto men;*
Knowing that of the Lord ye shall receive the reward of the inheritance: for ye serve the Lord Christ.
Colossians 3:17, 23-24

~~~~~

After Jesus ascended into Heaven, He sent His Spirit to live inside of the Church members so they could be His representatives in this earth. Paul said we were Christ's ambassadors, working in His stead to reconcile people back to God. Therefore, as His ambassadors, we've been given power of attorney to operate in Jesus' name. When we take His name in baptism and are filled with the Holy Ghost, we receive full authority to operate in His behalf. From that point forward, everything we do in word or deed, we do in His name. We pray, we heal, we baptize, we encourage, we minister, we give thanks, we teach, we sing in Jesus' name. Everything we do in life, is to be done exuberantly, thoroughly, and sincerely in the saving name of Jesus Christ. He is keeping records of our activities and will richly reward those who have represented Him well.

He has job openings. Have you applied for the position of exuberant ambassador of the King of Kings and Lord of Lords?
~~~~~

Gem #291 **October 17**

Blessed is the man unto whom the LORD *imputeth not iniquity,*
and in whose spirit there is no ***guile****.*
Psalms 32:2

Keep thy tongue from evil, and thy lips from speaking guile.
Psalms 34:13

Wherefore laying aside all malice, and all ***guile****, and hypocrisies,*
and envies, and all evil speakings, As newborn babes,
desire the sincere milk of the word, that ye may grow thereby:
1 Peter 2:1-2

For he that will love life, and see good days, let him
refrain his tongue from evil, and his lips that they speak no ***guile****:*
1 Peter 3:10

~~~~~

Guile is defined as character or behavior that is crafty or artfully deceptive; deceitful; fraudulent; insidious cunning in achieving a goal, which means operating in a seemingly harmless way, but actually with intent to trap, cheat, or mislead. The Psalmist warned against having an evil tongue that spoke with guile, and the Apostle Peter sounded a similar warning in the first epistle of his teachings. We know that lying is a grave sin, but we think we can get around lying by using little innuendos when discussing people or events. We may not actually tell a lie, but we insinuate something disparaging or derogatory that causes our hearer to think wrongly about the person or subject of discussion. Peter said that if we love living and want our lives to consist of good days, then it is imperative that we restrain our unruly tongue from the evil of saying anything that is misleading. Jesus commended Nathanael as *"an Israelite indeed, in whom is no guile,"* (John 1:47). What does Jesus see when He looks at your life and listens to your speech? Can He say, "That is my son, or that is my daughter in whom there is not one ounce of guile"?
~~~~~

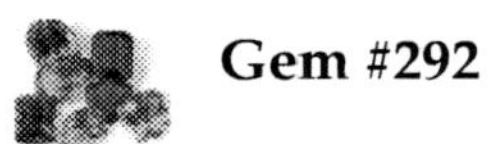

Gem #292 **October 18**

*...**IF** thou shalt hearken diligently unto the voice of the LORD thy God, to observe and to do all his commandments which I command thee this day, that the LORD thy God will set thee on high above all nations of the earth: [2] And all these **blessings** shall come on thee, and overtake thee, **IF** thou shalt hearken unto the voice of the LORD thy God. [3] **Blessed** shalt thou be in the city, and blessed shalt thou be in the field. [4] **Blessed** shall be the fruit of thy body, and the fruit of thy ground, and the fruit of thy cattle, the increase of thy kine, and the flocks of thy sheep. [5] **Blessed** shall be thy basket and thy store. [6] **Blessed** shalt thou be when thou comest in, and blessed shalt thou be when thou goest out. [7] The LORD shall cause thine enemies that rise up against thee to be smitten before thy face: they shall come out against thee one way, and flee before thee seven ways. [8] The LORD shall command the **blessing** upon thee in thy storehouses, and in all that thou settest thine hand unto; and he shall **bless** thee in the land which the LORD thy God giveth thee. [9] The LORD shall establish thee an holy people unto himself, as he hath sworn unto thee, **IF** thou shalt keep the commandments of the LORD thy God, and walk in his ways. [10] And all people of the earth shall see that thou art called by the name of the LORD; and they shall be afraid of thee. [11] And the LORD shall make thee plenteous in goods, in the fruit of thy body, and in the fruit of thy cattle, and in the fruit of thy ground, in the land which the LORD sware unto thy fathers to give thee. [12] The LORD shall open unto thee his good treasure, the heaven to give the rain unto thy land in his season, and to **bless** all the work of thine hand: and thou shalt lend unto many nations, and thou shalt not borrow. [13] And the LORD shall make thee the head, and not the tail; and thou shalt be above only, and thou shalt not be beneath; **IF** that thou hearken unto the commandments of the LORD thy God, which I command thee this day, to observe and to do them: [14] And thou shalt not go aside from any of the words which I command thee this day, to the right hand, or to the left, to go after other gods to serve them.*

Deuteronomy 28:1-14

~~~~~

The subject of blessing is a predominant theme throughout the Bible. Some form of the word bless occurs over 460 times in the KJV
~~~~~

Bible. One of the most familiar scriptures in the Old Testament gives a long list of the blessings that the Israelites could expect to receive from God IF they heard and obeyed all of God's commandments. Four times within the fourteen verses of pronouncing blessings on Israel, Moses inserted the condition that these blessings were only in force "IF" they kept all the commandments of the Lord. We enjoy receiving blessings from God and others, but are we willing to abide by all the "IFs" in the Bible in order to receive the blessings God has promised? His storehouse of blessings is never-ending, but He only hands out His best to those who have fulfilled the conditions of keeping all His commandments.

Gem #293 **October 19**

The righteous shall rejoice when he seeth the vengeance: he shall wash his feet in the blood of the wicked. So that a man shall say, Verily there is a reward for the righteous: verily he is a God that judgeth in the earth."

Psalms 58:10-11

~~~~~

"Someday God will set all things straight. The finale of a Beethoven symphony will seem inconsequential by comparison!"

Don Wyrtzen

~~~~~

In late summer of 2014, the residents in my neighborhood spent a day behind locked doors as helicopters flew overhead and policemen went door to door searching for a Federal felon who had eluded police arrest in our area. He was apprehended a day later, only a few blocks from my house. Sometimes frightening events occur around us, and it seems like evildoers in both government and society-at-large are prevailing over law-abiding citizens. But it is precisely these times that Jesus spoke of when He said in Luke 21:28, *"And when these things begin to come to pass, then look up, and lift up your heads; for your redemption draweth nigh."* My hope is in that promise.

 **Gem #294** **October 20**

For Herod himself had sent forth and laid hold upon John, and bound him in prison for Herodias' sake, his brother Philip's wife: for he had married her. For John had said unto Herod, It is not lawful for thee to have thy brother's wife. Therefore Herodias had a quarrel against him, and would have killed him; but she could not:

Mark 6:17-19

~~~~~

The story is told of Scottish missionary Alexander Mackay,[36] who arrived in Uganda in 1878 with the express desire of winning the heathen King M'tesa to Christ. His opportunity finally arrived on Sunday, January 26, 1879. He had an audience with the king and took his text from Matthew 11, stressing the fact that John the Baptist had been sent to prepare the way for the Messiah. During this Bible lesson, an Arab visitor was ushered into the king's presence. He brought fabric and guns to trade in exchange for slaves. As he negotiated with the king, King M'tesa's eyes glittered with the prospect of gaining guns to fight his enemies. As missionary Mackay watched the proceedings, a holy boldness rose up in him, and he confronted the king. He knew he was putting his life on the line, but he had to speak out against the evil practice of selling Ugandans into slavery. He said, "O King M'tesa, the people of this land made you their king and look to you as their father. Will you sell your children, knowing that they will be chained, put into slave-ships, beaten with whips; that most of them will die of mistreatment on the way and the rest be taken as slaves to some strange country? Can you be a party to these crimes, even for the sake of some guns? Will you sell scores or hundreds of your people,…for a few bolts of red cloth which any man can make in a few days?" There ensued some tense moments as the Arab scowled at the missionary while the king contemplated Mackay's words. The tension was finally broken as the king announced, "The white man is right. I shall no more sell my people as slaves." Later the king

---

[36] http://www.wholesomewords.org/missions/biomackay.html
~~~~~

sent a goat and a message to Mackay's hut. The message said, "It was a blessed passage you read today!"

∼∼∼∼∼

History contains hundreds of stories of other courageous men and women of God who dared to confront evil and speak the Word of Truth. Many like John the Baptist lost their lives because of their boldness, yet they refused to keep silent against evil practices. Today men are boldly declaring that evil is good, and good is evil. Christians are advised to keep their mouths shut against the evils of abortion, euthanasia, gay marriage and a host of other evils lest they be brought into court and fined for hate speech or thrown into jail. Where are the Jeremiahs and John the Baptists and Alexander Mackays who will fearlessly stand up for Truth even though it may cost their life? Lord, help us to not only believe and live the Word of God in our personal life, but to also fearlessly confront those who boldly reject it.

Gem #295 October 21

For though I preach the gospel, I have nothing to glory of: for necessity is laid upon **me***; yea, woe is unto me, if I preach not the gospel!*

1 Corinthians 9:16

∼∼∼∼∼

On January 26, 1879, Scottish missionary Alexander Mackay felt some measure of progress in his missionary work in Uganda when King M'tesa made a promise to quit selling his countrymen as slaves. Unfortunately, his promise was short-lived as influential foreigners with gold and guns persuaded him to recant. Before long he was trading people for weapons and other fine items. Thousands more were slaughtered on a whim. In a few years King M'tesa died, and his 18-year-old son, M'wanga came to the throne. He was more barbaric and evil than his father and quickly decided to exterminate all Christians from his kingdom. Over the ensuing years, hundreds of Christians were tortured and burned. King M'wanga ordered the execution of Missionary Mackay more than once, but God always protected him from death. Other missionaries were killed, and Alexander Mackay begged the Missionary Society in England to send more help. Unfortunately, the Missionary Society had strong reservations in sending more men to be slaughtered by the evil king and his aides. They even strongly urged Mackay to return to England for his safety. He replied, "What is this you write—'Come home?' Surely now, in our terrible dearth of workers, it is not the time for anyone to desert his post. Are you joking? If you tell me in earnest that such a suggestion has been made, I can only answer, *Never.* Tell me, ye faint hearts, to whom ye mean to give up the mission. Is it to murderous raiders like M'wanga, or to slave-traders from Zanzibar, or to English and Belgian dealers in rifles and gunpowder, or to German spirit sellers? All are in the field, and they make no talk of giving up their respective missions." Mackay continued laboring for the Lord until his untimely death at age 41 from the tropical fever. He had spent 14 years of his life laboring to build a "highway for the Gospel" amidst spiritual darkness and wickedness of every description. Was it worth the cost?

In 1922, Basil Matthews wrote: "Today the Prime Minister of Uganda is Apolo Kagwa, who as a boy was kicked and beaten by King M'wanga for being a Christian; and the King of Uganda, Kaudi, M'wanga's son, is a Christian. At the capital there stands a beautiful church. On the place where the boys were burned to death there stands a cross, put there by seventy thousand Waganda Christians in memory of the young martyrs." In addition, slave-raiding and slave-trading have been abolished; innocent people are no longer butchered to appease the gods; and the torture and burning of human beings to satisfy a mad king's lust for blood has ceased forever in Uganda. Mackay did not live to see these marvelous triumphs, but with the eye of faith he asserted: "The conquest of Africa has already cost many lives; but the end to be gained is worth the price paid. Let us not forget that the redemption of the world cost infinitely more."

~~~~~
~~~~~

God has called all of us to reach the world with the Gospel. As Paul said in his epistle, *"woe is unto me, if I preach not the Gospel."* Are you ready to run away at the least little bit of persecution or ridicule for your beliefs? Keep sowing and standing firm in your beliefs. A harvest will come in time if you don't lose hope.

Gem #296 **October 22**

For ***God so loved the world****, that he gave his only begotten Son, that whosoever believeth in him should not perish, but have everlasting life.*

John 3:16

As the Father hath loved me, so have I loved you: continue ye in my love. ***If ye keep my commandments, ye shall abide in my love;*** *even as I have kept my Father's commandments, and abide in his love.*

John 15:9-10

And I saw the dead, small and great, stand before God; and the books were opened: and another book was opened, which is the book of life: and the dead were judged out of those things which were written in the books, according to their works. And whosoever was not found written in the book of life was cast into the lake of fire.

Revelation 20:12, 15

~~~~~

Many of today's preachers attract thousands with the message of God's *unconditional love.* I recently spent over four hours researching God's love and mercy versus judgment, death and Hell. I found that there are approximately 250 scriptures that say He is a God of love and mercy, but there are more than 2,000 references to judgment, death and Hell *if we do not obey His commandments.* Yes, He loved me enough to provide atonement for my sins, but in order to continue in His love, I must obey His Laws. Lord, help me to love You and know Your Word so that I can obey Your commands and inherit eternal life with You after this life is over.
~~~~~

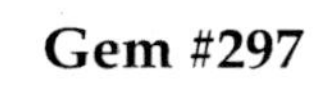 **Gem #297** **October 23**

*Many, O LORD my God, are thy …**thoughts** which are to us-ward: they cannot be reckoned up in order unto thee: if I would declare and speak of them, they are more than can be numbered.*

Psalms 40:5

How precious also are thy thoughts unto me, O God! how great is the sum of them! If I should count them, they are more in number than the sand…

Psalms 139:17-18

For I know the thoughts that I think toward you, saith the LORD, thoughts of peace, and not of evil, to give you an expected end.

Jeremiah 29:11

~~~~~

When I was a teenager, I met and fell in love with my future husband. I still remember the giddiness and excitement I felt when I would think about him and wonder what he was thinking about me. In my thoughts, I would remember conversations we had, and relived the excitement I felt during the times we were together.

In a similar way, Jesus, the Lover of our souls, constantly has us on His mind. The Psalmist said He thinks precious, peaceful thoughts about us, and His thoughts are so numerous that we can't even count them. I wonder if our thoughts about our Heavenly Lover are as numerous as His thoughts about us. I wonder if He sometimes feels disappointment because His love toward us is a little one-sided in that we don't think about Him as often as He thinks about us, and we don't spend as much time with Him as He wants to spend with us. He has great plans for our life together on this earth, and even greater plans for our eternal life with Him in Heaven.

He is thinking about you today and making plans for your life. Are you thinking about Him and anticipating those moments of togetherness in His presence?
~~~~~

Gem #298 **October 24**

*Make a **joyful noise** unto the LORD, all the earth:*
*make a loud noise, and **rejoice**, and **sing** praise.*
Psalms 98:4

*Serve the LORD with **gladness**: come before his presence with **singing**.*
Psalms 100:2

Moreover all these curses shall come upon thee…
*Because thou **servedst not the LORD thy God with joyfulness, and with gladness of heart**, for the abundance of all things;*
Deuteronomy 28:45, 47

~~~~~

"The aim and final end of all music should be none other than the glory of God and the refreshment of the soul."
Johann Sebastian Bach

~~~~~

Rejoice! Be glad! Sing! Give praise! Be merry! Be joyful! Be thankful! Be cheerful! Hundreds of times the Bible instructs us to celebrate the fact that we are chosen, called out, separated for the holy purpose of representing the King of Kings and Lord of Lords in this world! We shine as lights in this dark world, and God does not get the glory that is due Him if His chosen lights walk through their world with long faces and gloomy countenances. While it is true that life is full of hard trials, those who can be glad in the midst of sorrow, sickness, disappointment and betrayal give hope to others who are experiencing the tough places of life. Deuteronomy 28 gives a long list of blessings to those who diligently follow the Lord's commandments, but the same chapter pronounces curses on those who do NOT obey, and interestingly, one of the causes for receiving a curse from God is because they did not serve the Lord with joyfulness and gladness of heart.

Do you want God's best for your life? Then serve Him with joyfulness and gladness of Heart.

Gem #299 **October 25**

And there was a certain disciple at Damascus, named ***Ananias****; and to him said the Lord in a vision,* ***Ananias****. ...Arise, and go into the street which is called Straight, and enquire in the house of Judas for one called Saul, of Tarsus: for, behold, he prayeth, And hath seen in a vision a man named* ***Ananias*** *coming in, and putting his hand on him, that he might receive his sight. Then* ***Ananias*** *answered, Lord, I have heard by many of this man, how much evil he hath done to thy saints at Jerusalem: And here he hath authority from the chief priests to bind all that call on thy name. But the Lord said unto him, Go thy way: for he is a chosen vessel unto me, to bear my name before the Gentiles, and kings, and the children of Israel: For I will shew him how great things he must suffer for my name's sake. And* ***Ananias*** *went his way, and entered into the house; and putting his hands on him said, Brother Saul, the Lord, even Jesus, that appeared unto thee in the way as thou camest, hath sent me, that thou mightest receive thy sight, and be filled with the Holy Ghost. And immediately there fell from his eyes as it had been scales: and he received sight forthwith, and arose, and was baptized.*

Acts 9:10-18

~~~~~

God chose Ananias to be instrumental in the Apostle Paul's conversion. He is only mentioned twice in the book of Acts. Although Ananias faded from the scene of Christian history after these two mentions of him in scripture, his convert, Paul went on to become an evangelist to the world and wrote over half of the New Testament. Another well-known name in modern church history is Martin Luther, who is often called "The Father of the Reformation." He is most famous for his act of nailing his "Ninety-Five Theses" detailing unscriptural practices of the Roman Catholic Church to the door of the All Saints Church in Wittenburg, Germany. Although Luther's name is practically a household word in modern Christianity, there would've been no bold Luther to speak out against heresy in the church had it not been for his almost unknown mentor, Johann von Staupitz. During some low points in Luther's life, it was Staupitz's encouragement and teaching that influenced
~~~~~

Luther to study the scriptures and formulate the teachings that eventually became the foundational teachings of the Lutheran Church. Luther fully credited his conversion from Catholicism to Dr. Staupitz. We like to discuss the high-profile men and women in church history, but in reality there are far more unknown men and women whose prayer lives and consistent Godly lifestyles have had far more impact on the Kingdom than the ones whose names we recognize. Do you feel insignificant and unrecognized for your contributions to the Kingdom? Don't despair. I daresay that when rewards are handed out in Heaven, many of the unknown members of the Church may receive greater rewards than the high-profile members we wished to emulate. Just do your part!

Gem #300 **October 26**

Who ***satisfieth*** *thy mouth with good things;*
so that thy youth is renewed like the eagle's.
Psalms 103:5

For he ***satisfieth*** *the longing soul,*
and filleth the hungry soul with goodness.
Psalms 107:9

Thou openest thine hand, and ***satisfiest*** *the desire of every living thing.*
Psalms 145:16

"The fear of the Lord tendeth to life: and he that hath it shall abide ***satisfied****; he shall not be visited with evil."*
Proverbs 19:23

~~~~~

My morning devotional reading in Psalms 107 sent me on a search to see what the Bible has to say about finding my ***satisfaction*** in God. After reading a number of promises on that topic, my spirit is refreshed and ready to start my day. I am thankful for that Book which holds the keys to my ultimate satisfaction and fulfillment.
~~~~~

Gem #301 **October 27**

...the man whom the **LORD doth choose**, *he shall be holy...*
Numbers 16:7

But in the place which the **LORD shall choose...**
there thou shalt do all that I command thee.
Deuteronomy 12:14

...go unto the place which the **LORD thy God shall choose:**
Deuteronomy 14:25

Thou shalt in any wise set him king over thee, whom
the **LORD thy God shall choose:** *one from among thy brethren...*
Deuteronomy 17:15

When all Israel is come to appear before the **LORD** *thy God in the place*
which **he shall choose**, *thou shalt read this law... in their hearing.*
Deuteronomy 31:11

~~~~~

While doing some Bible research this morning about choices, my attention was drawn to the phrase, "the Lord shall choose," so I changed my search to find out what the Bible has to say about the things the Lord chooses. Moses instructed the Israelites to consult the Lord about His choice of places to sacrifice, where to eat their food, and who to select as their leaders. Israel was taught that decisions in life must be made after they had sought the Lord and learned what His choice was for them. After reading all those instructions, I did some soul searching. I try to start every day with prayer and Bible study, but I cannot say that I always consult the Lord for every decision I make throughout my day. During my meditation, one particular day from long ago came to mind. I had a lot of items on my to-do list that day, so I submitted my list to the Lord and asked Him to tell me what order to do them or if I should even do them at all. My eye was drawn to one item on the list, so I did it first. From that point forward, I continued to be prompted in
~~~~~

my mind for the next thing to do, and by the end of that day, I had accomplished much more than I dreamed was possible. I wonder how much more could be accomplished for the Kingdom if we would make a habit of asking the Lord what He would choose before decisions are made.

Gem #302 **October 28**

O give thanks to the Lord of lords:… To him who alone doeth great wonders:... To him that by wisdom made the heavens:... To him that stretched out the earth above the waters:... To him that made great lights:... The sun to rule by day:... The moon and stars to rule by night…

Psalms 136:3-9

...the earth is full of the goodness of the Lord.

Psalms 33:5

Be thou exalted, O god, above the heavens;
let thy glory be above all the earth.

Psalms 57:11

O Lord, how manifold are thy works!... the earth is full of thy riches.

Psalms 104:24

The earth, O Lord, is full of thy mercy:...

Psalms 119:64

Holy, holy, holy, is the Lord of hosts: the whole earth is full of his glory.

Isaiah 6:3

~~~~~

I spent time meditating this morning on the wonders and beauty of God's creation. When we look around us and see the variety of plants and animals, the majesty of the mountains and other amazing scenery on this earth, how can we not believe there is a God who created it all?
~~~~~

Gem #303 **October 29**

And the LORD *commanded us to do all these statutes, to fear the* LORD *our God,* ***for our good*** *always, that he might preserve us alive, as it is at this day. And it shall be our righteousness, if we observe to do all these commandments before the* LORD *our God, as he hath commanded us.*
Deuteronomy 6:24-25

...The hand of our God is upon all them ***for good*** *that seek him; but his power and his wrath is against all them that forsake him.*
Ezra 8:22

And I will give them one heart, and one way, that they may fear me for ever, ***for the good*** *of them, and of their children after them:*
Jeremiah 32:39

And we know that all things work together ***for good*** *to them that love God, to them who are the called according to his purpose.*
Romans 8:28

~~~~~

Our ideas of justice, fairness and equality are often in conflict with God's ways, and our ability to judge the rightness or wrongness of a situation is limited because of our inability to view all the pieces of the puzzle. That is why we must trust our Heavenly Father, who created all things and knows all things. He gave us laws to follow for our good. He put the Holy Ghost in the Church for our good so that we could have a unified heart to get His work done. And our calling and love for God gives us the security of knowing that everything that happens in our life works out for the greater good of His Kingdom.

Are you frustrated because things are not working out according to your ideas of fairness? Just keep loving God and walking in faith and obedience to His laws, and one day, He will return to right every wrong and reward those who have faithfully followed Him.
~~~~~

 **Gem #304** **October 30**

I am glad of the coming of Stephanas and Fortunatus and Achaicus...
For they have ***refreshed*** *my spirit and yours:*
therefore acknowledge ye them that are such.
1 Corinthians 16:17-18

...we were comforted in your comfort: yea, and exceedingly the more joyed we for the joy of Titus, because his spirit was ***refreshed*** *by you all.*
2 Corinthians 7:13

The Lord give mercy unto the house of Onesiphorus;
for he oft ***refreshed*** *me, and was not ashamed of my chain:*
2 Timothy 1:16

For we have great joy and consolation in thy love,
because the bowels of the saints are ***refreshed*** *by thee, brother.*
Philemon 1:7

~~~~~

Refreshing is defined as receiving new vigor and energy through rest, food, or encouragement from others; also to reinvigorate or bring cheer to another's mind or spirit.

In the above passages of scripture, Paul commended the church of Corinth along with Stephanus, Fortunatus, Achaicus, Onesiphorus, and Philemon because they had the unique ability of being able to offer refreshment to other saints who were overwhelmed by life's stressors.

We are living in perilous times in which violence, disrespect for authority, and diseases abound. Increasing prices make it difficult to pay the bills, and pressures to conform to worldly influences daily assault those who are trying to live Godly. How can a person keep themselves refreshed, let alone have enough refreshment left over to refresh someone else? The prophet Isaiah and the Apostle Peter taught that the Holy Ghost is that Spirit of refreshing that God
~~~~~

has provided for the Church.[37] Once a person has been filled with the Holy Ghost, their spirit receives refreshing on a continual basis as they spend time in God's presence through prayer, study of His Word, and fellowship with other believers.

Are you known as one who has the ability to refresh others when they spend time with you?

Gem #305 **October 31**

__Praise__ ye the L*ORD*. ***Praise*** *ye the* L*ORD from the heavens:* ***Praise*** *him in the heights.* [2] ***Praise*** *ye him, …angels: …hosts.* [3] *…sun and moon: …stars.* [4] *…heavens of heavens, and waters that be above the heavens.* [7] *Praise the* L*ORD from the earth, ye dragons, and all deeps:* [8] *Fire, and hail; snow, and vapours; stormy wind…:* [9] *Mountains, and all hills; fruitful trees, and all cedars:* [10] *Beasts, and all cattle; creeping things, and flying fowl:* [11] *Kings …and all people; princes, and all judges…* [12] *Both young men, and maidens; old men, and children:* [13] *Let them* ***praise*** *the name of the* L*ORD: for his name alone is excellent; his glory is above the earth and heaven.* [14] *…**Praise** ye the* L*ORD.*

Psalms 148:1-4, 7-14

Let every thing that hath breath ***praise*** *the* L*ORD.* ***Praise*** *ye the* L*ORD.*

Psalms 150:6

~~~~~

The Psalmist commanded that things in Heaven and earth should praise the Lord because His name is excellent and His glory is above the earth and Heaven. Everything that has the breath of life should give praise to their Creator. So on this day, I give praise to my Creator, my comforter, my deliverer, my friend, my healer, my provider, my protector, my Savior, my strength, and the lover of my soul. He is worthy to be praised!

---

[37] Holy Ghost is refreshing – Isaiah 28:12; Acts 3:19. Additional scriptures for study: Acts 27:3; Romans 15:32.
~~~~~

Gem #306 **November 1**

And as he entered into a certain village, there met him ten men that were lepers, which stood afar off: And they lifted up their voices, and said, Jesus, Master, have mercy on us. - And when he saw them, he said unto them, Go shew yourselves unto the priests. And it came to pass, that, as they went, ***they were cleansed****. And one of them, when he saw that he was healed, turned back, and with a loud voice glorified God, And fell down on his face at his feet,* ***giving him thanks****: and he was a Samaritan. And Jesus answering said, Were there not ten cleansed? but where are the nine? There are not found that returned to give glory to God, save this stranger. And he said unto him, Arise, go thy way:*

thy faith hath made thee whole.

Luke 17:12-19

~~~~~

The Bible discusses the subject of thanksgiving over 100 times. In this particular story, Jesus was asked to heal ten men who were lepers. While on their way to show themselves to the priest, they realized that they had been cleansed, yet only one, who was a Samaritan returned to say, "Thank you," to Jesus. His gratitude reaped the additional blessing of being totally healed as though he had never had the disease. I wonder if the Israelites had become so used to the miraculous provision of their God that they had developed an entitlement mentality that made them feel like Jesus owed them the favor of health because they were Israelites, but the Samaritan, an outsider, was so thrilled with what had been given to him that he eagerly expressed his thanks to Jesus and received an even greater blessing of total healing.

Has the Church developed the attitude that God owes them whatever they need from Him because they are His children? Could it be that He would hand out more blessings to His children if they would be more thankful?
~~~~~

Gem #307 **November 2**

*Then the **eyes of the blind shall be opened**,*
and the ears of the deaf shall be unstopped. Then shall
the lame man leap as an hart, and the tongue of the dumb sing…
Isaiah 35:5-6

*Jesus answered and said unto them, Go and shew John again those things which ye do hear and see: **The blind receive their sight**, and the lame walk, the lepers are cleansed, and the deaf hear, the dead are raised up, and the poor have the gospel preached to them.*
Matthew 11:4-5

*The Spirit of the Lord is upon me, because he hath anointed me to preach the gospel to the poor; he hath sent me to heal the brokenhearted, to preach deliverance to the captives, and **recovering of sight to the blind,** to set at liberty them that are bruised,*
Luke 4:18

*And these signs shall follow them that believe; In my name …they shall **lay hands on the sick**, and they shall recover.*
Mark 16:17-18

~~~~~

In 2007, I taught a Bible study to an elderly couple in their homes for an extended period of time, and they both received the Holy Ghost in their recliners during one of our early lessons. We took them to church, and they were baptized in Jesus' name. Several years later, they transitioned from home into a nursing care facility. In July 2014, the husband called me to ask for prayer for his wife who had developed an inflammation in her eyes which had left her totally blind. I went and had lunch with them a month later, and I felt such compassion for the wife as she tried to eat her food by touching everything while attempting to get it on the fork or spoon. When I talked with her afterward, she wanted to touch my hands or face or clothes to assure herself that it was really me. Before I left, I prayed with her and asked God to restore her eyesight so that she
~~~~~

could see during the time she had left in this life. I then asked her to believe that God would heal her and thank Him every day for hearing our prayer and restoring her sight. Two weeks later I received a phone call from her, and she said, "Guess what hunny-bunny! I can now see the clock on the wall, and it is ten minutes till seven!" I rejoiced with her, and said, "Thank you Jesus." God wants to do many miraculous works in the Church if we will only ask and believe.

Gem #308 — November 3

Now unto him that is able to do exceeding abundantly above all that we ask or think, according to the ***power that worketh in us,***
Ephesians 3:20

~~~~~

The world's leaders are obsessed with power and control, and they are constantly trying to dream up ways to tighten their reins of control over the populace. Sometimes we can feel so powerless as we watch evil rulers destroy the very foundations of morality and liberty upon which our nation was founded. Yet God never intended for His Church to be powerless. I am amazed at how many times the word ***power*** is used in the book of Acts and the Epistles to remind the Church of the great ***power*** that is available to the believers. Dozens of times we are taught about the ***power*** of the Holy Ghost, the ***power*** to preach, ***power*** to heal and perform miracles, the ***power*** of the Gospel to save, ***power*** to overcome, and ***power*** over fear. Why do we tremble in fear over the evils around us? God can do exceeding, abundantly, above all that we ask or think, but He is limited in His working to the amount of ***power*** that we allow to work through us.

It is time to quit being intimidated by the enemy. God wants to work in powerful ways through His Church.

Will you let Him work through you?
~~~~~

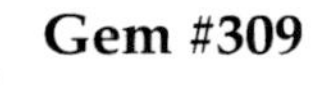

Gem #309 **November 4**

Who shall ascend into the hill of the LORD? or who shall stand in his holy place? He that hath ***clean hands, and a pure heart****; who hath not lifted up his soul unto vanity, nor sworn deceitfully. He shall receive the blessing from the LORD, and righteousness from the God of his salvation.*
Psalms 24:3-5

Blessed are the ***pure in heart****: for they shall see God.*
Matthew 5:8

Flee also youthful lusts: but follow righteousness, faith, charity, peace, with them that call on the Lord out of a ***pure heart****.*
2 Timothy 2:22

Seeing ye have purified your souls in obeying the truth through the Spirit unto unfeigned love of the brethren, see that ye love one another with ***a pure heart*** *fervently: Being born again, not of corruptible seed, but of incorruptible, by the word of God, which liveth and abideth for ever.*
1 Peter 1:22-23

~~~~~

God is handing out invitations for people to enter into His Holy Place, but certain requirements must be met before an invitation is issued. One of the requirements is having a pure heart. People with a pure heart have learned to repent often (Psalms 51:7, 10) so that their hearts are undefiled by worldliness, ulterior motives, or manipulation of circumstances and people. They are obedient. They love the Word and live by its teachings. Their love for others is unfeigned or genuine, and they have learned to view people through God's eyes and speak life and hope into broken, hurting lives.

For that gift, they are also **blessed** with the promise of seeing God in the life to come.
~~~~~

Gem #310

November 5

God is our refuge and strength, a very present ***help*** *in trouble.*
Psalms 46:1

Let us therefore come boldly unto the throne of grace,
that we may obtain mercy, and find grace to ***help*** *in time of need.*
Hebrews 4:16

~~~~~

Numerous times the Bible states that God is our help when we are in trouble or have a need. Too often we try finding our own solutions and only seek for His help as a last resort. I don't believe God is a magic genie that we can just snap our fingers and use as our servant to obey our every whim. He does expect us to be industrious and fruitful in our service to Him, our families and those who cross our path. However, in our times of distress, trouble or genuine need, we have the assurance that if we come boldly to His throne with our requests, we will receive the help that we need. Call Him today. He has solutions you never dreamed of, and His resources are unlimited.

Gem #311 **November 6**

Marriage is honourable in all, and the bed undefiled:
but whoremongers and adulterers God will judge.
Hebrews 13:4

Therefore shall a man leave his father and his mother,
and shall cleave unto his wife: and they shall be one flesh.
Genesis 2:24

Nevertheless, to avoid fornication, let every man have his own wife,
and let every woman have her own husband.
1 Corinthians 7:2
~~~~~

Marriage was the very first institution ordained by God for the protection and nurturing of the family, yet for many years this sacred institution has been under attack by evil people who have tried to change God's definition of marriage from the union of one man and one woman into man marrying man, woman marrying woman, or even man or woman marrying an animal. It is because of God's original plan for families to consist of one husband and one wife and their children that civilizations have remained stable throughout thousands of years. It is our responsibility as Christians to teach and model the Bible teachings concerning the sanctity of marriage and family to our children so that our grandchildren and succeeding generations will have safe homes in which to nurture their children.

Gem #312 **November 7**

Yea doubtless, and I count all things but loss for the excellency of the knowledge of Christ Jesus my Lord: for whom I have suffered the loss of all things, and do count them but dung, that I may win Christ, That I may know him, and the power of his resurrection, and the fellowship of his sufferings, being made conformable unto his death;

Philippians 3:8, 10

~~~~~

Saul of Tarsus had quite a pedigree before he was converted to Christianity. According to his own testimony, he was a Pharisee of the tribe of Benjamin, had studied the Law at the feet of the famous teacher, Gamaliel, and was blameless concerning his adherence to the Law. Yet when he became a Christian, he put behind him all the notable achievements from his past, and pursued God with everything inside him. He was willing to lose everything that had given him status and honor in men's eyes so that he could win the prize of knowing Christ, not only in the power of His resurrection, but also in the fellowship of His sufferings.

What are you willing to lose and suffer in order to know Christ?
~~~~~

Gem #313 — November 8

But I would not have you to be ignorant, brethren, concerning them which are asleep, that ye ***sorrow not, even as others which have no hope.*** *For if we believe that Jesus died and rose again, even so them also which sleep in Jesus will God bring with him. For this we say unto you by the word of the Lord, that we which are alive and remain unto the coming of the Lord shall not prevent them which are asleep. For the Lord himself shall descend from heaven with a shout, with the voice of the archangel, and with the trump of God: and the dead in Christ shall rise first: Then we which are alive and remain shall be caught up together with them in the clouds, to meet the Lord in the air: and so shall we ever be with the Lord. Wherefore* ***comfort one another*** *with these words.*

1 Thessalonians 4:13-18

~~~~~

Part of the package of human existence is the fact that we will eventually die. Whether that death is sudden and unexpected or drawn out through a prolonged illness, it nevertheless leaves a huge hole in the hearts of those who are left behind. My heart is grieved every time another loved one is taken from this life into the next.

However, the Bible tells us that we who are members of God's family do not sorrow in the same way as unbelievers who have no hope, for we know that those who die in Jesus will go straight into His presence, and Paul told us to comfort one another with these words. My husband has been in the presence of Jesus for over fourteen years, and I have grieved his absence at the weddings of all three of our sons and at the births of each one of my grandchildren. I have many other friends and family members who have left this world to be in God's presence. But while I miss them and often grieve over the fact that they are no longer with me, I know that one day soon, there will be a grand reunion of all of God's family, and from that day forward, we'll never be parted again. Happy Day!
~~~~~

Gem #314 **November 9**

Shew me thy ways, O LORD; teach me ***thy paths****.*
All the ***paths of the Lord*** *are mercy and truth unto*
such as keep his covenant and his testimonies.
Psalms 25:4, 10

And many people shall go and say, Come ye, and
let us go up to the mountain of the LORD, to the house of the God of Jacob;
and he will teach us of ***his ways****, and we will walk in* ***his paths****:*
for out of Zion shall go forth the law, and the word of the LORD
from Jerusalem.
Isaiah 2:3

~~~~~

The Bible teaches us many things about the *paths and ways* of the Lord. Just a few of the ones mentioned are:

1. The path of life (Psalms 16:11; Proverbs 2:19)
2. The paths of righteousness (Psalms 23:3; Proverbs 2:20; 12:28)
3. A plain path (Psalms 27:11)
4. The path of His commandments (Psalms 119:35)
5. Wisdom as the path of peace (Proverbs 3:17)
6. Right paths (Proverbs 4:11)
7. Old paths (Jeremiah 6:16)
8. Paths of judgment (Proverbs 2:8-9; Isaiah 40:14)
9. Paths of uprightness (Proverbs 2:13)
10. Strait [narrow] way (Matthew 7:13-14)

We understand that God is merciful, and we like to claim His mercy to cover our sinful ways. However, the Psalmist teaches us that God's mercy and truth are conditional and are extended only to those who keep God's covenant and testimonies.

Are you in need of God's mercy? Set your feet on His paths, and you will automatically receive the benefits of His mercy and His truth.
~~~~~

Gem #315

November 10

And we know that all things work together for good to them that love God, to them who are the called ***according to his purpose.***
Romans 8:28

Who hath saved us, and called us with an holy calling, not according to our works, but ***according to his own purpose*** *and grace, which was given us in Christ Jesus before the world began,*
2 Timothy 1:9

~~~~~

I often hear Romans 8:28 interpreted as God working all things for *my good*. There's even a popular Christian song that says, "He's working all things for my good." However, a closer inspection of that verse shows that God works for good in the lives of those who have been called according to ***His purpose***. What is His purpose? In the beginning, God enjoyed daily communion with Adam and Eve until the serpent's influence brought sin into their lives. Since then, God's ultimate purpose has been twofold. He loves people and will do whatever is necessary to save them from sin and prepare them for eternity with Him. He hates sin and will ultimately destroy it. God is longsuffering and not willing that any should perish (2 Peter 3:9), but when He has had enough of men's sins against Him, He sends judgment. The Bible gives numerous examples of judgment on men and nations for their sins. Often He allows bad things to happen to His people in His efforts to wake them up to their sins so He will not have to punish them. He even raises up pagan kings to perform His purpose (i.e. Pharaoh, Cyrus, Nebuchadnezzar).

The good and bad things that happen to us have less to do with God working for *our good*, but they have more to do with God's ultimate purpose of destroying sin in His people and perfecting and preparing a holy people to spend eternity with Him.
~~~~~

Gem #316 **November 11**

Bless ye the LORD, *all ye his hosts;*
ye ministers of his, that do his pleasure.
Psalms 103:21

Bless ye God *in the congregations, even the Lord,*
from the fountain of Israel.
Psalms 68:26

Sing unto the LORD, ***bless his name;***
shew forth his salvation from day to day.
Psalms 96:2

Thou art worthy, O Lord, *to receive glory and honour and power:*
for thou hast created all things,
and for thy pleasure they are and were created.
Revelation 4:11

~~~~~

God created the heavens and the earth and everything in the universe for His pleasure. He has all power and can do anything He chooses to do, yet there is one thing He cannot do for Himself. He cannot bless Himself for all His marvelous works. The angels were created to praise Him, and they have no choice except to praise God night and day. However, when God created man, He gave him freedom of choice. I can bless God or ask Him to bless me. Often we are more interested in serving God for the benefits we can receive from that relationship, i.e., forgiveness, health, redemption, love, mercy, satisfaction, renewal, etc. God loves to provide those things for His people, yet He hungers for us to compliment, praise and bless Him for the benefits He provides. At least 69 times the Bible instructs us to bless the Lord.

How about changing our requests today from those of "Bless Me, Lord" into those of "I will bless You, Lord" instead?
~~~~~

Gem #317 **November 12**

Jesus answered, Verily, verily, I say unto thee, Except a man be born of water and of the Spirit, ***he cannot enter into the kingdom of God.***
John 3:5

In whom we have ***redemption*** *through his blood,*
the forgiveness of sins, according to the riches of his grace;
Ephesians 1:7

...we have ***redemption*** *through his blood, even the forgiveness of sins:*
Colossians 1:14

In whom ye also trusted, after that ye heard the word of truth,
the gospel of your salvation: in whom also after that ye believed,
ye were ***sealed with that holy Spirit of promise,***
Which is the ***earnest of our inheritance*** *until the redemption*
of the purchased possession, unto the praise of his glory.
Ephesians 1:13-14

And grieve not the ***holy spirit of God,***
whereby ye are ***sealed*** *unto the day of redemption.*
Ephesians 4:30

~~~~~

Jesus taught Nicodemus that water baptism and Holy Ghost baptism were essential for entrance into the Kingdom of God. Paul reinforced that teaching when he spoke of redemption through Jesus' blood (which is accomplished in water baptism in Jesus' name) and being sealed by the Holy Spirit of promise. When I purchased my home, I included a deposit (earnest money) with my contract to "seal the deal" until I got a loan to pay for the entire purchase. In a similar way, the components of water baptism and Holy Ghost baptism are the deposits (or earnest) which "seal the deal" for our spiritual inheritance until Jesus returns to claim what belongs to Him. Have you been baptized in His name and filled with the Holy Ghost? If not, your "deal" is incomplete.
~~~~~

Gem #318 **November 13**

For unto you it is given in the behalf of Christ,
*not only to believe on him, but also to **suffer for his sake;***
Philippians 1:29

*Yea, and all that will live godly in Christ Jesus **shall suffer persecution.***
2 Timothy 3:12

And ye shall be hated of all men for my name's sake:
but he that endureth to the end shall be saved.
Matthew 10:22

Then shall they deliver you up to be afflicted, and shall kill you:
*and **ye shall be hated of all nations for my name's sake.***
Matthew 24:9

~~~~~

Modern Christianity is plagued with the erroneous teaching that those who live Godly will live in the best houses, build the most elaborate churches, drive the nicest cars, afford exotic vacations, etc. Americans especially seem to have adopted the idea that we do not deserve to suffer, but Jesus suffered horribly, and He warned His disciples that following Him came with the cost of suffering persecution for His name's sake. The people of God have suffered horribly at the hands of evil men since the beginning of time. It started when wicked Cain murdered righteous Abel, and the trend has continued throughout history until now. In an interview with World Net Daily on March 24, 2013, Christian Broham, an advocate for retaining religious freedom in America, made this statement: "A Christian is murdered somewhere every five minutes for simply believing in Jesus…" That adds up to approximately 288 people per day, over 8,600 per month and over 104,000 per year who are murdered for the name of Jesus! If suffering has not yet touched your life, then you must pray for those who are suffering, for not only is suffering part of the package of being a member of sinful humanity; it is also a part of the package of being a Christian.
~~~~~

Gem #319 **November 14**

Thus saith the Lord, Stand ye in the ways, and see,
and ask for the ***old paths, where is the good way,***
and walk therein, and ye shall find rest for your souls…
Jeremiah 6:16

Then said one unto him, Lord, are there few that be saved?
And he said unto them, Strive to enter in at the ***strait gate:***
for many, I say unto you, will seek to enter in, and shall not be able.
Luke 13:23-24

Enter ye in at the ***strait*** *gate: for wide is the gate, and broad is the way,*
that leadeth to destruction, and many there be which go in thereat:
Because ***strait*** *is the gate, and* ***narrow*** *is the way,*
which leadeth unto life, and few there be that find it.
Matthew 7:13-14

Not every one that saith unto me, Lord, Lord,
shall enter into the kingdom of heaven;
but he that doeth the will of my Father which is in heaven.
Many will say to me in that day, Lord, Lord,
have we not prophesied in thy name?
and in thy name have cast out devils?
and in thy name done many wonderful works?
And then will I profess unto them, I never knew you:
depart from me, ye that work iniquity.
Matthew 7:21-23

~~~~~

Jesus specifically said that the way that leads to life is narrow and restricted and only a few will be willing to unload the things that prohibit them from entering that narrow gate. Just because a teaching is popular doesn't mean it is right.

It is time to study the Book and learn its teachings and establish our feet on the narrow, restricted path that leads to life.
~~~~~

Gem #320 **November 15**

But ***seek ye first the kingdom of God****, and his righteousness;*
and all these things shall be added unto you.
Matthew 6:33

I exhort therefore, that, ***first of all****, supplications, prayers,*
intercessions, and giving of thanks, be made for ***all*** *men;*
1 Timothy 2:1

***Honour the* LORD** *with thy substance,*
and ***with the firstfruits*** *of all thine increase:*
Proverbs 3:9

~~~~~

Priorities! Priorities! As the holidays approach, it is easy to get caught up in the busyness of the season. There are menus to plan, groceries to purchase, house cleaning for guests, programs to plan and rehearse, parties to plan and attend, gift-buying, decorating, updating address lists, and mailing Christmas cards. Just contemplating the items on my schedule for the next six weeks is overwhelming. Most items on my schedule are good things, but what is the priority to fulfill in God's plan for my life? Jesus said to seek Him and Kingdom matters first, and everything else would fall into its proper place. Paul said that prayer should be a daily first priority, and Proverbs tells us that God is honored when we give to His cause before spending on ourselves. So before I blow the budget on holiday spending, I need to assess the priority of giving to God first. Does your end-of-the year schedule seem overwhelming? It is time to realign priorities. Seek God and His Kingdom first, then say no to things that do not answer back to that priority.

~~~~~

"When we put God first, all other things fall into their proper place
or drop out of our lives. Our love of the Lord will
govern the claims for our affection, the demands on our time,
the interests we pursue, and the order of our priorities."
Ezra Taft Benson

Gem #321 **November 16**

If any man ...consent not to wholesome words, even the words of our Lord Jesus Christ, and to the doctrine which is according to godliness; He is proud, knowing nothing, but doting about questions and strifes of words, whereof cometh envy, strife, railings, evil surmisings, Perverse disputings of men of corrupt minds, and ***destitute of the truth****, supposing that gain is godliness: from such withdraw thyself. But thou, O man of God,* ***flee these things****; and follow after righteousness, godliness, faith, love, patience, meekness.* ***Fight the good fight of faith****, lay hold on eternal life, whereunto thou art also called, and hast professed a good profession before many witnesses.*

1 Timothy 6:3-5, 11-12

Flee *also youthful lusts: but follow righteousness, faith, charity, peace, with them that call on the Lord out of a pure heart. But foolish and unlearned questions avoid, knowing that they do gender strifes.*

2 Timothy 2:22-23

~~~~~

Paul clearly instructed Timothy to ***flee*** from anyone who has abandoned Truth. Their lack of character and disputing of doctrines will influence those who spend time with them. Twice Paul mentioned that these people stir up strife with their words, creating discord and conflict in the Church. Solomon said that one of the seven deadly sins that God hates is the person who sows discord among brethren (Proverbs 6:16-19). Instead, we are instructed to follow the way of righteousness and put on Godly characteristics.

Those who hate lining up to God's "straight and narrow way" will viciously attack those who do. We must fight for our faith and never back down from the precious Truths that previous generations of saints have paid dearly to give us.

I am thankful today for the precious Word of God and the Truths passed to me from my elders.
~~~~~

Gem #322 **November 17**

Then I said, I will not make mention of him, nor speak any more in his name. But his word was in mine heart as a ***burning fire*** *shut up in my bones, and I was weary with forbearing, and I could not stay.*
Jeremiah 20:9

And of the angels he saith, Who maketh his angels spirits, and his ministers a ***flame of fire****.*
Hebrews 1:7

Let the priests, the ministers of the LORD, ***weep*** *between the porch and the altar, and let them say, Spare thy people, O LORD, and give not thine heritage to reproach, that the heathen should rule over them…*
Joel 2:17

~~~~~

Lord, set me a-fire, make me a flame for Thee.
Millions are lost, though You paid the cost
That they all might be free.
Lord I am yearning, set me a-burning,
Let me shine out for Jesus' name.
This my desire, set me a-fire, make me a flame.

~~~~~

I remember singing the above chorus as a teenager and weeping over the lost around me. My greatest desire was to be a burning light and testimony of the saving, healing power of God to my world. The world I live in today is doing its best to silence the voices of Christians, which makes my responsibility to weep and light the darkness around me even greater than ever. "

This my desire, set me a-fire, make me a flame."

Gem #323 **November 18**

Casting all your care upon him; for he careth for you.

1 Peter 5:7

~~~~~

I will cast all my cares upon You.
I lay all of my burdens down at Your feet.
Anytime I don't know just what to do
I just cast all my cares upon You.

~~~~~

This little chorus is one that I sing when life gets too stressful. As a single woman, sometimes it seems that problems descend like an avalanche and making decisions can seem overwhelming, but if I can just remember to give them to Jesus and spend quiet time in His presence, He has answers to every question and solutions to every problem.

Gem #324 **November 19**

Create in me a clean heart, O God; and renew a right spirit within me. Cast me not away from thy presence; and take not thy holy spirit from me. Restore unto me the joy of thy salvation; and uphold me with thy free spirit. ***Then will I teach transgressors thy ways;*** *and sinners shall be converted unto thee.*

Psalms 51:10-13

I beheld the transgressors, and was grieved; because they kept not thy word.

Psalms 119:158

~~~~~

If we want to teach God's ways to transgressors and see sinners converted, our example of living a lifestyle of repentance for our own transgressions will draw them to God.
~~~~~

Gem #325 **November 20**

*Then the people rejoiced, for that they offered **willingly**,*
*because with perfect heart they offered **willingly** to the LORD:*
and David the king also rejoiced with great joy.
1 Chronicles 29:9

*Whatsoever thy **hand findeth to do, do** it with thy might;*
for there is no work, nor device, nor knowledge, nor wisdom,
in the grave, whither thou goest.
Ecclesiastes 9:10

Every man according as he purposeth in his heart, so let him give;
*not grudgingly, or of necessity: for God loveth a **cheerful giver**.*
2 Corinthians 9:7

*And whatsoever ye do, do it **heartily**, as to the Lord, and not unto men;*
Colossians 3:23

~~~~~

"God does not want anything that
has to be pressed from an unwilling giver.
The prayer that is offered God from a sense of duty,
that work that is done just because we have to do it,
the word that is spoken because we are
expected to be ministers and to be consistent with our profession,
are dead, cold and comparatively worthless.
True service springs from a full and joyful heart,
and runs over like the broad and boundless river."
A. B. Simpson
~~~~~

Gem #326

November 21

***Delight thyself also in the Lord**: and he shall give thee*
the desires of thine heart. Commit thy way unto the LORD;
trust also in him; and he shall bring it to pass.
Psalms 37:4-5

If thou ...shalt honour [the LORD], not doing thine own ways,
nor finding thine own pleasure, nor speaking thine own words:
*Then shalt thou **delight thyself in the Lord**; and I will cause thee to ride*
upon the high places of the earth, and feed thee with the heritage of
Jacob thy father: for the mouth of the LORD hath spoken it.
Isaiah 58:13-14

~~~~~

I used to think that Psalms 37:4 meant that as long as I took delight in the Lord and in being involved in His work, then my desires would be granted. My personal desires included, among other things that my husband and I would work together in God's Kingdom, grow old together, and leave this world together in the rapture of the Church. Those ideas all changed when he died. For a period of time, I could not make any sense of that verse. One day my pastor told me that delighting myself in the Lord meant that His desires for me would become my desires. Eventually I discovered Isaiah 58:13-14, and I was able to understand what God was trying to teach me through my loss. As I honored the Lord with my lifestyle, found pleasure in the path He set my feet upon, and spoke the words He wanted me to speak, then I would know true delight and would be able to experience things I had never dreamed of doing before. As I review my life since my husband died, I can see that God has moved me into areas of ministry that I never would have considered pursuing. One of those areas that I had never considered pursuing was jail ministry, but an invitation over twelve years ago to play keyboard in a weekend ladies Bible study in our local jail, resulted in the start of a weekly Bible study, which eventually led to my current position as a volunteer Chaplain to the female inmates and staff. While it is important to set goals and
~~~~~

dream dreams, don't get so locked into your own desires that you miss out on the exciting high places in life that God wants to give you.

Gem #327 **November 22**

*Enter into his gates with **thanksgiving**, and into his courts with praise: **be thankful** unto him, and bless his name. For the LORD is good; his mercy is everlasting; and his truth endureth to all generations.*
Psalms 100:4-5

*And let the peace of God rule in your hearts, to the which also ye are called in one body; and **be ye thankful**.*
Colossians 3:15

"Thanks, thanks, I give you thanks
For all You've done.
I am so blessed, my soul has found rest,
Oh Lord, I give You thanks."
Carroll Mcgruder

~~~~~

During the month of November in which we celebrate the Thanksgiving holiday, this little chorus has become my theme song for the month. During recent morning devotions I have researched what the Bible says about being thankful. Over 100 times, reference is made to this virtue. One of my favorite references from 1 Chronicles 16 tells us that David appointed Levites to record the praises of the people. If we would write down the things we are thankful for and review them regularly, I think it would be easier to maintain an attitude of thankfulness. Today I am thankful for my Bible, the Holy Ghost, my Pastor and his wife, my children and grandchildren, and a host of Godly family and friends, working together to keep me on track in my journey toward my ultimate goal of spending eternity with my Savior.
~~~~~

Gem #328 **November 23**

And daily in the temple, and in every house,
*they ceased not to **teach** and **preach Jesus Christ**.*
Acts 5:42

Therefore they that were scattered abroad went every where
***preaching the word**.*
Acts 8:4

~~~~~

"Tell me the story of Jesus, Write on my heart ev'ry word
Tell me the story most precious, Sweetest that ever was heard.
Tell how the angels, in chorus, Sang as they welcomed His birth,
Glory to God in the highest! Peace and good tidings to earth."
Fanny Crosby

~~~~~

I opened up my hymn book and began singing this old song today. I want to know every story about the workings of Jesus in people's lives. Those stories are precious and faith-building. Many songs have been written as a testimonial of lessons learned, revelations received, or deliverance from dangerous situations. Joseph Scriven, a wealthy, educated Irishman wrote a familiar hymn in the mid-1800s because of deep sorrow in his life. The night before his wedding, his fiancée was thrown from a horse into a river and drowned. Grief-stricken, he moved to Canada and in time, met another lady and became engaged to be married, but before the wedding, this lady was stricken with pneumonia and died. He then gave himself to helping the elderly and those who were sick, often without charge. When his mother's health declined through grieving over her son's misfortunes, he wrote the words to the well-known song, ***What a Friend We Have In Jesus*** and sent them to her to encourage her. He had learned that when our hopes are dashed in this life, we have a friend who will never leave us or forsake us.

We all have stories to tell. Don't keep your stories to yourself. Tell them and bless someone today.

Gem #329 **November 24**

The Psalmist recognizes the need for leadership from God and asks on numerous occasions to be led into these 10 areas:

1. In Thy righteousness (Psalms 5:8)
2. Beside still waters (Psalms 23:2)
3. In the paths of righteousness (Psalms 23:3)
4. In Thy Truth (Psalms 25:5)
5. In a plain path (Psalms 27:11)
6. For Thy name's sake (Psalms 31:3)
7. In Thy light and Truth (Psalms 43:3)
8. To the rock (Psalms 61:2)
9. In the everlasting way (Psalms 139:24)
10. To the land of uprightness (Psalms 143:10)

Oh, that I would possess a teachable spirit and submit to the leading of God, His Word and the Godly people He puts in my life.

Gem #330 **November 25**

__Sing__ praises to God, __sing__ praises:
__sing__ praises unto our King, __sing__ praises.
Psalms 47:6

O __sing__ unto the Lord a new song: __sing__ unto the Lord all the earth.
Psalms 96:1

The subject of singing and praising is a key teaching of the Bible. The book of Psalms was the songbook of the ancient Israelites, but we know that Jesus and His disciples sang a hymn before going to pray at the Garden of Gethsemane. We do not have a lot of information about early hymns except we know they were different from Psalms according to Ephesians 5:19 and Colossians 3:16.

Hymns became popular in the 16th century as church reformers began writing songs about God and their experiences as a Christian.

The Israelites and the early Church sang songs on a variety of subjects, and as I glanced through the Bible, I found songs written on the following subjects:

1. Songs to the Lord (Judges 5:3; Psalms 13:6)
2. Songs of victory over enemies and life adversities (Exodus 15:1)
3. Songs of salvation (Psalms 96:2; Isaiah 12:1-3)
4. Songs about His blessings (Psalms 27:6)
5. Songs of determination (Psalms 57:7; 108:1)
6. Songs about His Word or Doctrine (Psalms 101:1)
7. Songs about His name (Psalms 61:8: 66:4)
8. Songs about His wondrous, marvellous works (1 Chronicles 16:9; Psalms 105:2; Revelation 15:3)

Although the Bible mentions the subject of singing and praise over 630 times, it only tells us to sing a new song nine times. Thousands of songs have been written through the centuries, and many of the old songs are rich in ***doctrine*** and ***testimonies*** of triumph in the face of severe adversities. It is important to maintain a balance between old music and new in order to keep our musical heritage alive and pass it down to succeeding generations so they will not forget God and His mighty works among His people.

~~~~~

"Powerful, life-changing music will never be initiated by monetary concerns or ego needs, for human genius without a focus on God is sterile. Until He does a deep work in our lives, we really don't have anything to write about!"

Don Wyrtzen
~~~~~

 **Gem #331** **November 26**

All the ways of a man are ***clean in his own eyes;***
but the LORD *weigheth the spirits.*
Proverbs 16:2

Be not deceived; God is not mocked:
for whatsoever a man ***soweth****, that shall he also* ***reap****.*
Galatians 6:7

~~~~~

Procrastination! The wrong place at the wrong time! Just one look! These actions set the stage for a lifetime of reaping regret, heartache and death in David's life and family. He was supposed to be in a battle with Joab and his army, but *"while he tarried,"* he just happened to get out of bed one night and take a walk on his rooftop. While gazing over the city, he just happened to see a beautiful woman named Bathsheba, bathing herself. His desire for her overcame his conscience, and he sent for her. That one little fling just happened to result in a pregnancy. David's attempts to hide his sin failed, so he ordered the execution of Bathsheba's husband. Then he married her. Yes, David repented, and God forgave him, but the seed of that sin produced a grievous harvest within David's family. The baby died. David's son Amnon, raped his half-sister, Tamar. Tamar's brother, Absalom, killed Amnon. Years later Absalom tried to steal the throne and kill his own father. Absalom was killed, and David was restored to the throne. Another son, Adonijah, rose up and tried to take the kingdom, but David installed Solomon instead.

How many marriages and children have been destroyed because of inappropriate meetings, conversations, or actions? Job said that he made a covenant with his eyes so he wouldn't think inappropriately about another woman (Job 31:1). That one glimpse or touch may start out innocently enough, but beware of the long-term consequences! The harvest is always greater than the seed. Is the momentary pleasure of the sin worth the long-term consequences?
~~~~~

Gem #332 **November 27**

I beseech you therefore, brethren, ...that ye present your bodies a living sacrifice, holy, acceptable unto God, which is your reasonable service.
Romans 12:1

By him therefore let us offer the sacrifice of praise to God continually, that is, the fruit of our lips giving thanks to his name.
Hebrews 13:15

~~~~~

When I was a teenager, we used to sing a little chorus that asked the question, "What can I offer the Lord?" The lyrics in the chorus stated that God already had everything I could offer, so the only thing I could give Him was my heart. While that is partially true, a closer inspection in the Bible of the words ***"give," "offer," "bring,"*** and ***"present"*** reveal that there are hundreds of recommended or even required items that God needs from His people. The two verses I chose above teach that God requires us to present our bodies as a living, holy sacrifice to Him, and then we continually offer sacrifices of praise and thanksgiving to Him. Sometimes our world is upside down, and we don't feel like praising. That's why it is called a "sacrifice." We offer it because it pleases God. While this following list is by no means comprehensive, here are several areas to get you a started on further study of the subject.

1. Bring an offering to God. (Psalms 96:8)
2. Bring presents to God. (Psalms 76:11)
3. Offer sacrifices of righteousness. (Psalms 4:5)
4. Offer sacrifices of joy. (Psalms 27:6)
5. Give glory to God. (Malachi 2:2)
6. Give thanks and praise. (Psalms 92:1; Colossians 1:3)

Jesus said, *"Thou shalt love the Lord thy God with all thy heart, and with all thy soul, and with all thy mind."* (Matthew 22:37). When our whole being is involved in the giving, it is done cheerfully rather than grudgingly. What can you offer to the Lord today?
~~~~~

Gem #333  **November 28**

Come unto me, all ye that labour and are heavy laden,
and I will give you ***rest****. Take my yoke upon you, and learn of me;*
for I am meek and lowly in heart: and ye shall find ***rest*** *unto your souls.*
For my yoke is easy,
and my burden is light.
Matthew 11:28-30

\~~~~~

My life seems to be one of constant busyness, overloaded schedules and never-ending to-do lists which leave me in a constant state of exhaustion. But when I come into His presence, that exhaustion drops off of me, and I am refreshed. Why is it that the activity that can benefit me the most often gets a low priority? As I start a new day, I crave to spend time in His presence and in His Word. That is at the top of my priority list because that rest will generate the energy and focus I need to accomplish the other items on my list.

Gem #334 **November 29**

And whosoever shall compel thee to go a mile, go with him twain.
Matthew 5:41

For, brethren, ye have been called unto liberty; only use not liberty for an occasion to the flesh, but by love ***serve*** *one another.*
Galatians 5:13

\~~~~~

Jesus is looking for people with a servant's heart, who, when asked to do something for someone else, will cheerfully and willingly do more than is asked or required.

Lord, help me not to be so caught up in my own little world that I am oblivious to the needs of others around me. Let me serve with love and humility.

Gem #335

November 30

...Walk in the Spirit, and ye shall not fulfil the lust of the flesh.
For the flesh lusteth against the Spirit, and the Spirit against the flesh:
and these are contrary the one to the other: so that ye cannot do the things
that ye would. But if ye be led of the Spirit, ye are not under the law.
Now the works of the flesh are manifest, which are these;
Adultery, fornication, uncleanness, lasciviousness, Idolatry, witchcraft,
hatred, variance, emulations, wrath, strife, seditions, heresies,
Envyings, murders, drunkenness, revellings, and such like:
of the which I tell you before, as I have also told you in time past, that
they which do such things shall not inherit the kingdom of God.
Galatians 5:16-21

But ***the fruit of the Spirit is*** *love, joy, peace, longsuffering, gentleness,*
goodness, faith, Meekness, temperance: against such there is no law. And
they that are Christ's have crucified the flesh with the affections and lusts.
If we live in the Spirit, let us also walk in the Spirit.
Galatians 5:22-25

~~~~~

Once we are born into the Kingdom of God, we begin to experience a continual tug-of-war between the desires of our fleshly nature and the desires of the Spirit that lives within us. The enemy of our soul wages all-out war to get us back. Paul warned that giving in to the desires of the flesh would produce works that would bar us from entering the Kingdom. But those who crucify the fleshly desires by living and walking in the Spirit produce fruit of the Spirit that identifies them with the God they serve.

Our life will either manifest ***works of the flesh*** or ***fruit of the Spirit***.

What are you manifesting to the world?
~~~~~

Gem #336

December 1

The law of thy mouth is ***better*** *unto me than thousands of gold and silver.*
Psalms 119:72

For the merchandise of [wisdom] is ***better*** *than the merchandise of silver, and the gain thereof than fine gold.*
Proverbs 3:14

How much ***better*** *is it to get wisdom than gold! and to get understanding rather to be chosen than silver!*
Proverbs 16:16

For wisdom is ***better*** *than rubies; and all the things that may be desired are not to be compared to it. My fruit is* ***better*** *than gold, yea, than fine gold; and my revenue than choice silver.*
Proverbs 8:11, 19

~~~~~

The Psalmist said that God's Word was better than gold and silver, and Solomon stated four times in Proverbs that the acquisition of wisdom was better than acquiring gold, silver, and rubies. The word ***better*** speaks of things that are superior in quality or excellence; things that are preferable or morally superior. Over 100 times the Bible speaks of the ***better things*** that God has reserved for His people. Here are a few of my favorites:

1. Obedience is better than rebellion and stubbornness (1 Samuel 15:22-23).
2. One day in Church is better than 1,000 days in the world (Psalms 84:10)
3. A good name is better than precious ointment (Ecclesiastes 7:1)
4. It's better to be poor and righteous than to be rich and wicked (Psalms 37:16; Proverbs 16:8; 28:6)

Will you settle for the mediocre things of life, or will you strive to achieve the ***better things*** God has reserved for those who belong to Him?
~~~~~

Gem #337 **December 2**

*Let the **words** of my mouth, and the meditation of my heart, be acceptable in thy sight, O LORD, my strength, and my redeemer.*
Psalms 19:14

*A **soft answer** turneth away wrath: but grievous **words** stir up anger.*
Proverbs 15:1

*Pleasant **words** are as an honeycomb, sweet to the soul, and health to the bones.*
Proverbs 16:24

~~~~~

"People may hear your words, but they feel your attitude."
John C. Maxwell

~~~~~

WORDS!! Those expressions of sound or text have enormous power to encourage or destroy. The little children's chant, "Sticks and stones may break my bones, but words can never hurt me" is seriously flawed and suggests that it is not okay to physically harm someone, but it is harmless to hurl vindictive words at them. I daresay that the topic of our speech, either verbally or in writing, is one of, if not the most important topics in the Bible as it is addressed thousands of times. James calls the tongue the most unruly member of our body, and he spends the entire third chapter of his book in discussion of that member.

Because I am constantly trying to guard against using my tongue to tear down others, my daily prayer to God when I open my eyes each morning is Psalm 19:14. "Lord, let my words and my thoughts be acceptable to you."

Who can you find today to speak a word of encouragement that will brighten their day?

Gem #338 **December 3**

We tend to use the word ***love*** to express our feelings for people and things. We ***love*** our God, our spouses, our children and grandchildren and others who are important in our life. We ***love*** our pets. We sometimes express ***love*** for certain types of food or items of clothing. We ***love*** attending church or certain types of events such as concerts or sporting events. But it is not often that we hear people talk about how much they ***love*** God's Word. Psalms 119 is the longest chapter in the Bible, and the key theme in every one of its 176 verses is the Word of God. In eleven of those verses, the Psalmist expresses his great ***love*** for God's Word. Consider these verses.

~~~~~

Vs. 47 - *And I will delight myself in thy* ***commandments, which I have loved.***

Vs. 48 - *My hands also will I lift up unto thy* ***commandments, which I have loved;*** *and I will meditate in thy statutes.*

Vs. 97 - *O how* ***love I thy law!*** *it is my meditation all the day.*

Vs. 113 - *I hate vain thoughts: but* ***thy law do I love.***

Vs. 119 - *Thou puttest away all the wicked of the earth like dross: therefore* ***I love thy testimonies.***

Vs. 127 - Therefore **I love thy commandments** above gold…

Vs. 140 - *Thy* ***word*** *is very pure: therefore* ***thy servant loveth it.***

Vs. 159 - *Consider how* ***I love thy precepts:*** *quicken me, O LORD, according to thy lovingkindness.*

Vs. 163 - *I hate and abhor lying: but* ***thy law do I love.***

Vs. 165 - *Great peace have they which* ***love thy law****: and nothing shall offend them.*

Vs. 167 - *My soul hath kept thy* ***testimonies****; and* ***I love them*** *exceedingly.*

~~~~~

Do you have that kind of love for God and His Word? It contains unlimited treasures to those who will take the time to dig for them. I dearly ***Love*** the Word of God. It is my most cherished possession.

Gem #339 **December 4**

But thou, O LORD, art a ***shield*** *for me; my glory,*
and the lifter up of mine head.
Psalms 3:3

The LORD is my strength and my ***shield****; my heart trusted in him,*
and I am helped: therefore my heart greatly rejoiceth;
and with my song will I praise him.
Psalms 28:7

Blessed be the LORD my strength which teacheth my hands to war,
and my fingers to fight: My goodness, and my fortress; my high tower,
and my deliverer; my ***shield****, and he in whom I trust;*
who subdueth my people under me.
Psalms 144:1-2[38]

~~~~~

The ***shield*** was an important piece of protective armor used in ancient warfare. They were typically large enough to shield the entire body and were worn on the left arm. They were made of metals or animal hides stretched over a wooden frame. Animal hides had to be anointed with oil frequently to keep them soft and to deflect any arrows that would come against the soldier. The Old Testament refers to God as our shield in seventeen places. Our enemy, the devil, would love for us to feel vulnerable and unprotected, but when we are born into God's Kingdom, He becomes our shield and our help, and there is no weapon the enemy can devise that will penetrate that holy, righteous shield (Isaiah 54:17). Do you feel assailed on every side by the fiery darts of the wicked? Just call on Jesus. He has promised to be your help and your shield.

---

[38] See also Genesis 15:1; Deuteronomy 33:29; 2 Samuel 22:3; Psalms 5:12; 33:20; 59:11; 84:9, 11; 91:4; 115:9-11; 119:114; Proverbs 30:5.
~~~~~

Gem #340 **December 5**

...O give thanks unto the LORD; ...for ***his mercy endureth for ever.***
Psalms 106:1

But the ***mercy of the LORD*** *is from everlasting to everlasting upon them that fear him...* ***To such as keep his covenant,*** *and to those that remember his* ***commandments to do them.***
Psalms 103:17-18

And shewing ***mercy*** *unto thousands of them that* ***love me, and keep my commandments.***
Exodus 20:6; Deuteronomy 5:10

I love them that love me*; and those that seek me early shall find me.*
Proverbs 8:17

If ***ye love me, keep my commandments.***
If ye keep my commandments, ye shall abide in my love;
even as I have kept my Father's commandments, and abide in his love.
John 14:15; 15:10

~~~~~

The phrase "his mercy endureth for ever" occurs 44 times in the KJV of the Bible. Strong's Concordance renders the meaning of the word "mercy" as "lovingkindness." So if we add that word to the list of scriptures, we add in another 29 times that we are reminded of God's enduring "love" and "kindness" to humanity. Because the theme of God's love is so prevalent in the Bible, there are some who teach that God loves unconditionally. However, there are 50+ verses in the Old Testament that teach God's love or mercy is extended to those who ***keep His commandments***. Jesus continued that theme in His teaching in John 14. While it is true that God's love for mankind compelled Him to the cross to make atonement for man's sins (John 3:16), and His love also draws men to Him so that their lives can be changed, God's ***abiding love*** and benefits belong to those who ***keep His commandments***.
~~~~~

Gem #341 **December 6**

Now unto him that is able to do exceeding abundantly ***above all*** *that we ask or think, according to the power that worketh in us,*

Ephesians 3:20

And ***above all*** *these things put on charity, which is the bond of perfectness.*

Colossians 3:14

And ***above all*** *things have fervent charity among yourselves: for charity shall cover the multitude of sins.*

1 Peter 4:8[39]

~~~~~

When we want to stress the importance of a statement, we use the idiom ***"above all."*** When someone says, ***"above all,"*** pay attention. You may be asked to do something that is above and beyond all other considerations. Several New Testament writers give us some important ***"above all"*** reminders. Paul asks us to remember that God's ability to grant our prayers is limited to the power that is working in us. Paul and Peter also address the importance of having charity to develop maturity in our Christian life and to overlook the shortcomings of others. If we place these admonitions above everything else in rank of importance, they will lead us to our ultimate destination of eternal life with our Lord and Savior, Jesus Christ.

An old chorus I grew up singing in church stresses the importance of being saved.

~~~~~

Above all else, I must be saved. For above all else, I must be saved.
So whatever you have to do to me, Don't let me lost for eternity.
Above all else, I must be saved.

Doug Davis

---

[39] For other "above all" reminders, see Ephesians 6:16; James 5:12; 3 John 1:2.

Gem #342 **December 7**

For great is the Lord, and greatly to be praised:
*he also is to be feared **above all gods.***
1 Chronicles 16:25

*For the LORD is a great God, and a great King **above all gods**.*
Psalms 95:3

*For I know that the LORD is great, and that our Lord is **above all gods.***
Psalms 135:5

One Lord, one faith, one baptism, One God and Father of all,
*who is **above all**, and through all, and in you all.*
Ephesians 4:5-6

~~~~~

Dozens of times the Bible reminds us that there is only one God, and He is superior to all other gods that men may invent. The prophet Elijah once challenged the false prophets of Baal to prove their god was real by praying for him to send fire from heaven and consume the sacrifice they had placed on an altar (1 Kings 18:19-39). After hours of praying, crying, and even cutting themselves until they drew blood, Elijah set them aside, repaired the altar, poured water on the sacrifice, and prayed a simple two-sentence prayer that brought the fire of Almighty God from heaven and consumed the sacrifice. Paul reminded the Ephesian Church that not only was there just one God, but He is also above everything, He works through every situation, and best of all, He lives in His saints.

The world promotes hundreds of imitation gods, but never forget that Jesus Christ is Lord of all, and one day soon…

" at the name of Jesus every knee should bow… And that every tongue should confess that Jesus Christ is Lord, to the glory of God the Father."
Philippians 2:10-11
~~~~~

Gem #343 **December 8**

Before I formed thee in the belly I knew thee;
and before thou camest forth out of the womb I sanctified thee,
and I ordained thee a prophet unto the nations.
Jeremiah 1:5

Thine eyes did see my substance, yet being unperfect;
and in thy book all my members were written, which in continuance
were fashioned, when as yet there was none of them.
Psalms 139:16

Trust in the LORD with ***all*** *thine heart;*
and lean not unto thine own understanding.
In ***all*** *thy ways acknowledge him, and he shall direct thy paths.*
Proverbs 3:5-6

~~~~~

God knew my name before I was ever conceived by my parents. He knows every intimate detail about me. I cannot hide anything from His all-seeing eyes. So I might as well give Him my wholehearted love and obedience, and plunge into His work with every ounce of energy and enthusiasm within me. I grew up hearing the saying, "If you live for God easy, then it's hard; but if you live for God hard, then it's easy." If you've been trying to do just enough to get by, try stepping up your level of consecration by giving God your very best. If you will make the commitment, He promises to direct the paths you take.

~~~~~

"If He has planned all my days, I should acknowledge Him in all my ways. That means developing the habit of deliberately pausing to ask God's will before making a purchase, giving an answer, writing a letter, making a decision, or taking an action. Acknowledge Him as Lord of that matter… Strategic pauses like that throughout the day would save us from many mistakes."
Robert J. Morgan

Gem #344 **December 9**

Great in counsel, and mighty in work: for thine eyes are open upon all the ways of the sons of men: to give every one according to his ways, and according to the fruit of his doings:
Jeremiah 32:19

And let us not be weary in well doing: for in due season we shall reap, if we faint not. As we have therefore opportunity, let us do good unto all men, especially unto them who are of the household of faith.
Galatians 6:9-10

~~~~~

The story has been told of an ex-serviceman, James Kilpatrick[40] who, while serving in France, shared his Army coffee and cakes from home each day with a hungry old French lady. Those acts of kindness came to the attention of Madame Jeanne Marshall, 83 of Baccarat, France whose seven sons had been killed by the Nazis, and she willed Kilpatrick $50,000 before her death. He was stunned to receive such recognition for his small acts of kindness.

Who do you know that needs encouragement, or an act of kindness to put a smile on their face? The eyes of the Lord are watching and are ready to give back to those who do not become weary in well doing.

~~~~~

"No one has ever become poor by giving."
Anne Frank

~~~~~

"Kindness is a language
which the deaf can hear and the blind can see."
Mark Twain

[40] Joy Haney, *When ye Give* (USA: Radiant Life Publications, 1992) 127.
~~~~~

Gem #345 **December 10**

***Blessed** are they that **mourn**: for they shall be comforted.*
Matthew 5:4

*I am troubled; I am bowed down greatly; I go **mourn**ing all the day long.*
Psalms 38:6

*The Spirit of the Lord GOD is upon me; because the LORD hath anointed me… to comfort all that **mourn**; To appoint unto them that **mourn** in Zion, to give unto them beauty for ashes, the oil of joy for **mourning**, the garment of praise for the spirit of heaviness; that they might be called trees of righteousness, the planting of the LORD, that he might be glorified.*
Isaiah 61:1-3

~~~~~

When my husband died unexpectedly of a heart attack at age 51, my whole world fell apart. I grieved deeply. I could relate to the Psalmist's comments about being bowed down and mourning all day long. During those years of grieving, I did not feel very **blessed**. In fact, I had lots of questions about why this had happened to me. Yet, my feelings were not true indicators of the **blessing** of God in my life. The Comforter, which is the Holy Ghost that was living in me, slowly and surely brought comfort to my hurting heart, and since then, I have been able to understand Isaiah's prophecy. Because I have experienced loss and mourned that loss, the anointing of God on my life allows me to understand the hurt of others who grieve the loss of a loved one, and I can comfort them in their grief and watch God turn their mourning into joy. Now, from a vantage point of many years after my loss, I can be thankful and bless God…

"Who comforteth us in all our tribulation,
***that we may be able to comfort** them which are in any trouble,*
by the comfort wherewith we ourselves are comforted of God."
2 Corinthians 1:4
~~~~~

Gem #346 **December 11**

[8] By faith ***Abraham****, when he was called to go out into a place which he should after receive for an inheritance, obeyed; and he went out, not knowing whither he went. [24] By faith* ***Moses****, when he was come to years, refused to be called the son of Pharaoh's daughter; [25] Choosing rather to suffer affliction with the people of God, than to enjoy the pleasures of sin for a season; [26] Esteeming the reproach of Christ greater riches than the treasures in Egypt: for he had respect unto the recompence of the reward. [32] And what shall I more say? for the time would fail me to tell... of the* ***prophets****: [33] Who through faith ...****stopped the mouths of lions.***

Hebrews 11:8, 24-26, 32-33

~~~~~

While the Bible lists only a handful of men who were called ***faithful***, three of those men, Abraham, Moses, and Daniel are notable names in Bible history. They are also listed in Hebrews 11 among the heroes of faith. What common characteristics would earn these men the distinction of being remembered as faithful men? The dictionary lists clues such as: thorough in the performance of duty; true to one's word or promises; loyal; reliable; trusted and full of faith. All of these men had the distinction of having to leave their homeland in order to fulfill God's call on their life. Abraham obeyed God's order to leave Ur. Moses fled Egypt because he had committed a murder. Daniel left Judah as a prisoner of war. In spite of strange customs among the heathen and opposition from others who did not understand their peculiarity, or were jealous of the favor they received from kings and priests, these three men remained obedient to God's laws. God trusted them, as did heathen kings and the priest of Midian. God is not looking for conceited, pampered people who expect a life of ease, fortune, and fame. He is looking for faithful men and women who will not lose hope when politics get dirty and they are caught in the fray. He needs someone who can be trusted to do a job and hold fast to their convictions regardless of what opposition comes their way. When God reveals His list of ***faithful*** men and women, will your name be on it?
~~~~~

Gem #347 **December 12**

And all the princes, and the mighty men, and all the sons likewise of king David, ***submit****ted themselves unto Solomon the king.*
1 Chronicles 29:24

Obey them that have the rule over you, and ***submit*** *yourselves: for they watch for your souls, as they that must give account, that they may do it with joy, and not with grief: for that is unprofitable for you.*
Hebrews 13:17

Submit *yourselves to every ordinance of man for the Lord's sake: whether it be to the king… Or unto governors, as unto them that are sent by him for the punishment of evildoers, and for the praise of them that do well.*
1 Peter 2:13-14

~~~~~

King David had many sons and daughters and no doubt, there were many conversations among the siblings as to who would inherit the throne upon their father's death. Absalom, who was son #3, developed quite a following and tried to force his dad off the throne, but he was killed. Some time later, Adonijah, who was son #4, decided to steal the throne from his aged father. David was alerted and swiftly moved to put favored son, Solomon on the throne. Solomon was one of David's younger sons, yet when he became king, all the hopes of his older siblings to inherit the throne were put aside, and all of them along with David's mighty men, ***submitted*** themselves to Solomon's rule. Sometimes elections do not go the way we want them to go, or another person is appointed to a position we had really hoped to receive. It is in these times of disappointment that we are instructed to ***submit*** to those who have authority over us and to pray for them (1 Timothy 2:1-3). Our pastors especially need our prayer covering because they will give account to God for every soul they pastor. That accounting can be given with joy for those who have cheerfully obeyed or with grief for those who were disobedient. Will the account of your life be given with joy or with grief?
~~~~~

Gem #348 **December 13**

And Lot lifted up his eyes, and beheld all the plain of Jordan, that it was well watered every where, before the LORD destroyed Sodom and Gomorrah, even as the garden of the LORD, like the land of Egypt, as thou comest unto Zoar. Then Lot chose him all the plain of Jordan; and Lot journeyed east: and they separated themselves the one from the other. Abram dwelled in the land of Canaan, and ***Lot dwelled in the cities of the plain, and pitched his tent toward Sodom****. But the men of Sodom were wicked and sinners before the LORD exceedingly.*

Genesis 13:10-13

~~~~~

After Lot's father died, his Uncle Abram took him in and treated him as his own son. Knowing Abram's consecration to God, it is surprising that when the time came for Abram and Lot to part ways because the land could not support both of their herds and flocks, Lot chose to pitch his tent toward Sodom even though the city was very wicked. In the beginning, Lot may have felt that his family was safe enough by living in the plain, but our next glimpse of Lot in Genesis 14 tells us that he actually moved his family into wicked Sodom. The influence of that city was so powerful over his family that when the angels came to remove Lot's family before God destroyed Sodom, two of his married daughters chose to remain there. As Lot, his wife and two unmarried daughters fled, his wife looked back and became a pillar of salt. Then the two remaining daughters decided to have a child by their dad. The two boys that were born, Ammon and Moab, became enemies of Abraham's descendants for all of time. I have often wondered why Lot did not flee to Uncle Abraham's house. There they would have been safe among people of God. Sometimes we do not realize how one decision will impact our family for generations to come. Lot's initial glimpse toward Sodom eventually drew him right into the midst of that wicked environment, and it cost him his whole family.

Does the world look appealing to you? Be careful! A seemingly innocent look could drive your family away from God for many generations into the future.
~~~~~

 **Gem #349** **December 14**

Say not ye, There are yet four months, and then cometh harvest?
behold, I say unto you, Lift up your eyes, and look on the fields;
for they are white already to harvest. And ***he that reapeth***
receiveth wages, *and gathereth fruit unto life eternal:*
that both he that soweth and he that reapeth may rejoice together.
And herein is that saying true, One soweth, and another reapeth.
John 4:35-37

~~~~~

One of the incentives for getting a job is to receive wages in return for services rendered. Jesus has promised wages for everyone who will get involved in reaping souls from His harvest field. In the natural world, there are many components involved in bringing in a harvest. There are companies that manufacture the seeds that are sown and people are employed in that company. Many people are employed in companies that manufacture tractors and other machinery used in tilling the ground, sowing the seed, removing the weeds, and harvesting the final crop. People are involved in manufacturing building materials for building silos for storing crops; others are involved in processing the crop for market. All people who participated in any portion of the manufacture of machinery, building materials, or the actual labor of sowing and reaping have an investment in the final harvest. Likewise, in the spiritual realm, soul winning and harvesting of souls occurs as a result of someone praying for the lost, someone witnessing to the lost, someone babysitting while someone else teaches a Bible study, someone extending hospitality or friendship, someone baptizing the new believer, or someone teaching the new convert to become a mature Christian. It takes *"all hands on deck"* to bring the harvest in, and everyone who has invested in any portion of that sinner's conversion will rejoice together and receive wages for their investment in souls.

What part can you play in winning a soul to Jesus? Every effort is needed to bring in the harvest.
~~~~~

Gem #350 **December 15**

[16] Shadrach, Meshach, and Abednego, …said to the king… [18]…be it known unto thee, O king, that we will not serve thy gods, nor worship the golden image which thou hast set up. [19] Then was Nebuchadnezzar full of fury… [23] And …Shadrach, Meshach, and Abednego, fell down bound into the midst of the burning fiery furnace. [24] Then Nebuchadnezzar the king was astonished, and rose up in haste, and spake, …Did not we cast three men bound into the midst of the fire?... [25] …Lo, I see four men loose, walking in the midst of the fire, and they have no hurt; and the form of the fourth is like the Son of God. [26] Then Nebuchadnezzar …said, Shadrach, Meshach, and Abednego, ye servants of the most high God, come forth, and come hither. Then Shadrach, Meshach, and Abednego, came forth of the midst of the fire. [27] And [all] …saw these men, upon whose bodies the fire had no power, nor was an hair of their head singed, neither were their coats changed, nor the smell of fire had passed on them.

Daniel 3:16, 18-19, 23-27

~~~~~

This story was always one of my childhood favorites, yet I couldn't imagine such a thing happening in today's world until I read LaJoyce Martin's November 6, 1962 testimony of being saved from a fire. She and her husband were visiting her in-laws to celebrate a birthday. When a fire developed on the stove, LaJoyce attempted to put it out by throwing water on it. An explosion sent sheets of fire above, below and on all sides of her. There was no way out of her fiery furnace, so in her desperation, she called, "JESUS!" Although she could not see her way out of the flames, she eventually found her way through a hallway that led to the outside door. Her clothes were not burned, her hair was not singed, and there was no smell of smoke on her clothing. She said, "The three Hebrew children have nothing on me! That same Jesus was in the fire with me, covering me with His asbestos suit and walking me right out to safety!" If it happened in the Bible, it can happen today, for *"Jesus Christ [is] the same yesterday, and to day, and for ever."*[41]

---

[41] Mary H. Wallace, *God Answers Prayer* (USA: Word Aflame Press, 1986) 23-27.
~~~~~

Gem #351 **December 16**

I beseech you therefore, brethren, by the mercies of God,
that ye present your bodies a living sacrifice, holy, ***acceptable*** *unto God,*
which is your reasonable service. And be not conformed to this world:
but be ye transformed by the renewing of your mind, that ye
may prove what is that good, and ***acceptable****, and perfect, will of God.*
Romans 12:1-2

~~~~~

Paul taught that God ***accepts*** the presentation of our bodies as a living, holy sacrifice to Him. Furthermore, our transformed and renewed minds give us insight into God's will for our lives. A journey through the Bible provides additional insight into things that are acceptable to God. In the Old Testament, we discover that God ***accepted*** Abel's blood sacrifice and rejected Cain's produce (Genesis 4:3-7). He ***accepted*** the sacrifices of Gideon (Judges 6:20-21), Elijah (1 Kings 18:38), and Solomon (2 Chronicles 7:1-3) by sending fire from heaven to consume the sacrifices. In the New Testament, Jesus instructed His followers to return to Jerusalem after His ascension to heaven and await the "promise of the Father" which was the baptism of the Holy Ghost and fire (Matthew 3:11; Luke 3:16). Their obedience was ***accepted*** by God with a baptism of fire on the Day of Pentecost to over 3,000 Jews. Later, God accepted the repentance and baptism of the Samaritans (Acts 8) and Gentiles (Acts 10) and baptized them with the Holy Ghost and fire. Since then, God continues to ***accept*** those who come to Him in repentance and obedience to His instructions for being born again of water and Spirit (John 3:3-8).

A common teaching in modern-day churches says that salvation is achieved through the avenue of *"accepting the Lord Jesus as one's personal Savior."* Since God has done all the accepting throughout the Bible, the closest teaching I could find to support the idea that man accepts God for salvation would be the acceptance of God's provision of salvation by obeying the Gospel message of the death, burial and resurrection of Jesus (1 Corinthians 15:1-4). Man accepts
~~~~~

Jesus' death by obeying the command to repent and die out to his sinful nature (Acts 2:38; 17:30; Luke 13:3). Man accepts Jesus' burial by obeying the command to be buried with Him in baptism in His name (Romans 6:3-4; Acts 2:38; 10:48; Mark 16:16). Finally, man accepts Jesus' resurrection by obeying the command to receive the "promise of the Father" which is the infilling of the Holy Ghost (Acts 1:4; 2:38; 5:32; 19:2, 6; John 7:38-39; Romans 6:4).

Have you ***accepted*** Jesus by obeying the Gospel?[42]

Gem #352 **December 17**

*God **setteth the solitary in families**:*
he bringeth out those which are bound with chains:...
Psalms 68:6

*Yet **setteth he the poor** on high from affliction,*
*and **maketh him families** like a flock.*
Psalms 107:41

~~~~~

Family ties have always been important in the Bible. The two books of Chronicles in the Old Testament are devoted to recording the genealogy of the Jews. Several other books contain detailed lists of family names and descendants. In America, we anticipate various holidays throughout the year and use those occasions to celebrate with our families. However, there are many people in the world who have no family connections, and holidays are difficult times of the year for them. God cares about those who are lonely and in a solitary state. His people are one huge spiritual family, and He desires to place the solitary, the poor, and the afflicted into a loving spiritual family. I believe it would please God for the Church to find someone who is alone or in financial need and include them in our end-of-year Church and family festivities.

---

[42] Comments based on a Bible lesson, "Who Accepts Who?" taught by Bethel Christian Ministries Pastor Elvin Anthony of Bellevue, NE in 2000.
~~~~~

Gem #353 **December 18**

[7] The law of the LORD is perfect, converting the soul... [8] The statutes of the LORD are right, rejoicing the heart... [9] ...the judgments of the LORD are true and righteous altogether. [11] Moreover ***by them is thy servant warned: and in keeping of them there is great reward.***
Psalms 19:7-9, 11

~~~~~

One of the most notable battles of the American Revolution occurred on Christmas night, 1776, when George Washington and his troops crossed the Delaware River and executed a surprise attack on the partying Hessian troops in Trenton, New Jersey. The Hessian commander, Johann Rall, received a note that night warning him of the approach of Washington's troops, but he was involved in a card game and placed the note in his pocket without reading it. He was mortally wounded in the ensuing battle, and the note that could have prepared his troops for battle was later discovered in his pocket.

The Bible contains hundreds of pages of instructions from God to acquaint us with His nature, His ways, His laws for people to live a life that pleases Him, His rewards for those who obey His laws, and His judgment and punishment for those who do not obey. God's ***warnings*** for disobedience are very clear in His Word, yet millions of people own Bibles that are rarely if ever opened, let alone studied. The specifics contained inside that book are never known. God has also appointed spokesmen to ***warn*** people and prepare them for eternal life or death after this earthly life, and yet, many fail to listen to God's messengers. According to the Bible signs around us, this age is coming to a close. Have you heeded the warnings and made the necessary preparations for the life to come? One day soon, God's record books will be opened, and everyone will receive either rewards or punishment for the way they have lived their lives.

Don't ignore God's warnings.
~~~~~

Gem #354 **December 19**

Keep me as the apple of the eye, hide me under the ***shadow of thy wings,***
Psalms 17:8

I will abide in thy tabernacle for ever:
I will trust in the ***covert of thy wings****. Selah.*
Psalms 61:4

He that dwelleth in the secret place of the most High
shall abide under the ***shadow*** *of the Almighty.*
Surely he shall deliver thee from the snare of the fowler, and
from the noisome pestilence. He shall ***cover thee with his feathers****, and*
under his wings shalt thou trust: his truth shall be thy shield and buckler.
Psalms 91:1, 3-4

~~~~~

God has given birds the ability to soar in flight when they spread their wings. The wings are covered with several types of feathers to provide various benefits to the bird. Two of the most important types of feathers are the *contour* and *covert* feathers. The *contour* feathers are the ones most visible and provide the color of the bird as well as give the bird its shape. They lie in layers much like shingles on a roof and shed rain and keep the bird's body well insulated. *Covert* feathers cover the *contour* feathers, and they provide additional insulation as well as a smoother surface to improve air flow over the wings during flight.

The Bible speaks of God's wings several times to give us a visual picture of the protection and covering that He provides for His children. Just as the bird's *contour* feathers protect from inclement weather, so do God's wings cover us during the raging storms of life, and the *covert* feathers help smooth out the turbulence brought on by life's hard trials. Are you being chased by the enemy of your soul and find yourself encountering one hardship after another? Flee to God's wings and burrow under His feathers of protection, safety and peace.
~~~~~

Gem #355 **December 20**

...Hide the outcasts, Do not betray him who escapes.

Isaiah 16:3 (NKJV)

~~~~~

Harriet Tubman was only 13 years old when she found her life's work. Born in slavery in the antebellum South, she was toiling one evening in the fields when she saw Jim, a fellow slave, slip away to the village store without permission. When she noticed his overseer take out after him, Harriet decided on the spur of the moment to make a dash through the fields to warn Jim. It was a futile attempt, and Jim was captured in the store. Looking at Harriet, the overseer demanded she help restrain Jim while he was being whipped. She refused; and when Jim darted out the door, she blocked the way, allowing him to escape. The enraged overseer grabbed an iron weight from the store's scales and threw it toward Harriet, striking her in the forehead. She crumpled to the floor, her scull fractured. For two months, Harriet lay in the corner of a room, her head wrapped in rags and in a state of delirium. No one expected her to survive, but her mother tenderly nursed her back to health. During those days of pain and convalescence, Harriet prayed earnestly that God would help her get rid of the awful institution of slavery. As a dedicated follower of Jesus Christ, Harriet believed God had called her to fulfill the command of Isaiah 16:3: *"Hide the outcasts, do not betray him who escapes."*

During the 80 years between her injury at age 13 and her death at age 93, Harriet Tubman made a ***difference***. She made thirteen hair-raising missions to rescue more than 300 slaves. When the Civil War erupted, she became a spy for the Union. She was the first woman to lead an armed expedition in the war, and she guided the raid on the Combahee River that liberated more than 700 slaves. Her nickname was "Moses." If a 13-year old slave girl with a fractured scull can make a difference in the world, surely God can use you, too.

What does it take to make a Difference? It only takes one.
~~~~~

Gem #356 **December 21**

*A **friend** loveth at all times, and a brother is born for adversity.*
Proverbs 17:17

*A man that hath **friends** must shew himself friendly:*
*and there is a **friend** that sticketh closer than a brother.*
Proverbs 18:24

Iron sharpeneth iron;
*so a man sharpeneth the countenance of his **friend**.*
Proverbs 27:17

~~~~~

"Friendship is a single soul dwelling in two bodies."
Aristotle

"There is a magnet in your heart that will attract true friends. That magnet is unselfishness, thinking of other first; when you learn to live for others, they will live for you."
Paramahansa Yogananda

"You can make more **friends** in two months by becoming interested in other people than you can in two years by trying to get other people interested in you."
Dale Carnegie

~~~~~

Friends are those choice people in my life who love me at my worst and applaud me at my best. Their honesty in alerting me to my shortcomings sharpens and improves my character. I'm thankful today for the choice people in my life who are my friends.

Gem #357 **December 22**

Ask, and it shall be given you; Seek, and ye shall find;
knock, and it shall be opened unto you: For every one that asketh receiveth;
and he that seeketh findeth; and to him that knocketh it shall be opened.

Matthew 7:7-8

~~~~~

I usually think of Thomas Edison when I think about the invention of the light bulb. Yet he was not the first one to invent a light bulb. Many earlier inventors had previously devised incandescent lamps, including Alessandro Volta, Henry Woodward, Matthew Evans, Humphry Davy, James Bowman Lindsay, Moses G. Farmer, William E. Sawyer, Joseph Swan, and Heinrich Gobel. Edison's public schooling only lasted three months because his teacher could not understand his insatiable desire to learn and called him addled. From then on, his mother educated him. He excelled in his studies and went on to invent the phonograph, the motion picture camera, and a long-lasting, practical electric light bulb. He is credited with numerous inventions that contributed to mass communication and in particular, telecommunications. These included a stock ticker, a mechanical vote recorder, a battery for an electric car, electrical power, recorded music and motion pictures. Mahen Theatre in what is now the Czech Republic was the first public building in the world to use Edison's electric lamps. What set Thomas Edison apart from these other men was his extraordinary desire to figure out a way to make his ideas work and share those ideas with the world. His wholehearted approach to finding answers gave him the distinction of being the fourth most prolific inventor in history, holding 1,093 US patents in his name as well as many patents in the United Kingdom, France, and Germany. Thomas Edison believed in a supreme being, but didn't consider himself religious. However, he learned to apply the Biblical principle of seeking answers with his whole heart, and he received what he sought after. He changed world history, but his motive was not Kingdom related. What are you seeking? God is looking for wholehearted seekers with a Kingdom-focus.
~~~~~

Gem #358 **December 23**

And ye shall seek me, and find me,
when ye shall search for me with ***all your heart****.*
Jeremiah 29:13

~~~~~

Harry Branding was the son of German immigrants who settled in Illinois, and they were faithful members of the Lutheran church. Harry married, had a family, and worked at various jobs to support his family. During a business trip to Florida in 1928, he visited a Baptist revival, and prayed through to an old-fashioned repentance experience. Hungry for more of God, he later began visiting other churches. Eventually he encountered Pentecost and began diligently studying the scriptures he heard taught in the services. In time he was baptized in Jesus' name and filled with the Holy Ghost. Eventually, God called him into the ministry. Rev. Branding was as fervent in his preaching as he had been in real estate and the other occupations he had pursued through the years. His preaching was enthusiastic and powerfully anointed, and people travelled long distances to attend the little mission church he pastored in St. Louis. He was a man of great faith and spent much time in prayer and fasting. He taught these principles to his church, and they also were people of prayer, fasting, and great faith. Healings and miracles were common. The little mission exploded with growth, and eventually they purchased a large Congregational Church at 13th and Gravois St. which they renamed the Apostolic Pentecostal Church. The church continued to grow and Rev. Branding's influence extended into many places through his mentoring of many young men who were called into the ministry. At least 22 daughter works were established and financed by the Apostolic Church. When needs would arise, Bro. Branding would seek God until he had an answer. He was instrumental in bringing about the merger between the two Pentecostal organizations which became the United Pentecostal Church. He served as District Superintendent of the UPC churches in Missouri for over 20 years. His dream of opening an Apostolic College in Missouri also was realized when
~~~~~

Gateway College of Evangelism was opened in 1968. He assisted in its dedication.[43] Many other stories could be told about this man who sought God with his whole heart, and only eternity will reveal the total extent of his Godly influence in this life. Are you wholeheartedly committed to changing history with the Gospel?

Gem #359 **December 24**

Then Nebuchadnezzar spake, and said, Blessed be the God of Shadrach, Meshach, and Abednego, who hath sent his angel, and delivered his servants that trusted in him… ***Then the king promoted Shadrach, Meshach, and Abednego,*** *in the province of Babylon.*
Daniel 3:28, 30

A man's gift maketh room for him*, and bringeth him before great men.*
Proverbs 18:16

~~~~~

The God-given wisdom of Hananiah, Mishael, and Azariah earned them prominent roles in the affairs of Babylon until the king learned of their refusal to worship his golden image. But after their trial by fire, the king acknowledged the superiority of their God and gave each of them a promotion. Sometimes it seems that others get the good jobs, the solo part in the choir, or the leading role in the Easter musical. Then the temptation comes to promote our skills, talents, or gifts to show off what we are capable of doing. The Psalmist warned against blowing your own horn or speaking arrogantly about your skills, because God is the one who allows a person to be exalted or abased (Psalms 75:5-7).

Just keep on working to improve your gifts, and as you fine-tune your skills, God will make room for your gifts to be used. Just wait on His timing.

---

[43] Mary Wallace, *Profiles of Pentecostal Preachers, Volume I* (Hazelwood, MO: Word Aflame Press, 1983) 27-46.
~~~~~

Gem #360 **December 25**

For unto us a child is born, unto us a son is given:
and the government shall be upon his shoulder:
*and **his name shall be called** Wonderful, Counsellor,*
***The mighty God, The everlasting Father,** The Prince of Peace.*
Isaiah 9:6

*And she shall bring forth a **son**, and thou shalt call his name **Jesus**: for he shall save his people from their sins. Behold, a virgin shall be with child, and shall bring forth a son, and **they shall call his name Emmanuel, which being interpreted is, God with us.***
Matthew 1:21, 23

In the beginning was the Word, and the Word was with God,
*and the **Word was God.***
John 1:1

*And **the Word [God] was made flesh**, and dwelt among us,*
(and we beheld his glory, the glory as of the only begotten of
the Father,) full of grace and truth.
John 1:14

Take heed therefore unto yourselves, and to all the flock,
over the which the Holy Ghost hath made you overseers,
*to feed the **church of God,** which*
he hath purchased with his own blood.
Acts 20:28

~~~~~

"The Father did not send a substitute to earth. HE came down.
That was Emmanuel in the manger. God with us.
Not a third of God. All of God."
Ken Raggio

God, the eternal Spirit, made Himself a body and came and shed His blood for my redemption. What a revelation!
~~~~~

Gem #361  **December 26**

Ye are our epistle written in our hearts, known and read of all men: Forasmuch as ye are manifestly declared to be the epistle of Christ ministered by us, written not with ink, but with the Spirit of the living God; not in tables of stone, but in fleshy tables of the heart.
2 Corinthians 3:2-3

Now then we are ***ambassadors*** *for Christ…*
2 Corinthians 5:20

~~~~~

We go through life and attend school, get a job, marry, raise a family, attend Church, and perhaps volunteer in our community. Very few of us achieve worldwide name-recognition because of the way we live our lives.

I started my Christian walk at the age of 9 and have tried to live in such a way that I represented my God well. After my conversion, I witnessed to my teachers and friends at school and after I started working, I also witnessed about God to my co-workers. I married young, raised a family, volunteered in my children's schools and in the community. My husband died unexpectedly when I was 45, and I moved across country to a new city and a new Church. I had to make a fresh start for being an ambassador for Jesus in a new area. I began volunteering with a group of musicians and music teachers and one day, one of the teachers nicknamed me "God's Girl." The name stuck and for several years now, that has been her pet name for me. You never know who you are influencing.

As you walk through your world, do others recognize you as "God's Girl" or "God's Guy"? I believe God is looking for those who will spend time with Him and learn, not only to recognize His voice, but also to surrender to His plan for their life. He longs for you to be "His Girl" and "His Guy."

Will you answer His call?
~~~~~

 **Gem #362**  **December 27**

Simon Peter, a servant and an apostle of Jesus Christ, to them that have obtained like ***precious faith*** *with us through the righteousness of God and our Saviour Jesus Christ: Whereby are given unto us exceeding great and* ***precious promises****: that by these ye might be partakers of the divine nature, having escaped the corruption that is in the world through lust.*

2 Peter 1:1, 4

That the ***trial of your faith, being much more precious than of gold*** *that perisheth, though it be tried with fire, might be found unto praise and honour and glory at the appearing of Jesus Christ: Receiving the end of your faith, even the salvation of your souls.*

1 Peter 1:7, 9

~~~~~

The word ***"precious"*** speaks of something that is very valuable, loved, or highly esteemed because of a spiritual or moral quality. We say that babies are ***precious*** and refer to their cute little antics as ***precious***. We sometimes say that valuable possessions we own are ***precious***. The Bible uses the term ***precious*** over 70 times to indicate the value of numerous things such as: precious stones, gold, silver, ointment, the dew and fruit of the ground, gifts, clothes, and substance gained through hard work. A premium is also placed on life, the soul, wisdom, knowledge, blood, and the death of God's saints. Peter spoke of the ***precious faith*** that has been given to God's people along with the great and ***precious promises*** that allow us to be partakers of God's divine nature. However, when God hands out His valuables to His saints, He always tests them to determine if they will keep His gifts, or exchange them for the world's gifts that do not cost so much. Peter reminded us that the trying of our faith is far more ***precious*** than gold because our successful journey through fire will strengthen our faith and result in the salvation of our soul.

Hold tightly to your ***precious faith*** and ***precious promises*** through every ***precious fiery trial***. In the end, your ***precious soul*** will be received into God's presence forever.
~~~~~

Gem #363 **December 28**

The LORD will give strength unto his people;
The LORD will bless his people with ***peace****.*

Psalms 29:11

Thou wilt keep him in perfect ***peace****, whose mind is stayed on thee:*
because he trusteth in thee.

Isaiah 26:3

~~~~~

During the four years my husband and I lived in southwest Iowa, we learned what it meant to live in a "Tornado Alley" state. I had never experienced so many tornado alerts in my entire life. One evening we hosted a Bible study in our home with about twelve of our neighbors in attendance. We were very intent on our discussion and did not have a radio turned on to alert us that severe weather was in the area. When our study was over, we walked outside with our guests as they were leaving and were surprised to see neighbors walking up and down the streets. We asked what was going on and were told that the house directly across a little creek from our house had taken a direct hit from a tornado and the roof was gone, as well as fencing in the yard. We had not heard any wind or noise during our Bible study. The next day when it was light, we were able to see the path of the storm. It had touched down in a field outside our subdivision, then lifted and passed over our house and touched down again at our neighbor's home. Then it lifted, crossed a major highway and touched down again, causing significant damage to a farm home and outbuildings. God has promised peace to His people in the midst of every storm IF we place our trust in Him, and keep our thoughts focused on Him.

Are you fearful of the natural and spiritual storms that surround you? Put your trust in Jesus. He offers peace in the midst of the storm.
~~~~~

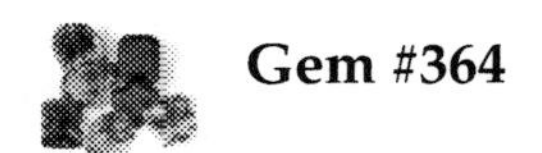

Gem #364 **December 29**

What time I am afraid, I will trust in thee.
Psalms 56:3

The Lord is on my side; I will not fear: what can man do unto me?
Psalms 118:6

And fear not them which kill the body, but are not able to kill the soul: but rather fear him which is able to destroy both soul and body in hell.
Matthew 10:28

∼∼∼∼∼

In a nation that is becoming increasingly hostile against Christianity, it is important to remember as we face a new year, that if persecution comes our way and we are jailed, tortured or even killed for the name of Jesus, we should not fear. As long as our trust is in God, He will be with us unto the very end of our days.

Gem #365 **December 30**

Wherefore he ***[Jesus] is able also to save*** *them to the uttermost that come unto God by him, seeing he ever liveth to make intercession for them.*
Hebrews 7:25

∼∼∼∼∼

Jesus is capable of saving to the greatest possible degree all who come to Him. No life is too messed up for Jesus to make new with His life-changing Spirit. As we close out this year, repentance and the forsaking of all our sins and shortcomings of the past year will allow Jesus to begin or continue the process of salvation in our lives, for we are not saved until we reach the end of our earthly journey. The day-by-day obedience to His commandments will result in our ultimate salvation. Make a commitment today to study His Word and meticulously follow its teachings every day. When you *"mess up, then 'fess up"* and keep walking. In the end, you will be saved.

Gem #366 **December 31**

It is of the LORD's mercies that we are not consumed,
because his compassions fail not.
They are new every morning: great is thy faithfulness.
Lamentations 3:22-23

~~~~~

On this last day of the year, my morning devotions include time for reflecting back over my life this past year. My journal for the past year highlights many moments of joy and gratitude that have been experienced while teaching a Bible class, praying with someone, receiving answers to prayers, helping others, spending time with family or those who need a little attention, and remembering God's provision for unexpected needs and His protection in my travels and daily life. Although I have tried to live my life with Kingdom priorities in mind, I often fall short of the pattern given to us by the book of Acts Christians. My hunger for the coming year is to be less focused on the physical, temporary matters of life and to become even more focused on things that have eternal value. I want to make a difference in the lives of those whose paths cross mine. My reflections bring to mind a chorus to an old song we used to sing often in Church when I was very young. It says:

~~~~~

"Is He satisfied? Is He satisfied? Is He satisfied with me?
Have I done my best? Have I stood the test? Is He satisfied with me?"
A. Hamblen

~~~~~

My consolation for my shortcomings comes from the scriptures in Lamentations 3:22-23. If I have not quite measured up to God's standard, I can repent and make the required changes. After repentance, God wipes my slate clean of my sins and failures, and I have a brand new slate every day to fill with God's plans for my life. If you have fallen short of fulfilling His purpose in your life this past year, now is a good day to repent and change.

A New Year is a good time to make a fresh start.
~~~~~

About the Author

Pam Eddings has more than twenty years of experience in writing, editing, and proofreading Christian literature, and has assisted in the making of dozens of books and hundreds of articles by both Apostolic and secular writers.

She draws from a lifetime of teaching Sunday School classes, and speaking at seminars, retreats and special events. As a licensed minister and prison Chaplain, she has taught weekly Bible studies for more than twelve years to thousands of men and women inmates.

Pam is also a skilled singer, musician, and music instructor, and plays active musical and teaching roles in her local Church. She has three sons, three daughters-in-law, two grandsons and three grand daughters. Her home is in Springfield, Missouri.

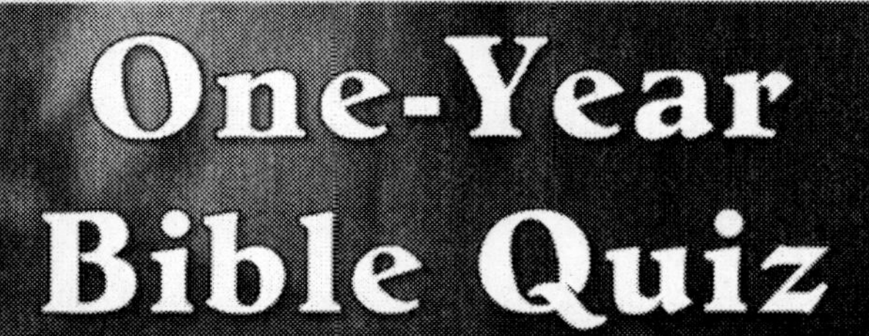

In This Book...

One-Year Bible Quiz

The ENTIRE BIBLE has 1189 Chapters. ONE YEAR has 52 weeks.

Pam Eddings has prepared an extraordinary resource for Weekly Bible Studies, Sunday School Classes, or Parent-Child Lessons.

She has prepared ONE QUESTIONAIRE PER CHAPTER. All 1189 Q & As are divided equally into 52 WEEKS.

Each week, you will find just enough BIBLE QUESTIONS AND ANSWERS to cover the entire Bible in ONE YEAR.

An OUTSTANDING TEACHING AID!

PAM EDDINGS

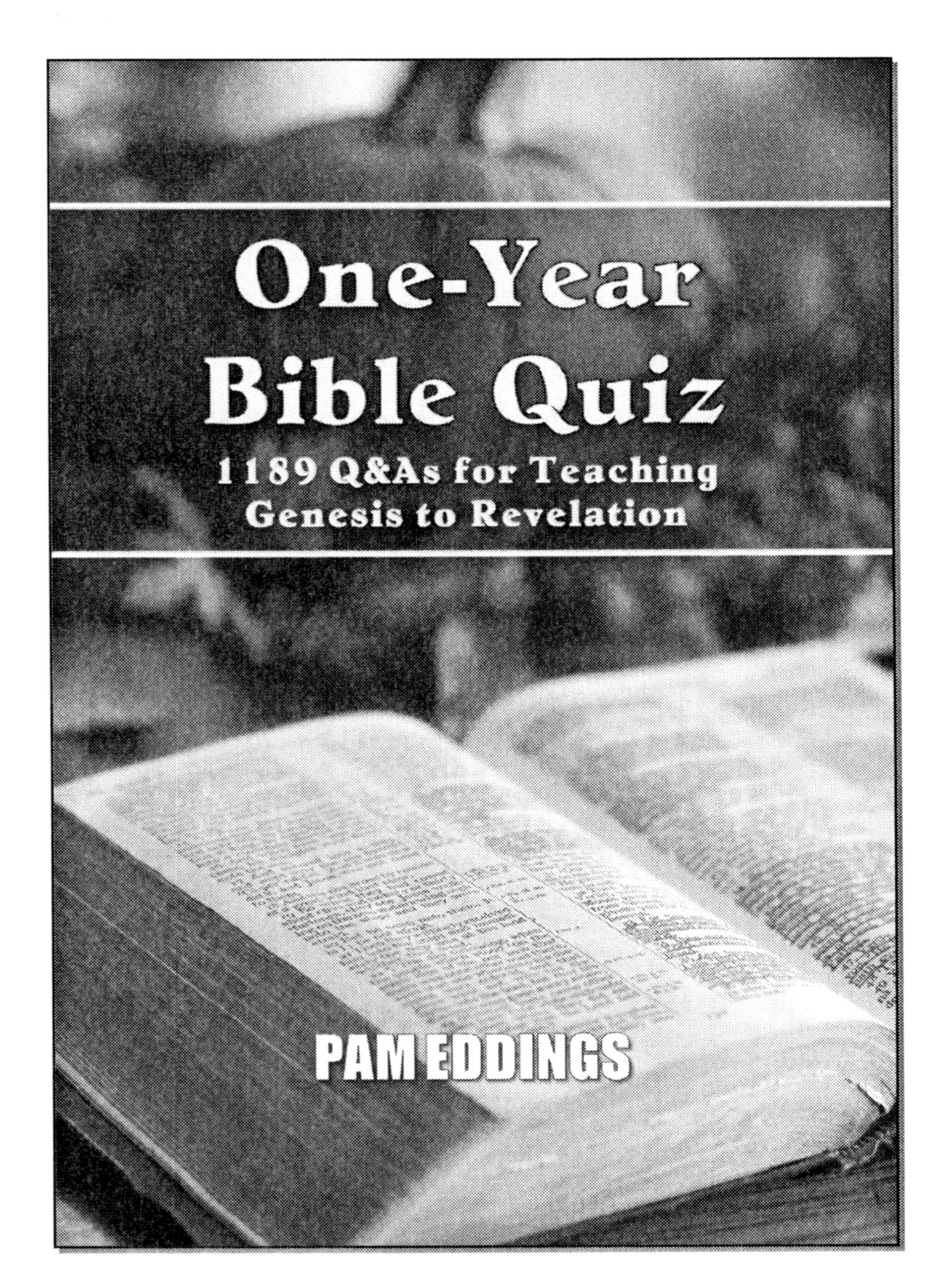
One-Year
Bible Quiz
1189 Q&As for Teaching
Genesis to Revelation
PAM EDDINGS

To Order Additional Copies of

ONE YEAR BIBLE QUIZ

Or

BIBLE GEMS

By Pam Eddings

Please EMAIL her at:

eddingspam@gmail.com